BECOMING ADULT

BECOMING
ADULT

{ How Teenagers Prepare
for the World of Work }

Mihaly Csikszentmihalyi

and Barbara Schneider

BASIC
BOOKS

A Member of the Perseus Books Group

Published by Basic Books,
A Member of the Perseus Books Group

Librar of Congress Cataloging-in-Publication data
Csikszentmihalyi, Mihaly.
    Becoming adult : how teenagers prepare for the world of work / Mihaly Csikszentmihalyi and Barbara Schneider.
    p. cm.
    Includes bibliographical references and index.
    ISBN 0-465-01540-9
    1. Teenagers—Vocational guidance—United States.   2. Teenagers—Employment—United States.   3. Teenagers—United States—Attitudes.   I. Schneider, Barbara.   II. Title
HQ796.C892   2000
305.235'0973—dc21   00-028908

FIRST EDITION

00 01 02 03 / 10 9 8 7 6 5 4 3 2 1

CONTENTS

TABLES

FIGURES

ACKNOWLEDGMENTS

We greatly appreciate the intellectual contributions of our co-principal investigators, Professor Charles Bidwell and Professor Larry Hedges. Throughout the six years of this study they consistently made meaningful and significant contributions to our work. We deeply thank them for their support and collegial spirit, which made this effort possible.

PREFACE

In the summer of 1991, the Alfred P. Sloan Foundation provided the University of Chicago with a grant to study career formation among adolescents. A research team of Charles Bidwell, Mihaly Csikszentmihalyi, Larry Hedges, and Barbara Schneider designed a national longitudinal study of adolescents in grades six, eight, ten, and twelve. A pilot study was conducted in 1991–1992, and the full-scale study was launched in the fall of 1992 and continued through 1997. This effort was unusual in that it brought together a diverse academic team of educators, psychologists, and sociologists to think about a problem commonly researched by scholars in career guidance and vocational development. Taking a different approach, the team decided that to understand how young people form ideas about future schooling and work, it is important to consider not only what the adolescents' aspirations are but also how they are influenced by family, peer groups, schools, and the communities in which they live. It was assumed that this broad perspective would provide new insights into how today's teenagers think about the future and how much influence others have in helping them formulate their plans.

This is one of very few longitudinal studies of career development involving adolescents. The majority of previous studies on career development were not longitudinal, so it was difficult to ascertain how young people's career aspirations and ideas of work changed over time. These types of questions were rarely asked of students in middle school, yet we had reason to believe that early experiences with work shaped attitudes and values that could be sustained into adulthood. Our study focused on populations typically under-represented in research on career development. Previous career studies focused primarily on males. With more women entering the labor force and obtaining higher levels of education, we decided to include equal numbers of young women in our sample. Teenagers from low-income families and minority groups were also frequently excluded from previous studies. Therefore, we deliberately sought school populations that would give our sample significant numbers of racial and ethnic minorities and adolescents from low-income families.

We also believed that to understand more about work in the lives of adolescents, we would need to use different methods than those used in more conventional studies of career development. Rather than investigate how personal attributes might predict occupational choice, we wanted to know what conditions enhanced knowledge about different occupations and career interests. To learn more about this we relied on the Experience Sampling Method (ESM) to obtain daily accounts of how students spend their time and how they feel from moment to moment throughout the day. We also created our own Career Orientation Survey (COS) to determine which students had more knowledge about the world of work and what factors seemed to contribute to it. The survey measures job knowledge in unique ways and examines adolescent experiences and activities related to particular job choices. To gain a deeper understanding of the influence of others on career knowledge, we also developed a peer sociometric questionnaire that identified whom adolescents relied on for advice about their futures.

This book describes the experiences of adolescents as they were reported in the first few years of data collection. Longitudinal data on the base-year high school graduates are used to examine the association between high school experiences and student decisions to enter postsec-

ondary school or the labor force. Through interviews, surveys, time di-
aries, and other data sources, a picture emerges of how adolescents spend
their time, how they feel about their relationships with their parents and
friends, and what images they have of work and their future lives.

This book is organized into three parts. Part 1, "Adolescent Views of
Work," discusses how the nature of adult work has changed, how young
people form ideas about adult work, and how teenagers envision adult
work. Part 2, "Learning to Work," describes how teenagers distinguish
between work and play activities, which factors contribute to enjoyable
work, how families shape teenagers' perceptions of work, and what activities students find most beneficial to their future. Part 3, "Transitioning
from High School," explores how high schools influence student career
paths after graduation; why students take different paths; and finally,
how schools and parents can help their adolescents develop creative
problem-solving techniques and the ability to seek engaging, challenging
activities that promote productive adult lives.

Each of the investigators took responsibility for specific chapters, and
in some instances they worked in teams. The teams of graduate students
who worked with each of the principal investigators are noted under each
chapter title. Professor Csikszentmihalyi was responsible for chapters 1, 3,
4, and 5. Professor Schneider was responsible for chapters 2 and 8. Profes-
sors Csikszentmihalyi and Schneider worked together on chapters 6, 7, 9,
and 10. Professor Kevin Rathunde from the University of Utah also played
a major role in the development of Chapter 6.

A project of this complexity requires a great deal of coordination, and
the four principal investigators worked collaboratively on the design, in-
strumentation, and analyses of the data. But the core of the project was
really built on the enormous effort and energy of University of Chicago
graduate students from anthropology, education, human development,
and sociology, who assisted in all aspects of the study. The Sloan Foundation explicitly requested that this project be carried out by graduate students at the University of Chicago. Aided by the excellent facilities and
staff of the National Opinion Research Center (NORC), a series of training materials and data quality management systems was put into opera-
tion to train students involved with this project. These training activities

proved to be very helpful, and we are proud to report that data from the pilot and first year of the study served as the basis for two undergraduate honor's papers, three master's papers, and four doctoral dissertations. Two of these students deserve special thanks. Dr. Jennifer Schmidt was invaluable in the conduct of this study. In all phases of the work, from creating field manuals, training students, and developing instrument items, to analyzing data and writing reports, she played a central and essential role. Her careful attention to detail and her awareness of the importance of maintaining confidentiality made her the "keeper of the data." Throughout the years of this study, she has been a true leader and colleague, whose cooperative and caring spirit strengthened and benefited our team. Lisa Hoogstra also deserves our thanks. She has been our in-house editor and lead coder. Few errors escape her attention. Both of these individuals helped to create a single voice for this manuscript rather than a cacophony of conflicting voices.

There are many people to whom we owe a debt of gratitude for helping us in our work. We would like to thank the superintendents, principals, teachers, parents, and the wonderful students who allowed us to assess their lives repeatedly, asking what we are sure seemed like endless questions. The cooperation of the students and the schools was remarkable, and we are extremely grateful for their enthusiastic participation. A special thank you goes to each of the school coordinators who helped us contact students and organize our data collection efforts. In several of the sites, interviews were conducted with local businesses and community college personnel, and we are very appreciative of the time they gave us to learn more about how community resources can influence career formation.

We also recognize the important contributions of colleagues who worked with us on several different components of the study. We would like to thank Dr. Kevin Rathunde of the University of Utah, who spent several summers with us analyzing the family data. His analyses form the argument of Chapter 6. Dr. Kathryn Borman of the University of South Florida spent a summer instructing us on new ethnographic techniques. Her wisdom helped us to formulate our field observation protocols. The case materials used in several of the chapters were developed in consultation with her. During the pilot year, Dr. Samuel Whalen, Senior Research Associate at the Chapin Hall Center for Children, University of Chicago, spent considerable time and effort in training students in the ESM and in developing the COS. Dr. Jeylan Mortimer of the University of Minnesota provided us with her recent findings on adolescent work and offered helpful advice on the preparation of our instruments.

We also benefited from an advisory team of leading experts that provided useful advice, particularly at the initial stages of our work. We thank Dr. Lawrence Bobo of Harvard University, Dr. Ellen Greenberger of the University of California at Irvine, Dr. Kenneth Hoyt of the University of Kansas, and Dr. Alan Kerckoff of Duke University. The selection of our sample was guided in part by the thought-provoking suggestions of our advisory panel. The panel offered several new interpretations of the pilot data that were very useful for designing the full-scale study.

Several graduate students worked diligently in the field, including Anthony Berkley, Joseph Hermanowicz, Jeanine Hildreth, Lori Hill, Frederic Hutchinson, Jeffrey Link, Harriet Morgan, Douglas Novotny, Michael Karesh, Daniel McFarland, Lauren Song, and George Wimberly. A special thanks to Cheryl Sutherland, who helped organize the fieldwork, and Nicole Couture, who carefully monitored the quality of our data management system. Throughout the course of this work we also employed several undergraduate students. Special thanks go to Jennifer Pals and Sonya Geis. Several recent graduates from the University of Chicago and other institutions were also employed as interviewers, transcribers, and coders. We thank Barbara Camp, Steven Cass, Dr. Jennifer Clodius, Christopher Falls, Dr. Eleanor Hall, Michael Kamen, Rebecca Kamen, Hanh Lam, Marili Pooler, Miguel Remon, and Phillip Weiss. We frequently shared our ideas with the Sociology of Education Workshop at the University of Chicago and various graduate classes in education, human development, and sociology. We thank the individuals in these organizations for their helpful comments.

This project was housed at NORC, and the many people who work in that organization often helped in the preparation of our materials. Many individuals provided continuing assistance in the management of this enormous undertaking. We are especially thankful to Ms. Isabel Garcia, who kept track of hundreds of receipts from the field. We also were fortunate to have the services of Deborah Kulyukin, who, as the project administrator, made this project work even when we had research teams on both sides of the United States at the same time. We offer special thanks to Dr. Phillip DePoy, president of NORC, and Dr. Norman Bradburn, vice president for research at NORC, for their continued support throughout this project and for helping us find ways to follow our longitudinal sample into the next millennium.

We are indebted to the Alfred P. Sloan Foundation for selecting us to conduct this important work, and we are particularly indebted to our project director, Vice President Hirsh Cohen. Dr. Cohen kept us on track, nudged us along, and challenged our assumptions. He not only provided directional guidance but also listened carefully to the findings of our graduate students, whose stories from the field are reflected in the results presented in this book.

{ **Part One** }

ADOLESCENT VIEWS OF WORK

THE EVOLVING NATURE OF WORK

THIS BOOK describes how American teenagers develop attitudes and acquire skills to achieve their career goals and expectations. From 1992 to 1997, our group of researchers followed the progress of more than a thousand students from thirteen school districts across the United States. These students came from both wealthy communities in which a young person could expect to move without effort into professional occupations and inner-city neighborhoods rife with unemployment and crime. Study sites included a magnet high school famous for training some of the best scientific talent in the country as well as high schools having the goal of preparing teens for community college.

Students in these schools recorded at random moments their thoughts and feelings about what they did; filled out questionnaires concerning their families and school, their peer relationships, and career aspirations; and told us about their lives in extensive interviews. Their friends, parents, and teachers were also interviewed. A team of graduate students spent time becoming familiar with the schools and communities and spoke to teachers and school counselors about their schools' educational aims and their students' future prospects. The detailed results of these inquiries provide a window on the future of our society through which we can glimpse how adolescents today are preparing themselves for the lives they will lead in years to come.

The need for such knowledge is pressing because our ideas about educating young people are still shaped by tradition, whereas the realities they have to confront are changing rapidly. Families are not as stable as they were a generation ago, the information needed to thrive in our culture differs greatly from what was necessary forty years ago, and the kinds of jobs that will be available a decade from now are hard to imagine and even harder to predict. Yet families, schools, and the broader cultural environment that supposedly prepares youth for the future still operate with an outdated understanding of what it takes for a child to reach a productive adulthood. This book presents information crucial to updating our knowledge for a new age.

For most of human history, young people were not faced with deciding what to do when they grew up. Adult careers were few and predictable, and the division of labor was simple: women gathered, men hunted (Lee and DeVore 1975). "In a small group like the hunting band . . . all men learn the same activities, such as the skill in the hunt or in war" (Washburn and Lancaster 1975, 298). From the earliest years, children rehearsed the productive roles they would play as adults. At about the age of two, Inuit boys were taught to shoot ptarmigan with tiny bows while their sisters helped their mothers find berries and cure leather. In herding societies, small children first learned to tend goats, then sheep, and finally cattle. Most adolescents followed the path their parents did. The transition from childhood play to adult work did not require any change in attitudes, values, or knowledge; moreover, no questioning or complex decisions were involved.

The situation has changed dramatically in the past few centuries, and the change is accelerating. Young people no longer live in a world where adult productive roles are predictable. They have little idea of what they will actually do when they grow up, and they do not know which role models, if any, are valid. They do not know what expectations are realistic, what skills are useful, or what values are relevant to their future. Most youth of high school age—as many as 80 percent by some measures—say that they would like to be professionals; this expectation is bound to be unfulfilled for the great majority.

Now more than ever young people must learn the skills and values necessary to build successful careers. We have delegated to our schools the responsibility for preparing youth for the future, yet few would claim that schools are well equipped to prepare youth for realistic careers even in the present, let alone in the years to come. Somehow we must find better ways to inform youth about the kinds of opportunities that will be available to them when they grow up, as well as the habits, skills, and values they should acquire in preparation for those opportunities.

This book addresses three sets of questions pertaining to the preparation of young Americans for the world of work. The first set is the images and expectations that teenagers have about their future careers. What do young people mean by "work"? What activities do they think of as being like work as opposed to play? What images do they associate with things that are like work? How do they experience work-like activities? What kind of work do they imagine doing as a career? Do these concepts of work differ by age, gender, social class, and ethnicity, and if so, how? The manner in which young people learn to think about work will likely affect the enthusiasm and optimism with which they will face their occupational future. Positive associations with work activities will help students have positive expectations and eagerly seek work opportunities. Conversely, if they learn that work is boring and meaningless, a creative and motivated approach toward future career options will be harder to come by.

The second set of questions deals with what impact the social environment has on young people's career expectations and work ethic. How does the family help teenagers develop habits and values that will be useful in their careers? What is the role of schools in providing academic preparation and career counseling? How does the peer group—that network of interaction among friends and acquaintances—affect teenagers' views of the working world? There is no question that differences in child-rearing patterns have a crucial effect on adolescents' preparation for the opportunities and demands of the workplace. We all approach our careers with different amounts of useful knowledge, or "cultural capital," inherited from our families. We also invest different amounts of time and energy in the development of this capital: Some spend most of their time hanging out with friends, while others prefer to spend time studying or developing complex skills. The social milieu of family, schools, and friends greatly determines how cultural capital will be invested.

The third set of questions explores the actual work experiences teenagers have and their transition into occupational roles one or two years after graduation from high school. What kinds of jobs do young people take at different ages? What types of experiences do they report when working? Who enjoys work, and why? How do different jobs affect self-esteem? After high school, how is the passage to adult work status accomplished?

Because of the increasing pace of technological and social change, it is imperative to begin collecting hard facts about how young people prepare for a productive and engaged adult life. We are fortunate that this study allows us to answer, at least tentatively and provisionally, some of the questions necessary to an understanding of how teenagers find their way into the world of work.

Images and Expectations of Work

It could be argued that teenagers' values and attitudes about work are largely irrelevant to the determination of their future occupations. According to this perspective, a career is predetermined by social position and unfolds according to the opportunities afforded by the economic system. Individual values matter little in comparison with environmental realities. For instance, the elite who can afford to attend select private preparatory schools such as Phillips Academy or Andover will learn the social skills common to those at the top of the socioeconomic pyramid (Cookson and Persell 1985). After a stint in a prestigious college, these young people will start predictable careers in the banks and corporations where their families have prospered in the past. At the other end of the scale, the children of single-parent, poor families will attend schools where little learning may occur. Many of these young people can look forward to a future of unemployment, job insecurity, or menial work. Between these two extremes, the great majority of young people will find their places in the occupational structure according to family background and regardless of their individual values and beliefs about work.

Another determinant of occupational outcomes is the macroeconomic environment in which young people live. Respect for hard work makes little difference if the community cannot provide a job. A strong work ethic was of little help to the Irish farmers of the mid-1800s when the potato crop failed. The once-bustling industrial cities of northern England are now increasingly obsolete; in the 1990s the unemployment rate in Liverpool was 15 percent, and one out of three young men between the ages of eighteen and twenty-four was out of work (Morrison 1994). In the United States, unemployment rates vary dramatically by region and race, approaching 40 percent for young African-American males (U.S. Department of Commerce 1997).

The extreme consequences to society of environmental deterioration were documented by Turnbull (1972) among the Ik of Uganda. In that culture, the inability to produce enough food to support the population led to a general breakdown in values and social ties that approached the Hobbesian nightmare of a "war of all against all." Similar situations are all too familiar in Cambodia, Somalia, and parts of South America. Clearly, personal attitudes about work will make little difference if a society loses its capacity to produce. It also appears that people's attitudes affect both their own opportunities and society's ability to adapt to changing environmental conditions. Psychologists such as David McClelland (1961) have argued that individuals with a strong need to achieve will find better jobs and advance further occupationally. Moreover, societies in which the need for achievement is more widespread will be more economically viable because they will favor technological innovations and entrepreneurship.

The Role of a Work Ethic

The classic formulation of the effects of personal values on the economy was Max Weber's *The Protestant Ethic and the Spirit of Capitalism*, first published in 1922. Weber argued that communities that prospered in Europe and the Americas did so because, in adopting Protestantism, they had been compelled by the logic of their beliefs to place a high value on work and on material accomplishments. The Reformation's rejection of the Roman Catholic Church and its sacraments left Protestants without the comfort of absolution and the assurance that their souls would be saved for eternity. John Calvin found a solution: It was unlikely that God intended to damn for eternity a person to whom He had given success in this life. Prosperity became a sign of inclusion among God's elect, and hard work and wealth signified His grace. Weber claimed that this conflation of material and spiritual success enabled those parts of the world that adopted Protestantism to prosper. Because Protestants literally found salvation in their work, they worked harder than people from cultures in which salvation hinged on church-administered forgiveness.

The current status of the Protestant work ethic has been widely debated. It seems clear that the early spiritual fervor that prompted Puritans to toil toward proof of election is no longer a strong source of motivation, as Weber himself had recognized by the first third of the twentieth century. This does not mean, however, that the value of work has necessarily diminished in our society. Many surveys attest to the fact that we still consider work to be one of the most central concerns in our lives (W. E. Upjohn Institute 1973). Yankelovich (1981), for example, found that 84 percent of men and 77 percent of women said that they would continue to work even if a large inheritance made a job unnecessary.

However, the reasons that people value work seem to have changed considerably in the past few decades. Whereas the early Puritans may have seen work's dividends as a sign of divine goodwill, by World War II most people saw work almost exclusively as a means of material advancement and security. It was not until the 1960s that young people began to think of work as a way to achieve personal fulfillment (W. E. Upjohn Institute 1973; Featherman 1980). Recently, material concerns have become relatively more salient again, with an added twist: Young people value work because it provides the means to indulge expensive leisure and consumption habits.

The value attributed to work has changed over time. In the earliest stages of a hunting-and-gathering economy, work could scarcely be said to exist because it was so undifferentiated from the rest of life. A hunt was partly a necessity, partly a binding tradition, partly a social occasion and a religious ritual, as well as a sporting event where personal prowess could be established and expressed. Each activity seems to have had these multiple functions and could not be considered as exclusively work or play. In such situations it does not make much sense to speak of the value of work because it cannot be separated from the value of life as a whole.

Rhythms of work and leisure began to diverge after large-scale farming was introduced about ten thousand years ago. Although singing, ritual, and sociability were still strong elements of agricultural work, the new farming technology made forced labor possible and thus introduced the experience of work alienation. Still, however, farmers viewed their work as a natural necessity, an unquestioned part of living on a par with breathing and sleeping.

Another consequence of the agricultural revolution was that as it progressed it made the division of labor possible. Five thousand years ago, people living in the early cities could, for the first time in history, learn and practice different occupations. Young people could see streets full of millers, bakers, masons, weavers, teamsters, scribes, and priests, each using different skills and knowledge. A person's job began to define his or her identity. In choosing an occupation, a individual took on an entire way of life. Work became valued as an means of acquiring a sense of self as well as status in society.

The relationship between identity and occupation became even closer after the Reformation. As a result of the equation of worldly success with divine grace, work became a sign of the vocation that a person was called to fulfill within God's design. It was this spiritual value placed on work that is supposed to have made the Protestant work ethic such a powerful force for economic change (Weber 1930). The view of work as a calling further served to transform occupations from a natural necessity into a much more personalized and individualistic undertaking.

Until quite recently, however, free occupational choices were still relatively rare. Sons and daughters usually followed in their parents' footsteps. As recently as two centuries ago, laborers in many parts of the world were forbidden to leave the estate where they were born, and strict guild regulations excluded newcomers from practicing hereditary crafts. Although even today doctors are often doctors' children and farmers tend to be the children of farmers, explicit barriers have been drastically reduced. We have entered an era in which work has become a personal choice. Rather than drawing one's identity from the job, a job is now more and more perceived as an extension and a fulfillment of individual potential, and therein lies its main value.

As our attitudes toward work become increasingly reflective, and personal freedom and satisfaction in work become more essential, our increased awareness has resulted in an ever-harsher duality. On the one hand, work that is freely chosen and that allows personal growth and expression is valued more than ever; on the other, work that is obligatory and alienating is felt to be a burden. The fact that our historical attitudes toward work have changed as a result of technological transformations and an increased capacity to reflect on the human condition does not guarantee that this line of development will continue. Reversals are always possible. A severe economic downturn or a protracted technological stagnation following the exhaustion of natural resources may again change the value of work for our grandchildren or their descendants. If security and survival once again become paramount considerations, personal fulfillment on the job will have to yield to more immediate concerns. Still, if material progress continues on its present course, without major stoppages or reversals, the value of work will inevitably change in ways that are difficult to predict. If, for example, the development of nanotechnologies results in tiny electronic robots doing all the production and maintenance work traditionally done by humans, work might turn into purely mental operations or might refer to something that people do just for enjoyment.

In the meantime, however, a certain positive evaluation of work—a positive work ethic—seems to be necessary to socialize children into adulthood. Without it we might expect an increasingly inefficient, demoralized, and passive population unable to exploit opportunities. But upon what would such an ethic be based? We cannot assume that our children will grow up with the belief that work is a natural necessity. Nor is the idea of work as a vocation tenable any longer: Jobs change too quickly, employers feel diminished responsibility for their workers, and religious motivations are less common than they once were. Valuing work as a means of personal expression is a possibility, but one that at present is open to few. Most young people will be severely disappointed if they expect their jobs to be interesting and creative.

Intrinsic Rewards and the Experience of Work

Most people have no choice but to work. Adults spend roughly 40 percent of their waking lives working, not because they want to but because they must. Survival needs and self-respect dictate that they must invest the most substantial portion of their energy in productive activities. It is generally thought that because work is necessary it must always be alienating. Even the Bible tells us that Adam and Eve did not need to work so long as they were in God's favor but were cursed to do so after the Fall. It is an axiom of modern life that one works only to make enough money to pay the mortgage, put the children through school, take pleasant vacations, look forward to a secure old age, and perhaps leave some of it behind. "Thank God It's Friday!" has become a mantra for workers in all classes who can hardly wait for the weekend to begin.

Yet, despite all the prejudices we learn in our culture, men and women still say they would keep working even if they did not have to. It is also true that workaholism, or an excessive dedication to one's job, is just as real as alienation from work. Furthermore, a careful look at how adults feel in their everyday lives shows that they report being more satisfied, strong, creative, active, and happy when they are working than when they are not (Csikszentmihalyi and LeFevre 1989). How is this possible?

It is clear that, contrary to popular wisdom, most jobs are *intrinsically rewarding*. In other words, work usually provides the same kind of enjoyment as sports, games, music, or painting. This is true not only of elite professions such as surgery or management, where workaholism is most rampant, but also of such maligned jobs as assembly-line work or filing. True, most of the time when people work they do not realize that they feel better than when they are not working; they are too busy waiting for the day to be over so they can go home.

The reason work is intrinsically rewarding is that jobs are like games. They have clear goals and rules. They provide feedback about how well we are doing. They allow us to match our abilities with challenges. They make it possible for us to concentrate, to become so involved that the problems of daily life are no longer on our minds. They give us a sense of control together with a chance to forget ourselves temporarily. These are the most important reasons that people enjoy playing sports, music, or slot machines, and why many people feel compelled to work sixty hours a week or more. Work's game-like qualities make it less of a paradox that most jobs provide more rewarding experiences than many leisure activities in which one has no clue what to do or how well one is doing.

It appears that, as a species, we have evolved to make optimal use of two opposite sets of genetic instructions. On the one hand, we seek relaxation, comfort, and ease, which are ways to save energy and to recuperate. Our nervous system is built to derive pleasure from inertia. This is a conservative strategy that presumably helped our ancestors survive. On the other hand, we also enjoy exerting ourselves toward a goal, body and mind fully stretched to meet a difficult challenge. Both of these strategies are useful and necessary for survival. The first prompts individuals to seek contentment. The second ensures that they will be motivated to go beyond the status quo and explains how some can invest so much effort, and even risk their lives, in exploring the unknown, creating and discovering new ideas and technologies, and developing their skills to the utmost. No society can prosper when it no longer finds hard work rewarding.

Preparing Teenagers for Work

Most psychologists and sociologists would agree that learning to enjoy the intrinsic rewards of hard work is essential to successful development. In their classic survey of American youth, James Coleman and his co-authors wrote that one of the essential objectives our society should strive for is to

> develop in youth the *capabilities for engaging in intense concentrated involvement in an activity*. The most personally satisfying experiences, as well as the greatest achievements of man, arise from such concentration, not because of external pressure, but from an inner motivation which propels the person and focuses his or her attention. Whether the activity be scholarship, or performance (as in dramatics or athletics), or the creation of physical objects, or still another activity, it is the concentrated involvement itself, rather than the specific content, that is important. (Coleman et al. 1974, 4)

Despite the accuracy of this prescription, it does not seem that in the quarter century since it was given we have taken this message to heart. In fact, there may now be fewer opportunities for such intense involvement. Few children have the background to experience academic tasks with this kind of intensity. The more readily accessible activities, such as music, art, drama, and even athletics, are disappearing from the repertoires of more and more schools because of pedagogically uninformed budget decisions. Changing family structures and new residential areas formed in sprawling suburban communities contribute to teenagers' isolation. Agencies that once offered opportunities for engagement, such as the YMCA and the Boy Scouts, have lost touch somewhat with the youth culture and suffer from limited budgets and image problems.

On the other hand, passive leisure and consumption have increased among children and teens. Television absorbs the greatest part of our youths' psychic energy, and it rarely produces the kind of concentrated involvement that Coleman and his colleagues saw as necessary preparation for a happy and productive adulthood (Kubey and Csikszentmihalyi

1990). The other staples of youth culture, such as video games, listening to music, and mall cruising, are not much better.

Learning from Models

An essential ingredient for growing up with sensible attitudes toward work is the availability of adult models who can teach by example what a young person needs to do to become a productive member of society. Here, too, the current situation leaves much to be desired. As the psychologist Urie Bronfenbrenner pointed out long ago, our society is characterized by age segregation to an extent unparalleled in the past. Young people are isolated from adults and tend to congregate with their peers and thus are rarely exposed to role models who are involved in meaningful activities (Bronfenbrenner 1961). Compared with young people in other industrialized societies such as Italy or South Korea, American adolescents spend about twelve hours more per week in each other's company, for a total of about thirty-five hours a week. This is in addition to time spent at school, where despite the presence of a teacher the peer group culture also tends to prevail (Csikszentmihalyi and Larson 1984; Won 1989). When they are with peers, teenagers feel significantly happier but are also less able to concentrate and are less in control of their actions. It is the hedonistic values of the peer culture that are transmitted in such contexts, rather than more realistic prerequisites for a productive adulthood.

The fragmentation of the modern family makes it even more difficult for children to get the support and guidance they need. Bumpass and Sweet (1989) estimated that over half of the children born in the late 1970s would live in a single-parent family at some point before reaching the age of eighteen. Even for those lucky enough to have a father, it has been estimated that the average teenager now spends less than half an hour a week alone with his or her father (Csikszentmihalyi and Larson 1984). Moreover, half of this time alone with the father is spent watching television, a situation that does not readily lend itself to quality parent–child interaction. And no matter how "quality" that time may be, three to four minutes per day are not enough to transmit the knowledge, values, attitudes, and skills that adult males should pass on to their children.

Meaningful models outside the home are also in short supply. Up to the early years of the twentieth century most biographical articles in popular magazines described the lives of inventors, businessmen, statesmen, and religious figures. Today, however, the media mainly provide profiles of entertainers, athletes, and celebrities of doubtful standing as role models. When asked which public figure they would like to be like, teenagers usually mention athletes such as Michael Jordan, who are difficult to emulate for those who lack superior athletic ability. In the imagination of our children, the pendulum has clearly swung away from instrumental models involved in productive activity to expressive models admired for their entertainment value.

Such expressive role models are attractive not the least because our culture presents them as people who enjoy what they do and whose lives are well rewarded and free of care. While engineers and accountants are presumed to lead lives devoid of variety and excitement, rock singers and star athletes have it all. Our culture conspires to reinforce this image and to disguise the reality: how few media stars out of the innumerable aspirants actually succeed and how few of those who succeed lead happy and contented lives. Teenagers build shrines in their bedrooms to movie stars and singers in the hope that they too will become rich and famous; few surround themselves with the likenesses of successful engineers or accountants.

Learning from Expectations

Few things are as crucial in preparing a teenager for the future as parental expectations. However, there are two reasons why communicating expectations to children may be getting more difficult. The first emerges from the new forms of family life that are becoming endemic in our society. If it is true that up to half of our children will be living in single-parent or reconstituted families as they grow up, the question is, who will care enough to prepare them for the future? The task is difficult under ideal conditions, and the evidence suggests that nonbiological parents, even those with the best of intentions, are usually not as concerned with their children as are biological parents (Schneider and Coleman 1993).

The second reason is that rapidly changing economic and technological requirements are calling into question long-established values. Until just one or two generations ago, parents could feel that they were helping their children by teaching them to save and to work hard. Even wealthy families prided themselves on teaching their children self-reliance and moderation: to make their own beds, study at home, and go to sleep early. Today it is difficult to have unquestioning faith in these guidelines. When the entire economy rests on credit and on increasing consumption, what is the point of learning to be thrifty? When the most visibly successful people create wealth by manipulating phantom paper transactions, what is the point of learning a difficult craft? When it is so easy to turn on a television set or compact disc player, what is the point of learning art or music to amuse oneself? Even if the parents still have faith in these values, it is entirely possible that their children, full of the messages the media dispense with such abandon, will turn a deaf ear to their advice.

Learning Work Skills

Values, attitudes, and expectations are not the only things young people must learn to become productive adults. It is also important for them to learn what job opportunities will be available to them and to practice the appropriate skills to take advantage of these opportunities. In this respect, young people in the United States have some advantages over their contemporaries in comparable societies. American teenagers start part-time jobs earlier, and keep them for a much longer time, than is usual in other countries. The average urban high school student works about five to seven hours per week (less as a freshman, more as a senior), whereas in countries such as France, Italy, and Russia, the average is around one hour per week. Similarly, teenagers in the United States spend much more time doing chores around the house than is typical for their middle-class counterparts around the world (Third International Mathematics and Science Study, 1998).

Some believe that this early exposure to work experiences helps teens develop the responsibility, social skills, and disciplined habits that will be useful to them in their careers (Mortimer et al. 1995). Others argue that the low-level, routine jobs teens typically find, such as babysitting, delivering papers, or working in fast-food restaurants, only serve to disillusion them about future work prospects (Greenberger and Steinberg 1986).

The difficulty in teaching young people relevant occupational skills is that, to a degree unprecedented in American history, nobody quite knows what these skills might be. As the economy changes, skills can rapidly become obsolete and knowledge useless. In the seventeenth century, the Cheyenne in Minnesota built log cabins and cultivated fields, perfecting a fairly sophisticated farming technology. As white settlers began to press inland from the Atlantic seaboard, the Cheyenne were pushed onto the Great Plains, where their agricultural knowledge was useless and was forgotten in a few generations, except in myths. In American cities a hundred years ago, thousands of young blacksmiths found that their long training in forging and ironworking was no longer of any use as automobiles became the favored form of transportation.

Even such seemingly safe, state-of-the-art skills as computer programming, robotics, or genetic engineering may not exist in their present form by the time our children are ready to enter the labor force. While it is probably true that training in medicine, law, and the basic sciences will not change drastically, the number of openings in such fields will inevitably be few. Most young people have to think about more ephemeral options. Some trends in employment statistics are downright ominous: Among the fastest-growing job opportunities are those for armed guards, truckers, cleaning personnel, and fast-food and other service workers (U.S. Department of Labor 1995). Ironically, as production is becoming ever more technologically complex, the expansion of labor opportunities is greatest for the least-skilled and least-desirable positions.

Learning Meta-Skills for a Productive Adulthood

Given the difficulty of predicting which expectations are realistic and what skills will be useful to the next generation of productive adults, the best approach to preparing teenagers for the world of work may be to provide them with two essential learning strategies, the first of which is to learn the fundamental principles on which a scientifically based society rests. This must include more than the separate disciplines of mathematics, physics, chemistry, and biology. Young people must also acquire an integrated, systemic understanding of how processes interact in the real world (Murnane and Levy 1996). What are the consequences for the water table of neighboring communities of manufacturing microchips in Silicon Valley? What impact does the quality of life in one part of the world have on the quality of life elsewhere? What are the social costs of a culture's personal, consumer, and lifestyle choices over time? These issues have been treated as ethical problems in the past, but they are amenable to scientific analysis; if they are not treated as such, the next generations will grow up in dangerous ignorance. By "scientific" we do not mean simply the application of the existing hard sciences, but rather the generation of a new perspective that integrates the knowledge accumulated in the social sciences with the wisdom of the humanities.

The second strategy requires that young people develop an equally important set of meta-skills: the values and attitudes that will be necessary to meet the challenges of the future no matter what they turn out to be. Here we can do no better than to call for what James Coleman's team found so important: the opportunity for young people to experience intense concentration in any activity that requires skill and discipline, regardless of its content. Learning to get along with customers and co-workers in a fast-food franchise could be a useful experience, but unless the young worker feels enthusiasm and challenge in such an occupation, an essential ingredient for future growth will be missing. When Charles Darwin was a boy, he had a collection of insects in which he took great pride. One day, as he was walking in the woods a good distance from his home, he saw a large beetle, a specimen missing from his collection, hide under the bark of a tree. Darwin started stripping the bark to get at the creature, and to his delight he found not one, but three of the large beetles. Since he could not hold more than one in each hand, he popped the third in his mouth and ran all the way home with his catch. Examples of such involvement are typical in the childhood of most people who carve out creative and productive lives for themselves.

While not every child will develop interests as fascinating as Darwin's, without the enthusiasm that leads to intense, concentrated activity, a child will likely lack the perseverance to develop the skills and habits needed to face the future successfully. We may not know what jobs will be available to young people ten years from now; we do not know what knowledge they require to ensure they will have a productive, lifelong career. But to the extent that teenagers have had experiences that demand discipline, require the skillful use of mind and body, and give them a sense of responsibility and involvement with useful goals, we might expect the youth of today to be ready to face the challenges of tomorrow.

This book not only investigates what adolescents expect to do in the future, what their parents expect of them, how they are doing in school, and what their counselors do to help them step from the world of school into that of work; it also examines adolescents' beliefs, values, and experiences. We compare how teenagers feel in school with how they feel at home, at their part-time jobs, and in the company of their friends, to find out how well they are internalizing the values and habits they will need in the future. We investigate the impact of their peer groups on their values and expectations. We also look for similarities and variations across communities and schools to understand the range of educational strategies and opportunities available to young people.

Growing up to be a happy, productive adult gets more and more difficult as occupational roles become more vague and ephemeral with each passing decade. Young people can no longer count on a predictable future and cannot expect that a set of skills learned in school will be sufficient to ensure a comfortable career. For this reason we need to take a long look at the conditions that prepare youth for a changing, uncertain future, including the experiences provided by the family, the peer group, the school, and the community as a whole. Only by a painstaking analysis of how adolescents can draw useful knowledge and habits from these varied social networks can we understand what it will take to prepare our youth for the future. This book takes a modest first step in that direction.

{ 2 }

THE DESIGN OF THE STUDY: SAMPLE AND PROCEDURES

Lisa Hoogstra

T HE SLOAN STUDY of Youth and Social Development has collected data in four waves: 1992–1993, 1993–1994, 1994–1995, and 1996–1997. This book analyzes the first wave of data to understand how parents, friends, teachers, schools, and communities affect adolescent development and career formation. These data allow us to examine variations among students according to age, parent education, and other demographic characteristics, as well as in different school and community settings. How do young people of various ages and family backgrounds differ in their conceptions of work? What learning opportunities do families with different economic circumstances provide for their children with respect to work and careers? How do schools influence educational expectations and career formation? By reviewing cross-sectional results across age cohorts (students in grades six, eight, ten, or twelve) we can draw cautious inferences about patterns of developmental change in teenagers. Comparing students from different family, school, and community environments allows us to explore the effects of these contexts on students' quality of experience, their values and attitudes regarding work, their opportunities to learn about jobs, and their aspirations for the future. We can thus estimate the strength of relationships between adolescents' developing values, occupational images, capabilities, and expectations and the social and normative components of the worlds in which they live. Data from the study's subsequent waves will enable us to evaluate these inferences from the base year.

Sample Selection: Sites and Schools

We selected our sample in three stages: localities, public schools within each locality, and students within each school. We sought communities that differed significantly in economic condition and the makeup of the labor force, assuming that adolescent conceptions of work would likely be influenced by community resources. Therefore, we selected places that differed in level of urbanization, racial and ethnic composition, labor force characteristics, and economic stability. The twelve localities that we chose are widely distributed geographically and include urban, suburban, and rural communities, as well as two of the country's three largest urban populations. The sites differ in the degree to which their local economies are concentrated in manufacturing or service sectors as well as in their trend toward economic growth, stability, or decline over the 1990s. (See Appendix A for descriptions of the sites.)

To achieve a sample of adolescents whose racial and ethnic composition would be representative of the U.S. population from ages twelve to eighteen, and also to ensure racial and ethnic diversity across localities, we chose some sites in which certain racial or ethnic groups were overrepresented in comparison with the national population. In this way, fifteen potential communities in twelve states were identified. It was possible to make dual comparisons across these communities because the sites were similar in demographic characteristics but not in labor market characteristics. Final selections depended upon the cooperation of the schools within these potential sites.

Because we could study only a small number of schools at each locality, we limited our work to public middle schools and high schools. Once a site was selected, we contacted the local school superintendent and invited him or her to participate in the study. A small honorarium for each year of participation was offered to each school. Twelve area superintendents in nine states agreed to participate. We then contacted the high school principals and asked for their schools' participation in the study. Upon their consent, we also asked the principals to identify the major feeder elementary or middle schools of their respective high schools.

Our twelve selected sites included thirty-three schools (twenty middle schools and thirteen high schools; the names of all localities and schools have been changed). To increase the diversity of the high schools, we included two specialized schools: one a mathematics and science high school located in Bridgeway, the largest urban area that we studied, and the other, in Central City, a magnet language academy that the area superintendent requested we include in the study. The remaining high schools had comprehensive curricula. In the smaller localities, the high school selected for study was the only one in the community. In larger communities we chose high schools that drew from local attendance areas with adult populations that closely resembled the locality's total population with respect to race, ethnicity, and labor force participation. One or two of the principal feeder middle schools associated with each of the comprehensive high schools were also selected for study. Students from these middle schools comprised between 30 and 60 percent of the high schools' 1991 freshman classes.

School Types

The Curie School of Science in Bridgeway graduates a high proportion of students interested in careers in science or mathematics. Curie selects students citywide on the basis of rigorously competitive entrance requirements. It is substantially oversubscribed and therefore can choose students who have demonstrated high levels of academic ability. Curie's students come from all parts of Bridgeway. In contrast, the magnet school in Central City was created to assist in desegregation. It enrolls students on the basis of their test scores in seventh grade. These students enter the high school in eighth grade. The magnet school's curriculum offers a wide range of courses in languages, the humanities, science, and mathematics. A second high school in Central City was also selected and, like the remaining high schools in the study, is a more traditional comprehensive high school. The remaining high schools are located in communities we call Bayside, Betton, Cedar, Crystal Port, Del Vista, Feldnor, Forest Bluff, Maple Wood, Metawa, and Middle Brook.

On the basis of such indicators as family income, education level, and occupational status, the populations of Forest Bluff can be characterized as upper class; of Maple Wood and Middle Brook as upper middle class; of Feldnor and Del Vista as middle class; of Betton, Metawa, and Central City as lower middle class; of Cedar and Bayside as blue collar; and of Crystal Port as severely economically depressed. There is also substantial socioeconomic heterogeneity in the schools we sampled. For example, the correlation between parental education and community social class as described above is only .39 (p > .001), indicating that there is substantial socioeconomic variation within communities. Both of the specialized high schools draw students from a wide range of socioeconomic backgrounds. This heterogeneity is also characteristic of Feldnor's high school, where students come from extremely wealthy families as well as from families who receive public assistance.

The localities and schools provide complementary combinations of economic and demographic characteristics that allow systematic comparisons of one locality or school with another. For example, Cedar and Metawa are demographically similar in their racial composition and the proportions of the population whose education includes advanced degrees and who work in manufacturing or service jobs. However, Cedar is experiencing serious decline in manufacturing, whereas Metawa is relatively stable. By comparing the career formation process experienced by teenagers in Cedar and Metawa—young people who are otherwise similar in key psychological traits and socioeconomic circumstances—we can specify ways in which differences in economic opportunity affect such matters as beliefs about work and expectations for adult employment.

Student Selection

For each elementary or middle school and for each high school we selected two student samples: focal students and cohort students. The focal students were chosen from school-prepared enrollment lists of the students then in grades six, eight, ten, and twelve. Criteria for student selection at each grade level included gender, race, ethnicity, and level of academic performance, so as to be representative of students in the school. Based on student records, teachers rated each of these students as being academically successful, working at grade level, or having academic problems. These ratings allowed us to include high-, medium-, and low-ability students in the sample, from which we drew panels of twenty-four teenagers from each grade. The core longitudinal data on career formation to be used at later stages of our study were collected only for focal students.

Each cohort student sample represents one of the school grades in which a panel of focal students was enrolled. These cohort samples are not longitudinal panels and have been selected anew for each wave of data collection. Information collected from the cohort samples is used primarily to measure characteristics of the focal students' school environments and peer friendship networks. In addition, for certain cross-sectional analyses, data about the focal and cohort students can be combined. If a school grade enrolled no more than 150 students, the cohort sample consisted of the entire grade. Otherwise, a random sample of 150 students was chosen from the grade enrollment list, which was stratified like the focal panel, by gender, race, and achievement level.

We obtained a focal sample of 317 sixth graders, 347 eighth graders, 279 tenth graders, and 271 twelfth graders. The cohort sample includes 3,602 students: 487 in sixth grade, 837 in eighth grade, 1,352 in tenth grade, and 926 in twelfth grade. The cohort numbers are smaller in the middle school grades because at some sites more than the one or two sampled middle schools sent students to the sampled high schools. In addition, because the magnet schools drew from the entire community, it was not possible to isolate middle schools that sent students specifically to those schools.

The demographic characteristics of the focal and cohort base-year samples are strikingly similar (see Table 2.1). For example, the percentages of students who are Asian-American, African-American, and Native American are quite similar within the focal and cohort samples. In both samples males and females are represented equally, with only slightly

TABLE 2.1   DEMOGRAPHIC CHARACTERISTICS OF THE BASE-YEAR SAMPLE

	Focal		Cohort	
Total	1,215		3,604	
Gender				
Male	565	47%[a]	1,661	46%
Female	648	53%	1,870	52%
Grade level				
Middle school	664	55%	1,324	37%
High school	550	45%	2,278	63%
Race/ethnicity				
African-American	267	22%	664	18%
Asian	70	6%	266	7%
Hispanic	190	16%	342	9%
Native American	13	1%	53	1%
White	699	58%	1,916	53%
Parent education				
No college	284	23%	782	22%
Some college	82	7%	381	11%
Four-year college	193	16%	543	15%
Advanced degree	247	20%	739	21%
Community SES				
Poor	194	16%	173	5%
Working class	190	16%	847	24%
Middle class	458	38%	1,625	45%
Upper middle	256	21%	906	25%
Upper class	117	10%	53	1%

[a] Categorical percentages that do not total 100 are due to rounding. In the case of parent education and race/ethnicity, percentages that do not total 100 are due to missing data.

more females than males. Percentages of students whose parents have no college education, some college education, or bachelor's or advanced degrees are also similarly distributed within each of the samples.

Instruments

In the first year of the study, data were collected from the focal students by three methods: the Experience Sampling Method (ESM), an in-depth interview, and a battery of questionnaires. The questionnaires included the Teenage Life Questionnaire, a modification of instruments used in the National Education Longitudinal Study of 1988–1994 (NELS:1988–94); a Friends Sociometric Form (Friends Form), which provides information regarding the respondents' peer groups and certain other social ties; and a questionnaire called the Career Orientation Scale (COS), which measures the respondents' job knowledge and their occupational expectations. Cohort students completed the questionnaires but were not interviewed and did not participate in the ESM.

The Experience Sampling Method

The ESM is especially useful for eliciting the subjective experiences of persons interacting in their natural environments (Csikszentmihalyi and Larson 1987). It allows the respondent to report his or her specific activities as they occur at various times throughout the day and to describe the cognitive and affective states associated with the reported activities. ESM data make it possible to investigate how differences in location, time, and physical and social environments affect the quality of experience. For instance, our ESM data allow us to report whether adolescents are happier when they are doing paid work as opposed to studying, or when they are talking with friends as opposed to family members. Thus the ESM makes it possible to identify day-to-day continuities and discontinuities in adolescent lives as well as the range of adolescents' activities and experiences in socially diverse settings.

In this part of the study, preprogrammed wristwatches signaled the focal students randomly eight times each day at different intervals from 7:30 A.M. through 10:30 P.M. over the course of a normal week.[1] The predetermined schedule of signals was designed to be unpredictable to the students, thus providing a representative sample of each person's moods and activities for that day and week. Students were asked to fill out a one-page form each time they were signaled. The form took only a few minutes to complete. The respondent reported the activity in which he or she was engaged, his or her location, any other persons who were present, and his or her thoughts and feelings at the time.[2] Those students who responded to fewer than fifteen signals over the course of the week were dropped from analyses of ESM data because the data obtained for these students were unrepresentative of the students' experiences during the week.

In the study's first year, the focal respondents gave more than 28,000 ESM responses during the week of experience sampling, or about 30 responses per person. In most statistical analyses of ESM data, mean values are calculated for each person's responses to any given item, and these means, rather than the specific responses, are used in analysis. Thus, the unit of analysis is the person, not the response. For example, to test whether young men or young women reported greater happiness, the appropriate comparison is between the mean happiness scores of males and females.[3] (For examples of the growing body of literature on the reliability and validity of the ESM, see Csikszentmihalyi and Larson 1987; Hormuth 1986; Moneta and Csikszentmihalyi 1996. For other analyses of ESM data, see Csikszentmihalyi and Csikszentmihalyi 1988; Csikszentmihalyi and Larson 1984; Csikszentmihalyi, Rathunde, and Whalen 1993; Kubey and Csikszentmihalyi 1990; and Larson and Richards, 1994.)

The Teenage Life Questionnaire

The Teenage Life Questionnaire incorporates a series of questions from the eighth- and tenth-grade student questionnaires of the NELS:1988–94, a longitudinal survey based on a nationally representative sample of students and of their schools, parents, and teachers. The inclusion of questions from NELS:1988–94 enables us to make comparisons between the responses of students in our focal and cohort samples and those in a large-scale, national sample.

Like NELS:1988–94, the Teenage Life Questionnaire focuses on the determinants of academic performance, postsecondary educational plans, and occupational choices. The questionnaire provides information about the respondent's ethnic and religious background, family composition, the educational background and occupations of the parents and other adults in the household, family socioeconomic status, parental involvement, academic and social guidance, and family expectations for postsecondary schooling. Items regarding patterns of family decision making focus on the distribution of responsibility for career decisions, such as whether the respondent may drop out of school, take a paying job, enroll in certain courses, or apply to college. A significant portion of the questionnaire is devoted to students' school experiences and activities, including information about their present high school courses, homework, and extracurricular activities. The survey also includes questions about friends and role models, current work experiences, and the amount of time the student spends on various activities. (See Hafner, Ingels, Schneider, and Stevenson 1990 for a detailed description of the NELS:1988–94 design, purpose, and base-year results.)

The Friends Sociometric Form

The Friends Form asks respondents to list as many as fourteen friends and to indicate the nature of their relationship to each person listed, such as family member, neighbor, classmate, teammate, or church member (see Appendix B). The form also asks respondents to note how often they talk with the friends (from "every day" to "less than once a week") and which of them are "best friends." Finally, it asks respondents to identify which friends they go to for advice, which ones ask them for advice, and whether there are persons other than those already listed from whom they seek advice. Respondents typically listed parents, siblings, or teachers as persons they went to for advice, but some respondents included peers as well.

The Career Orientation Scale

In an effort to capture the complex nature of teenagers' thoughts about their future careers, we designed the Career Orientation Scale (COS) to measure respondents' knowledge of work and career aspirations. The COS also asks respondents to identify role models and to state why these persons are important to them. Other questions concern activities in which the respondent has been involved that relate to his or her long-term life goals. The COS also contains a leadership scale, an optimism scale, and a time line on which respondents are asked to indicate when they expect such key events in their lives as beginning full-time work, getting married, having a baby, and retiring to take place.

Interviews with Students

The first-year interview was designed to elicit detailed information about focal students' educational and career goals. Questions regarding aspects of each student's family life, friendships, and future expectations were also asked. Interviews typically lasted from thirty minutes to an hour. Questions about adult work focused on how respondents' life goals related to possible careers they envisioned. Interviewers also probed for respondents' degree of understanding of the type of adult work they would like to do, as well as their ability to recognize potential obstacles to attaining these goals. Respondents were also asked whether they had any occupational role models and what kind of work they would like to do if there were no constraints on their choice. If the respondent had been employed in the past year, either over the summer or during the school year, the interviewer asked about the nature of the job, the respondent's main reason for working, the job's relation to longer-term goals, what steps the respondent had taken to secure the job, and what steps would be necessary to find another job if one were to be sought in the next year or two.

Most interviews were conducted after the student had completed the week of experience sampling. In such cases the interviewer read through the student's completed ESM forms before the interview and selected three situations—one dealing with friends, one with future goals, and one with family—that could be related to the questions. At the beginning of each section of the interview, the interviewer showed the respondent his or her ESM form and asked that the situation be described in more detail and connected with broader aspects of the respondent's life. This procedure proved to be an effective means of eliciting detailed interview responses.

Interviews with Parents

Approximately one-third of the focal respondents' parents were interviewed. In the first year, we interviewed the parents of eight students in each school. The parent interviews sought information about family composition and structure, especially relationships between the parents and the students. Some of this information amplified data provided by the adolescent respondents when they completed the Teenage Life Questionnaire, while other topics extended coverage of the family context. Major topics were the job histories of adults in the household, the parents' evaluation of the quality of the student's schooling, the parents' educational and occupational expectations for the student, and the parents' thoughts about the student's plans after graduating from high school. (See Appendix B for a copy of the parent interview protocol.)

Interviews with School Staff and Supplemental School Information

Information about school contexts is crucial to an understanding of students' postsecondary expectations and career formation. We wanted specifically to learn how high school administrators, counselors, and teachers influence students' understandings or conceptualizations of work and postsecondary education. We were also interested in studying how curricular differences between and within schools lead to different occupationally relevant experiences for students, and how the participation of students in work-study programs influences their behaviors and attitudes toward work.

Administrator and Counselor Interviews

At every high school we interviewed an administrator (either the principal or a curriculum coordinator) and a counselor with primary responsibility for advising students about postgraduation opportunities such as college and careers. These interviews were designed to elicit information about the school's mission and the administrators' and counselors' expectations for the students. Questions included what these staff members expected students to do after graduation, what obstacles they thought these students might face, and what kinds of students they thought would most likely be particularly successful or unsuccessful after graduation. We also asked about students' families and their expectations for their children, the goals of the counseling program, and the school's role in guiding students toward their postsecondary educational and occupational objectives. School administrators were also asked for their opinions of special programs such as internships with local area businesses that were specifically designed to help students make the transition from school to work. Counselors were asked more detailed questions about contacts with colleges and how they helped students with their college applications. They were also asked to describe a recent counseling session and were questioned regarding the extent to which individual differences were taken into account when advising students.

Teacher Interviews

At least four teachers per grade were interviewed at each school. Teacher interviews provided information about what opportunities students had to discuss and explore the relationship between school and work and their plans for future education and adult employment. For example, we asked whether the teachers ever discussed with students how their current academic progress might affect their lives as adults and about the effect of part-time employment on students' school-work. Teachers were also asked whether they encouraged students to investigate particular fields in which they displayed a special interest or talent. Finally, we inquired into the role that teachers play in helping students to select a college or find employment both during high school and after graduation. In addition to this main line of questioning, we asked teachers to give us their views of the persons their students chose as role models and their assessment of the obstacles facing these students upon leaving school.

Supplemental Information About the School

The administrator, counselor, and teacher interviews were supplemented in several ways. From the schools, we received materials such as student/parent handbooks, curriculum guides (or courses of study), mission statements, school yearbooks, and lists of faculty. We also collected data about the school population and the opportunities available to students through a school questionnaire that was completed by either the principal or the curriculum coordinator. We observed student life and classroom activities and obtained verbatim records of conversations and activities that occurred during an hour spent in the guidance or the attendance office of each school. A photographic record of the high schools was assembled to help us gain familiarity with each school's environment and atmosphere; this record focused especially on common areas such as hallways, cafeterias, and main offices, as well as areas outside the schools where students typically congregated.

Data Collection

The main data collection activities began in October 1992 and continued through June 1993. Nine-member teams of interviewers visited each site

over an initial two-week period. The teams obtained student class schedules and learned of any special activities or events in the school during
the data collection period; scheduled the interviews and survey administration; oriented the focal students who wore watches for the ESM; administered the Teenage Life Questionnaire, COS, and Friends Form to the
focal and cohort students; collected such ethnographic data as school
documents, descriptions of special events, and interviewer observations;
and conducted interviews with focal students, parents, teachers (a minimum of four per grade), administrators (at least two per school), and
counselors (at least one per school).[4] At some sites teacher and parent
meetings were held to explain the design of the study and to answer questions about procedures. In those cases interviewers received special training to ensure that they did not reveal the exact nature of the study; if
known, such information might have biased the responses.

During the winter of 1993 we piloted telephone interviews with twelve
Metawa focal students who had graduated from high school in June 1992.
A review of the resulting data encouraged us to conduct telephone interviews in the winter of 1994 with those students who had graduated from
high school in June 1993. Information from these interviews provides the
basis for Chapter 9, in which we consider sources of differences in the experience of moving from high school to college, a key transition in career
formation.[5]

Base-Year Findings

In examining adolescents' preparation for the world of work, we focus on
several key questions and variables. How much formal education do
teens expect to obtain? How much time do they spend in productive activities such as studying and attending class versus time spent socializing
with friends or engaged in leisure activities? In turn, how do students' expectations and use of their time vary by age, gender, ethnicity, and parents' level of education?[6]

We found that the majority of students expect to reach high educational goals (see Table 2.2).[7] Overall, 80 percent of students expect to

complete four-year college or advanced degrees. These expectations are fairly consistent across grades. Most middle and high school students plan to receive four-year college or advanced degrees (87.9 percent of sixth graders, 84.5 percent of eighth graders, 73.4 percent of tenth graders, and 81.2 percent of twelfth graders). The younger students have the most ambitious educational aspirations; the percentage of students who expect to receive college or advanced degrees decreases from sixth to

TABLE 2.2   EDUCATIONAL EXPECTATIONS BY SELECTED DEMOGRAPHIC VARIABLES

	N	< Four-Year Degree	Four-Year Degree	Advanced Degree	χ^2
Grade					
Sixth	388	12.1[a]	30.2	57.7	
Eighth	697	15.5	32.1	52.4	
Tenth	930	26.6	31.8	41.6	
Twelfth	649	18.8	24.5	56.7	72.81***
Gender					
Male	1,144	22.0	31.6	46.3	
Female	1,519	17.8	28.6	53.6	14.67***
Race/ethnicity[b]					
Hispanic	304	31.3	27.6	41.1	
African-American	428	20.8	25.2	54.0	
White	1,686	17.6	32.2	50.2	
Asian	208	11.5	26.4	62.0	73.22***
Parent Education					
No college	833	30.9	30.9	38.3	
Some college	429	27.5	26.3	46.2	
Four-year college	554	12.1	39.7	48.2	
Advanced degree	726	6.3	23.4	70.2	263.68***
Percentages overall		20%	30%	50%	

*** p < .001

[a] Categorical percentages that do not total 100 are due to rounding. In the case of parent education and race/ethnicity, percentages that do not total to 100 are due to missing data.

[b] The base-year sample included a small number of Native American students. These students have been excluded from the present analysis because of the small size of this subsample.

tenth grade, but then slightly increases at twelfth grade. Female students (82.2 percent) are more likely than male students (77.9 percent) to expect to obtain higher degrees, and most students plan to obtain at least a bachelor of arts or science degree regardless of race or ethnicity (68.7 percent of Hispanic, 79.2 percent of African-American, 82.4 percent of Caucasian, and 88.4 percent of Asian students). Although higher parent education levels are associated with students' higher educational expectations, most students expect to receive bachelor's or advanced degrees regardless of their parents' educational level (69.2 percent of students whose parents have a high school diploma or less, 72.5 percent of students whose parents have completed some college work, 87.9 percent of students whose parents have a four-year college degree, and 93.6 percent of students whose parents have an advanced degree). Further, across all these variables—grade, gender, race or ethnicity, and parent education—more students expect to pursue advanced degrees than foresee completing their education with a bachelor's degree.

As students enter the higher grades, they tend to spend more time engaged in productive activities (see Table 2.3). Compared to sixth and eighth graders, tenth and twelfth graders spend more time on classwork, homework, and jobs. Older students also spend less time socializing and participating in active leisure, that is, extracurricular activities, games, sports, and hobbies. Sixth graders are more likely than eighth, tenth, and twelfth graders to socialize and engage in active leisure. Regardless of gender, race and ethnicity, or parents' level of education, students spend similar amounts of time engaged in productive activities. Outside of such productive time, socializing is more common among female students than male students and less common among Asian students than Caucasian, African-American, and Hispanic students. Female students also spend more time than males on maintenance, including personal care and household chores, while male students spend more time on leisure. Participation in leisure activities does differ across parent education levels. Students whose parents have advanced degrees are more likely to spend time in active leisure and less watching television and movies than students whose parents have a high school degree or less.

TABLE 2.3 MEAN TIME SPENT IN ACTIVITIES BY SELECTED DEMOGRAPHIC
VARIABLES*

	N	Productive	Social	Active Leisure	Passive Leisure	Maintenance	Other
Grade							
Sixth[a]	245	25.1[a]	10.64[a]	16.39[a]	17.52[a,b]	25.99[a]	4.36[a]
Eighth	243	24.35[a]	13.72[b,c]	11.31[b]	19.21[a]	26.2[a]	5.2[a]
Tenth	207	29.98[b]	15.95[b,c,d]	9.83[b]	15.45[b,c]	24.43[a]	4.36[a]
Twelfth	168	29.19[b]	17.89[c,d]	9.98[b]	12.78[c]	26.1[a]	4.06[a]
Gender							
Male	357	27.32[a]	10.83[a]	14.22[a]	18.26[a]	24.53[a]	4.84[a]
Female	506	26.53[a]	16.57[b]	10.67[b]	15.39[b]	26.51[b]	4.33[a]
Race/Ethnicity							
Asian	55	29.69[a]	9.99[a]	15.47[a]	14.57[a]	26.03[a,b]	4.25[a,b]
White	500	27.55[a]	14.95[b]	13.46[a]	15.71[a]	24.35[a]	3.99[a]
African-American	164	24.95[a]	14.57[b]	9.64[b]	17.6[a,b]	27.55[b]	5.69[b]
Hispanic	136	25.87[a]	12.17[a,b]	8.83[b]	19.48[b]	28.22[b]	5.33[a,b]
Parent Education							
High school or less	251	26.46[a]	13.68[a]	10.23[a]	18.11[a]	26.28[a]	5.23[a]
Some college	104	28.11[a]	15.96[a]	10.98[a,b]	16.57[a,b]	24.34[a]	4.04[a]
College degree	173	27.12[a]	14.4[a]	13.4[b,c]	15.48[a,b]	25.79[a]	3.8[a]
Advanced degree	224	26.67[a]	14.16[a]	14.36[c]	15.23[b]	25.07[a]	4.51[a]

* Means, within each category and activity type, with the same superscripts are not significantly
different from each other at the p < .05 level. For example, looking at the comparison of time spent in
productive activity by grade, the *a* superscript indicates that sixth and eighth graders differ from tenth
and twelfth graders, but do not differ from one another in time spent in productive activities. Likewise,
the *b* superscript indicates that tenth and twelfth graders do not differ from one another but do differ
from sixth and eighth graders in time spent in productive activities.

What emerges from these descriptive analyses is that most adolescents, regardless of background, have very high educational aspirations.
The overwhelming majority of adolescents expect to get at least a bachelor's degree, and half of these expect to earn some kind of advanced degree. They spend most of their time, particularly as they get older, on
productive activities such as schoolwork and jobs rather than socializing
and engaging in leisure activities. What these figures fail to tell us is how

adolescents experience these different activities. How focused, happy, and motivated are they when they are in class, at a paid job, or engaged in other work-like activities? How do adolescents' positive or negative experiences of work influence their ideas about the kind of work they will do as adults?

{ 3 }

ENVISIONING THE FUTURE

Kiyoshi Asakawa, Joel Hektner,
and Jennifer Schmidt, with the assistance
of Rustin Wolfe and Desiree Henshaw

How teenagers visualize their futures influences the kinds of adults they will grow up to be. As they move through school and try out part-time jobs, they begin, at first with little regard for reality but then with increasing earnestness, to fantasize about the kind of work they would like to spend their lives pursuing. Such expectations often act as self-fulfilling prophecies: A young person who sees few opportunities ahead is likely to settle for less than one who has more optimistic beliefs about the future. Some have argued that families, schools, books, and television programs encourage girls to pursue traditional female occupations, thereby restricting their ambitions (Vondracek 1995). Others have claimed that lower class families and communities tend to place minimal emphasis on academic and professional achievement (Hannah and Kahn 1989). But these stereotypes were not borne out by our study, nor were they present in the larger National Education Longitudinal Study of 1988–1994 (NELS:1988–94). Although differences still exist, it would appear that neither gender nor social class is as great an obstacle to occupational aspirations as each once was. Unrealistically high expectations can also be detrimental: Adolescents who expect too much may set themselves up for disappointment in adulthood.

Though we do not know what the "right" level of expectations might be, or even if there is such a thing, the extremes of hoping for too much or too little seem likely to limit optimal development in later years. In this chapter we first review what teenagers imagine their future careers will be like, both in terms of specific jobs and of the rewards they think such jobs will provide. Next we discuss how social circumstances influence the development of adolescents' occupational expectations as well as their exposure to job opportunities through high school. Finally, we review some of the students' more general dispositions toward the future, such as optimism and pessimism, which will be important in realizing these young people's dreams.

Expectations of the Future

To get an idea of what our teenagers expect of the future, we looked at several questions in the Teenage Life Questionnaire that centered on academic aspirations, future jobs, and more general lifestyle expectations (see Table 3.1). Responses suggest a rather positive, optimistic outlook. If anything, it appears that our teens may have expectations that are too high.

At least seven out of ten of these adolescents believe that they have a better than even chance of attending college, of having an enjoyable job that pays well, and of owning their own homes. They have less confidence that their lives will be better than their parents' lives. Overall, the pattern suggests that teenagers are sanguine about their future prospects, but they might be setting their sights a bit too high. Jobs that pay well and are enjoyable are a rarer commodity than our youth imagine. Presumably many of these teenagers' expectations will not be realized, and they may have to adjust their definition of jobs that are "well paying" and "enjoyable" to correspond to the realities of the labor market. Expectations about the future are bound to be influenced by demographic factors, such as race and ethnicity, gender, and age. A young woman born to a poor Hispanic family may anticipate a future that is very different from that of a Caucasian boy whose parents are highly educated. Therefore, it is essential to examine how various demographic characteristics relate to teenagers' views of the future.

Age Trends

Generally, older students are more confident of finishing high school and going on to college. This is understandable because in a certain sense they are the survivors. They have not dropped out of school and can be more confident that their educational expectations will be realized. In contrast to the pattern found for educational expectations, older students and younger students do not differ substantially in their general occupational expectations. It is true that older teens become more realistic about their chances of entering some occupations, such as professional

TABLE 3.1   EXPECTATIONS ABOUT THE FUTURE

Think about how you see your future, *What are the chances that you…* [a]	Percentage indicating chances are…		
	Very High	*High*	*50% or Less*
N = 2759			
Educational			
…will graduate from high school	77%	14%	9%
…will go to college	63%	20%	17%
Occupational			
…will have a job that pays well	42%	35%	23%
…will have an enjoyable job	45%	33%	22%
Living			
…will own a home	42%	32%	26%
…will have a better life than your parents	34%	30%	36%

[a] The question was originally scored on a 5-point scale, where 1 = chances are very low and 5 = chances are very high. Responses to a "50 %" chance, a "low" chance, and a "very low" chance were combined to form the category "50% or less."

athlete or entertainer, which younger students anticipate with great enthusiasm. Although younger teens expect to have enjoyable and high-
paying careers just as much as older teens do, they are less aware of the
need to obtain higher levels of education to begin most of their desired
careers. With age, then, we see a trend of increasing realism in educational and occupational expectations.

Gender Differences

Interestingly, boys and girls hold similar outlooks on their academic, occupational, and lifestyle chances. The only significant gender difference
can be found for "enjoyment": Girls expect their future jobs to be more
enjoyable than boys do. Despite the current inequalities in the labor market, girls believe that their chances of getting a well-paying job are as high
as boys' (Schneider and Schmidt 1996).

Racial and Ethnic Differences

Educational expectations do not vary significantly by students' ethnic
and racial background, with the exception of Hispanics, who have low
educational expectations: More of them expect only to complete high
school.[1] Occupational aspirations, also, do not vary by racial and ethnic
groups. Roughly the same proportion of Hispanic and African-American
students expect to have well-paying and enjoyable jobs as do Asian-American and Caucasian students. But the first two groups do not believe as
strongly as the latter two that they will end up owning their own homes.

Social Class Differences

Two measures are used to assess the social class of our respondents. The
first measure is the highest academic degree of either parent in the
household. While this gives an indication of economic resources at the

family level, it does not provide an index of the opportunities and re-sources available in the broader social context—the community. This concept is tapped in our second measure, which is based on the census characteristics of the neighborhoods in which students live. We refer to this as the Social Class of Community (SCC) indicator. Both of these measures show a pattern similar to that found for ethnic and racial trends. Students whose socioeconomic status and community social class backgrounds are more advantageous expect better educational outcomes but do not have more positive occupational expectations. Contrary to what previous studies suggest (Hannah and Kahn 1989), teenagers from the inner city and those whose parents failed to complete high school are as confident of having a well-paying and enjoyable job as those living in the affluent suburbs and whose parents have advanced graduate degrees.

Advantaged students are significantly more confident than less-ad-vantaged students that they will end up owning a home, but they are sig-nificantly *less* confident that their lives will be better than those of their parents. Teenagers from higher social classes are possibly becoming aware of a ceiling effect in terms of their own standard of living, while the less-advantaged teens see their opportunities relative to their origins in a more positive light. All in all, these results suggest two generalizations about current teens' views of their future. First, *the average teenager has quite positive educational, occupational, and lifestyle expectations.* Despite rapid technological changes, the tightening of economic opportunities, and the social malaise of the past decade, there is little indication of widespread worries about the future among these adolescents. Demo-graphic characteristics appear to play a smaller role in how teenagers view their futures than one might expect. Second, *neither age nor gender is asso-ciated with what teenagers expect their future to be like.* Boys and girls, twelve- and eighteen-year-olds, see very similar outcomes when they look ahead. Even ethnicity and social class make relatively little difference and do not seem to be related to how teens see their future jobs and lifestyle.

These teenagers seem to have a rather upbeat attitude toward their fu-ture prospects. But this same optimism may produce disillusionment later, when the expected professional jobs fail to materialize and many young adults have to settle for less desirable occupations. In our sample, lower-class minority teens are more likely to sense that they are unlikely to go as far in school as their more advantaged peers. Both groups, however, expect their jobs and lifestyles to give them similar rewards and satisfaction in their adult lives. Whether this belief in the equalizing effect of occupations is destined to be frustrated by later experience is an important question that bears on the future viability of our society.

Expectations for Specific Careers

The results of the study so far give us a general idea of the future occupational outlook of American students and their confidence about their desired goals of a college education, a good job, and a secure lifestyle. To gain a deeper understanding of the jobs that are likely to produce these intrinsic and extrinsic rewards, we need to take a more specific look at exactly which jobs these students expect to have. To determine what kinds of work and careers young people look forward to, we developed the Career Orientation Scale (COS). On this instrument, students respond to open-ended questions about what jobs they *expect to have* when they finish school, what jobs they *would like to have,* and whether they are doing anything now that is somehow related to the jobs they expect to have in the future.

One of the main differences between growing up at the end of the twentieth century and growing up in generations past is that young people now have less concrete experience with adult occupations. Moreover, the occupations to which they are likely to be most exposed—those of their parents—are probably not the ones they will have. Fewer than one in five teens in our sample expects to have an occupation in even the same general category as either parent's occupation.

The occupations adolescents do choose are changing so rapidly that even the best informed among them may have to adjust to a different job when they are ready to enter the labor market because of shifts in technology and demand (Schorr 1988; U.S. Department of Labor 1994). So it should be difficult for adolescents to visualize with any sense of clarity and confidence the jobs they will be doing in the future. Despite these structural uncertainties, it seems that many teenagers still have very specific ideas of the kinds of jobs they hope to have when they grow up.

Table 3.2 lists the twelve jobs students most frequently mentioned that they *expect* to have and *would like* to have. In addition to these most popular jobs, others are mentioned. For instance, out of 4,281 students who provided responses, 71 mentioned wanting to be cashiers and 35 said they expect to be truck drivers. The jobs listed in Table 3.2 suggest a mixture of realism and wishful thinking.

On the realistic side, the list includes few ballerinas or astronauts. By sixth grade, these students seem to have outgrown obviously romantic childhood fantasies. Yet more than 15 percent of this representative cross-section of teenagers expects to be either a doctor or a lawyer, when, according to the 1990 U.S. Census, the actual percentage of physicians and attorneys in the labor force is slightly over 1 percent. In fact, the list is top-heavy with professional jobs that will be obtained by very few among

TABLE 3.2 FREQUENTLY MENTIONED OCCUPATIONS

Occupation	Expect to Have		Would Like to Have	
	Rank	% of Sample	Rank	% of Sample
N		3,891		4,281
Doctor	1	10	2	11
Businessperson	2	7	5	6
Lawyer	3	7	3	9
Teacher	4	7	6	4
Athlete	5	6	1	15
Engineer	6	5	8	3
Nurse	7	4	9	3
Accountant, CPA	8	3	-	2
Psychologist	9	3	10	3
Architect	10	3	-	2
Musician, composer	-	2	7	4
Actor, director	-	2	4	6

this cohort of teenagers (Schneider and Stevenson 1999). It must come as a surprise to the American Psychological Association, for instance, that more than 3 percent of America's youth expects to enter its distinguished ranks. Much as one might like psychologists, three million of them would surely be too many. The ranking of expected jobs by these secondary school students corresponds quite closely to a ranking given by college freshmen in 1994 (Astin 1997). The only jobs that made the top ten for college students, but not for our respondents, were computer programmer and skilled tradesperson. Conversely, the two jobs included in Table 3.2 that were not mentioned by college students were athlete and psychologist.

Other evidence of the struggle between romantic and realistic ideas about the future can be seen by comparing desires and expectations. The job most wanted by teenagers is "athlete." The glamour of sports figures in our society is too enticing for youth to ignore. A smaller number, however, *expect* to become professional athletes than *would like* to: More than half of those who say that they would like to become athletes do not include "athlete" in their list of expected jobs. The trend for the job of "fashion model" is similar: Many more *would like* to have this job than *expect* to have it. These gender-stereotyped occupations—the strong athlete and the gorgeous model—still exert a strong pull on adolescents' imaginations. In fact, 12 percent of the younger students and 3 percent of the older ones expect to become professional athletes, when the actual frequency of athletes in the labor force is only seven in ten thousand. So, although the tenth and twelfth graders are more realistic than the sixth-graders, they still overestimate their chances for an athletic career about five hundred-fold.

Although many teens recognize the improbability of becoming professional athletes or fashion models, it appears that most believe they can achieve the more standard professional and semiprofessional careers that they overwhelmingly would like to have. The rankings for these professional jobs—doctor, lawyer, teacher, engineer, nurse, and psychologist—in terms of expectations and desires are similar. However, the types of occupations that young people consider pursuing are mediated by the sociodemographic factors of age, gender, race and ethnicity, and social class.

Age Trends

Many older teens are more realistic than their counterparts in middle school about their future jobs. Athlete, doctor, and lawyer are mentioned much less frequently by high school students than by younger teens, while accountant, businessperson, and engineer are mentioned more frequently. This pattern may also reflect an increasing awareness and knowledge about these jobs, which are not portrayed as frequently in the media and are therefore less well known to younger teens. Other widely recognized jobs, such as police officer, nurse, secretary, and teacher, are mentioned fairly evenly across the age groups.

Gender Differences

There is a clear pattern of gender-stereotyped expectations regarding occupations that have traditionally been dominated by one sex. Boys list "athlete," "engineer," and "police officer" significantly more often as expected jobs, while girls more often mention "nurse," "secretary," "social worker," and "teacher" as their future occupations. However, boys and girls tend to mention professional jobs such as "accountant" and "businessperson" with about the same frequency, and girls more often mention "doctor," "lawyer," and "psychologist" as expected jobs than do boys.[2]

Racial and Ethnic Differences

Adolescents from different racial and ethnic groups differ from one another in the types of jobs they expect to have as adults. African-Americans mention "athlete" and "lawyer" as expected jobs significantly more often than do other groups. The high visibility and success of African-American professional athletes is no doubt a strong influence on many of these teens. Hispanics, by contrast, mention "police officer" and "nurse" more often than do other teens. Finally, Asians mention "architect," "businessperson," "doctor," and "engineer" more frequently and mention "athlete," "lawyer," "police officer," and "teacher" less frequently than do other students.

Social Class Differences

With higher social class and levels of parental education, the number of students expecting to be doctors and musicians significantly increases, while the number anticipating occupations such as police officer or secretary decreases. Other differences appear to be more complex. "Athlete," for example, is mentioned most often by students from working class and middle class communities and by students whose parents have only a high school degree than by other students. "Lawyer" is mentioned in roughly equal numbers by all except those in lower class communities and those whose parents have less than a high school education; these students less frequently expect to become lawyers, perhaps reflecting an accurate assessment of their lack of opportunity. A similar pattern is seen with "psychologist," which is mentioned most frequently by students whose parents have college or advanced degrees and by students from upper and upper middle class communities.

Occupational Values

On the COS, students were also asked to indicate how important each of sixteen values was for the job they expected to have in the future. The value profile obtained may indicate, for example, whether teenagers who plan to become physicians prioritize different payoffs from their expected jobs than, say, those who plan business careers. Each of the ten most frequently mentioned occupations provides a distinctive set of rewards in the eyes of the teenagers who aspire to that particular job (see Table 3.3). Even more surprising is the fact that the value profile of each job corresponds quite closely to the cultural stereotypes for those occupations, suggesting that secondary school students have already internalized notions of the kinds of values each job is supposed to realize. They may not

TABLE 3.3 VALUES OF OCCUPATIONS

"How important are the following to you?" The ranks were obtained by standardizing scores first for each individual, then top and bottom ranks were ordered out of 16 possible values in response to the stem: "For the job you expect to have in the future," across the average standardized score for each value.

Expected Careers	Top 3 Values	Bottom 3 Values
	(Each of the three values in each career category is significantly higher than in rest of career categories)	*(Each of the three values in each career category is significantly lower than in rest of career categories)*
Doctor	1. Helping people	14. Having much free time
	2. Improving society	15. Expressing yourself
	3. Working with others	16. Working outdoors
Businessperson	1. Making money	14. Not having desk job
	2. Being ethical	15. Working with animals
	3. Having much free time	16. Working with your hands
Lawyer	1. Improving society	14. Not having desk job
	2. Helping people	15. Working outdoors
	3. Expressing yourself	16. Building, creating things
Teacher	1. Teaching others	14. Working with your hands
	2. Helping people	15. Being famous
	3. Expressing yourself	16. Making money
Athlete	1. Being famous	14. Being ethical
	2. Working outdoors	15. Improving society
	3. Working with your hands	16. Helping people
Engineer	1. Building, creating things	14. Teaching others
	2. Working with your hands	15. Working with animals
	3. Learning new things	16. Helping people
Nurse	1. Helping people	14. Teaching others
	2. Working with others	15. Building, creating things
	3. Improving society	16. Being famous
Accountant	1. Making money	14. Building, creating things
	2. Having much free time	15. Working outdoors
	3. Working with others	16. Not having desk job
Psychologist	1. Helping people	14. Being famous
	2. Working with people	15. Making money
	3. Teaching others	16. Working with your hands
Architect	1. Building, creating things	14. Working with animals
	2. Working with your hands	15. Teaching others
	3. Working outdoors	16. Helping people

be very clear about what a job entails, how much education it requires, or how much it pays, but they are quite clear about what values are more and less important in each job.

For instance, students who intend to be doctors list helping people, improving society, and working closely with others as the most signifi- cant factors in their career choice and list having free time, expressing themselves, and working outdoors as the least important. Aspiring busi- nesspersons and accountants turn out to give the highest relative rank to making money, while engineers-to-be and architects-to-be are much more interested in being able to build and create with their own hands. Those who expect to become teachers and psychologists end up giving top rankings to the same three values: teaching others, helping people, and working with people. Future doctors and nurses share the same three top values: helping people, working with people, and improving society. Those who expect to become professional athletes (and who tend to be younger males of disadvantaged backgrounds) are the outliers among the top ten expected occupations. What is relatively most important to them is being famous, working outdoors, and working with their hands—val- ues that tend to rank among the lowest for the other groups. Conversely, aspiring athletes rank lowest some of the other students' most cherished values: helping people, improving society, and being ethical.

If only the raw rankings had been used, the various career groups would not have been greatly different from one another. Most would have given the highest importance ratings to altruistic values such as helping people, improving society, and working with people. While it is good to know that American teenagers hold these values, the lack of differentia- tion provides little additional information. The raw scores were recoded twice into standard scores to establish the importance of the value rela- tive to the other fifteen values for each student and to establish the im- portance of the value for each student relative to other students.[3] The pattern in Table 3.3 suggests that while teenagers hold people-oriented values paramount as far as their intended careers are concerned, they are quite sensitive to fine discriminations in what different jobs might offer. For instance, those who want to become lawyers, accountants, and busi- nesspeople quite rightly do not mind having desk jobs; future teachers don't value money or fame highly; and aspiring doctors have already re-signed themselves to not having much free time.

Learning About Future Careers

We have suggested that young people today are not fully able to develop a firm occupational identity because they rarely have access to the kinds of jobs they are likely to hold. Whereas twelve-year-old children of farmers or artisans in the nineteenth century typically knew and had practical experience with what their parents did, the children of insurance salespeople or computer chip assemblers may have little idea and no direct experience of what their parents do for a living.

We coded students' descriptions of what they were learning about their expected adult job ("Learn"), the kind of skills they were practicing that were relevant to that job ("Do"), and the context within which this learning and experiencing occurred, namely, school, community, family, and friends. A learn-do score was calculated by adding these two subscales. Each subscale measure was given a value from 0 to 3. The higher the value, the more the student was learning about or practicing skills related to his or her intended job. For example, an adolescent who wants to be a nurse and does not list any learning experiences related to her future job would be given a "0" on the "Learn" subscale. Another student with the same career goal who says he learned first aid in health class is given a score of 1 on the same subscale. One who takes a course in biology is given a 2. One who trains to be a certified nurse's aide is given a 3 on learning. In terms of the "Do" subscale, a student who takes care of her little sister when she is sick would get a score of 1; one who works at a day care center would get a score of 2; and one who works at a hospital a score of 3. Adding these subscales, a student's total score on the learn-do scale could vary from 0 to 6.

Using this method, we find that although students may have very clear occupational goals, most have very little preparation, either in terms of knowledge or experience, for their intended adult careers. Some adolescents seem to take advantage of opportunities to learn about or to be involved in work they hope to have as adults. The majority, however, either do not have or choose not to take advantage of such opportunities. While we find no significant differences in learn-do scores by gender, there are significant differences in these scores by age, race and ethnicity, and socioeconomic status.

Age Trends

When learn-do scores are analyzed, it is clear that age, as expected, plays a significant role in the acquisition of knowledge and experience about one's intended career. For each succeeding grade level of the students, average learn-do scores are significantly higher than those of the preceding grade. The largest jump in scores occurs between the eighth and tenth grades, as might be expected given the vast amount of change and development that occurs in the lives of adolescents as they pass from junior high to high school. The increase in scores with grade level shows a robust pattern among all ethnic groups and social classes.

The pattern of responses suggests that practical work-related knowledge and experience is difficult to come by prior to about age fifteen. Sixth and eighth graders are rarely involved in anything resembling the adult version of the job they look forward to. At best, what they do can be construed as anticipatory socialization, or the practice of related roles and values that help the teenager acquire the actual occupational roles at a later time. By tenth, and especially twelfth, grade, the opportunities to practice real-life skills increase appreciably, although they are still relatively infrequent.

Table 3.4 gives a condensed summary of the kind of learning about adult jobs available to teenagers and the social environment in which such learning is likely to occur. Most career-related learning and experience starts at home. At first, children who wish to become lawyers may spend time arguing with their family, those who aspire to become models put on fashion shows with their siblings, and those who want to be mechanics learn from their parents how to fix their bikes. More often than not, the adult role-related behavior is first practiced in the context of spontaneous play. A family where future job skills can be learned and practiced provides numerous enriching experiences to a growing child.

When a child reaches eighth grade, the school starts to play an increasing role in such skills learning, although the opportunities offered by the family remain extremely important. Students who aspire to be doctors or scientists begin to see the relevance of biology and chemistry classes to their long-term aspirations. Those who wish to be teachers or writers may start to take English more seriously. The aspiring computer

TABLE 3.4 EXAMPLES OF RESPONSES FOR LEARNING AND DOING FOR THREE OCCUPATIONS BY GRADE

Grade[a]	Architect	Businessperson	Doctor
Grade 6	Play with Legos at home	Help aunt in store	Play doctor with toys
	Make models of dream house	Sort out sibs' money problems	Take care of sick family
Grade 8	Draw house plans	Work for dad	Take biology in school
	Ask mother (architect) how she does things	Sell tapes of my band	Read *Physicians' Desk Reference*
Grade 10	Design brick barbecue pit and friend's bedroom	Sound engineer and treasurer for small record company	Work as X-ray technician and receptionist
	Enter drawings in contests	President of Little Boys' Inc.	Take AP biology
Grade 12	Work on building projects	Manager of workplace	Work in hospital
	Take classes, internship in firm	Business intern program	Medical intern, work in doctor's office

[a] This table was compiled from several different student responses. Based on the responses we have, this table may be said to represent the *optimal developmental pattern.*

programmers focus on math and computer classes. Others practice in the school orchestra hoping for a career in music, write for the school paper to acquire journalistic skills, or do special science projects. At this stage of a young person's development, an impoverished curriculum and a limited choice of extracurricular activities will curtail learning about future vocational options.

The first opportunities to actually practice adult skills arise in mid-adolescence. Tenth graders typically describe these opportunities as occurring through a network of contacts in the family and the community. For instance, a cardiologist's child was taken to the hospital to see his mother perform a catheterization. An aspiring architect got a chance to work on designs for an addition to the family home, an artist-to-be was asked to design a neighbor's business cards, a future biologist joined a local biology club and became a member of his city's aquarium, and a computer enthusiast joined the computer section of the Boston Museum of Science. At this stage, personal contacts and community resources begin to play an increasingly important role in the career socialization of adolescents. A young person who has no exposure to people who can facilitate entry into the practice of a skill, or who lacks access to institutions that might facilitate learning, will be greatly disadvantaged in developing a future vocational identity.

By twelfth grade the adolescent on the verge of young adulthood may have the opportunity to join formal programs of transition into adult occupational roles. Internship programs are available, though rare, in accounting, architecture, business, drama, journalism, medicine, politics, and teaching, to name just a few mentioned by our students. Of course, there is also the even more frequent opportunity of serious part-time, summer, or even full-time work in line with one's ultimate career plans. Aspiring archaeologists go on summer digs, programmers work for computer firms, mechanics apprentice in local repair shops, and future managers start climbing the job ladder at shops in the mall or start their own shoestring companies. At this point of transition between adolescence and adulthood, it is the broader community that is mainly responsible for offering chances to learn and practice one's intended career. A severely depressed economy may not have jobs available for young people.

A community that lacks internship options restricts the kind of apprenticeship that may give a young person a realistic foreshadowing of the positives and negatives of an intended career.

Racial and Ethnic Differences

Race and ethnicity appear to be important factors influencing the amount of learning and experience students report. Caucasians and Asians generally report activities rated as more complex on our scales, while Hispanics and African-Americans have lower average learn-do scores. These differences reflect at least in part the differing opportunities and resources available to students in each of these groups.

Social Class Differences

The effects of differing levels of resources are more evident when we compare average learn-do scores of students from different socioeconomic backgrounds. Students whose parents have a high school education or less have lower learn-do scores than students whose parents have completed at least some college. A similar pattern emerges when we look at the average learn-do scores of students from each of the communities in our sample. Students from communities with the highest social-class characteristics report activities that have the highest average ratings on our scales; those from the most disadvantaged communities have the lowest average learn-do scores. The largest jump in learn-do scores occurs between the lowest levels of community social class and the next-lowest group, suggesting that even a small quantity of community resources is enough to make an important difference in the types of learning experiences available to students.

The difference a community makes becomes more pronounced as a student gets older. For sixth graders the most salient learn-do context is the family, but by eighth and tenth grade the school is the primary source of opportunities for career preparation. Finally, we see from the responses given by the high school seniors that community becomes the predominant setting. Overall, seniors more often report multiple contexts, suggesting that they are beginning to take advantage of a more integrated network, which includes family, school, and community.

The importance of social context in determining access to productive occupations can hardly be overestimated. First the family, then the neighborhood network, and finally the more formal community institutions will either provide an expanded menu of choices or restrict the range of knowledge available to young people. Not many youngsters have the chance to witness their parents performing difficult heart surgery, building a house, repairing a car, or defending a complicated legal case. But it is not just by acquiring concrete knowledge and skills that young people prepare for their lives as workers. Perhaps equally important is the kind of work-related motivations they develop and whether they look forward to the future with a general sense of optimism or pessimism.

Work-Related Motivations and Future Orientation

If one took a psychological, person-centered approach to explaining why some teenagers go on to have satisfying and productive adult jobs while others do not, one might say that what counts is how motivated the teenager is. A good attitude can overcome any obstacle. Certainly, there are people who achieve brilliantly despite all sorts of early handicaps. Linus Pauling, who was awarded the Nobel Prize in two different fields, grew up as the orphan son of a poor pharmacist in an undistinguished neighborhood of Portland, Oregon. Many businesspersons and politicians (recent American presidents such as Richard Nixon, Ronald Reagan, and Bill Clinton come to mind) attained great eminence after disadvantaged childhoods.

A more sociological approach, however, might suggest that many of the attitudes and motivations that help children overcome obstacles or hinder their pursuit of goals are themselves the product of social contexts. One acquires these orientations by interacting with parents, family, friends, teachers, and neighbors. It is easier to be optimistic and highly motivated if the people one knows are successful and secure. So despite occasional and highly dramatic exceptions—which in fact may not be exceptions at all, since one can usually find a positive social influence in the life histories of even the most deprived overachievers—one should expect that internalized attitudes will conform to one's social context. Our perspective involves an attempt to integrate the psychological and sociological approaches. Its fundamental assumption is that individual agency is no less real and important to career formation than external circumstances. Throughout this book we endeavor to show how personal attitudes, habits, and motivations interact with social conditions in a reciprocal process of career formation.

To gauge motivation we asked students what kind of rewards they seek when they are involved "in a difficult task" and what they feel about the future. Three main kinds of rewards emerged (see Table 3.5). The first of these are *intrinsic* rewards, those that are inherent in the activity itself. One pursues sports, music, art—and often even math,

TABLE 3.5 TASK MOTIVATION AND FUTURE ORIENTATION

	Mean	Standard Deviation
N = 4,518		
Task Motivation[a]		
Intrinsic	4.18	0.67
Extrinsic	4.10	0.69
Social	3.19	0.91
Future Orientation[b]		
Optimism	4.92	1.34
Openness to experience	5.30	1.33
Pessimism	2.62	1.12

[a] Range = 1–5

Intrinsic: mean of enjoying, being interested, learning something new, taking on a challenge, being good at it

Extrinsic: mean of secure job, making money, parents' expectations, not falling behind, learning something useful

Social: mean of impressing friends, doing better than others, getting respect

[b] Range = 1–7

Optimism: mean of powerful, confident.

Openness to experience: mean of curious, enthusiastic

Pessimism: mean of empty, angry, lonely, doubtful, worried

science, bricklaying, or farming—primarily because one enjoys the activity, is interested in it, and is driven by curiosity, not because of any rewards that will follow later. The second kind of rewards are *extrinsic,* which include the money or status one gets for doing something, whether one likes the work or not. Most jobs in our society are done primarily for extrinsic rather than intrinsic reasons. Finally, *social* rewards provide the third main source of motivation. These include doing things to achieve the respect and approval of other people. The pressure to conform is strong in most Eastern cultures, and it is perhaps stronger in the United States than we care to admit.

These three sources of reward often operate simultaneously. For example, surgeons get many intrinsic rewards from their jobs, but they also get a great deal of money and respect for what they do. In a healthy society, work should provide all three sorts of rewards. Intrinsic rewards are necessary so that a person feels that what he or she does is enjoyable and worth doing for its own sake, extrinsic rewards to satisfy the material requirements of life, and social rewards to fulfill our deep-seated desire for approval from our fellow beings. Interestingly, in our sample, extrinsic and intrinsic rewards are rated on average as almost equally important sources of motivation, while social rewards are held to be much less important.

Another way to look at the data is to focus on the proportion of students rating each source the highest: 52 percent of the sample rate intrinsic motives as more important than the other two, while 40 percent favor the extrinsic, and 8 percent the social ones. Older students are significantly more likely than younger ones to mention intrinsic rewards as motivating them, while girls are more likely than boys to respond to extrinsic rewards. Caucasians, compared to the other ethnic groups, are likely to favor intrinsic rewards over extrinsic ones. The same was true of students from more affluent communities and more educated families.

In a crude fashion this pattern reflects Maslow's (1971) contention that a hierarchy of needs underlies human motivation. When a person's livelihood and survival are threatened, the main goal is to stay alive and remain secure. If these more basic needs are satisfied, then one begins to respond to community pressure and the need to achieve self-esteem. If all the previous necessities are taken care of, one then begins to be motivated by the desire to explore and expand one's potentialities—the need for self-actualization. The extrinsic rewards satisfy the more basic needs, the social rewards the intermediate ones, and the intrinsic rewards correspond to the higher-order needs that begin to motivate a person when the more immediate necessities are taken care of.

The second set of findings concerns students' future orientation. Students were asked to indicate the extent to which different adjectives reflect their feelings about the future. Analysis of their responses again uncovered three main factors. The first, which we called *optimism,* includes the adjectives "powerful" and "confident." The second comprises a set of positive attitudes about the future, which seem to describe *openness to experience,* such as "curious" and "enthusiastic." The third factor, which brings together all the negative attitudes about the future such as "empty," "angry," and "doubtful," we called *pessimism.* As Table 3.5 shows, American teenagers' attitudes about the future are best characterized by openness to experience, then by optimism, and finally—much more weakly—by pessimism. These findings are certainly encouraging. They confirm the earlier patterns of results that show the great majority of these teenagers as having hopeful and positive attitudes about almost every aspect of the future. To a degree, the demographic analyses qualify this positive picture. We find significant differences on these measures by age, gender, race and ethnicity, and socioeconomic status.

Older students scored significantly lower than younger ones in terms of openness to experience and scored significantly higher on the pessimism scales.[4] Curiosity and enthusiasm appear to decline throughout adolescence, while doubts about the future tend to increase. Differences between boys and girls show the pervasive power of gender stereotypes. Boys score significantly higher on optimism; they attribute to themselves greater power and confidence than girls do. Girls, however, score significantly higher on openness to experience; that is, they look at the future with greater curiosity and enthusiasm.

Ethnic and social-class analyses suggest an unexpected pattern concerning attitude about the future. The less advantaged groups—African-Americans, ethnic minorities, and students whose communities rank lower in social class—tend to have the highest optimism scores.[5] The more

advantaged groups—Caucasians, those whose communities rank higher
in social class, and those whose parents have more education—have
higher scores on openness to experience.[6] Post hoc comparisons found
that Caucasian students and other more advantaged students—those
who ranked higher in terms of SCC and parent education—had significantly higher openness-to-experience scores than students from other
groups. Apparently, feelings of power and confidence are less important
to those who are already relatively secure in their futures, whereas curiosity and enthusiasm are more of a luxury for those who are more likely to
have to struggle to succeed. Pessimism seems to be tied more to cultural
than to socioeconomic conditions. Hispanic students look at the future
with significantly greater pessimism than do either the African-American or Caucasian students. Yet less advantaged students, as identified by
the social class of their communities or by their parents' level of education, are no more pessimistic than their more advantaged peers.

The overall impression, however, is that American teenagers enjoy un-
tempered optimism. Again and again the responses indicate high expectations for and enthusiasm about the future. Although such optimism is
encouraging, some of our findings may be cause for concern. Many
teenagers at present do not have the opportunities to engage in activities
relevant to the careers they wish for. Moreover, in light of the current proportions of professional occupations in the labor market, it seems inevitable that at least some of our participants have unrealistic
expectations.

The Good News

It is encouraging that close to seven out of ten of these American
teenagers expect to have jobs that pay well and that they will like. These
positive attitudes carry over to the specific jobs they look forward to
doing as adults. The similarity between the kinds of jobs teenagers expect
to have and the kinds of jobs they would like to have is very striking. Although these youths in general are rather isolated from learning about
and experiencing adult work, they are exposed to a wider range of oppor-

tunities for learning about and for practicing their intended vocations with each passing year.

Teenagers are quite clear about what values they expect to satisfy through different occupational choices. Their highest values are altruistic: helping others and improving society. At the same time, each job has a corresponding pattern of values that is quite specific to that occupation. Students who aspire to be veterinarians, for example, rank working with animals and working outdoors as much more important than do students anticipating any other career.

In terms of motivation, teenagers seem to be responsive to a great range of potential rewards in their environment. They report a good balance between strong extrinsic and intrinsic motivation. Teenagers' affective outlook seems to be very strong and positive. Fear, doubt, and other signs of alienation lag far behind expressions of enthusiasm and confidence in the future. Teens score almost twice as high on optimism and openness to experience as they do on pessimism.

Other positive findings concern the fact that gender, ethnicity, and social-class differences are not as strong as one might have feared. Boys and girls look forward to similarly fulfilling jobs, and their motivations and future orientations are more similar than they are different. Ethnicity and social status are associated with differences in educational expectations, but they make no discernible difference in terms of occupational expectations, and their effect on motivation and future expectation is mixed.

The Not-So-Good News

Are these teenagers being too optimistic? Do they expect too much from the future, and will they be disillusioned as working adults? Will the gender, ethnic, and social-class differences increase with time, resulting in a society that is deeply divided along occupational lines? There are signs in the data pointing toward these possibilities.

In the first place, it might be unrealistic for 70 percent of a given cohort to expect well-paying and enjoyable jobs. The "might" refers to the fact that "well-paying" and "enjoyable" are subjective concepts, so it might indeed be possible for the majority to find satisfying occupations even though objectively these are not well remunerated or interesting. But it is clearly unrealistic for most teenagers to expect professional careers in medicine, law, teaching, sciences, athletics, the arts, and so forth. Here we come up against the stubborn fact that most jobs in any known society so far have been in the less desirable extracting, manufacturing, and service sectors. No matter how far we have advanced technologically, it is still true that there are far more openings for miners, truckers, factory workers, and office clerks than there are in the glamorous professions that teenagers expect to enter. What will happen when these hopes fail to be realized? It is possible that these disillusioned young adults will reconcile themselves easily to their situation, realizing that their earlier expectations had been unrealistically inflated. Or they may nurse the failure of their dreams with increasing bitterness.

A disquieting sign in this direction is the fact that, with age, teenagers tend to express significantly less curiosity and enthusiasm about the future and more doubts and worries. It is unlikely that these findings reflect cohort rather than age effects, given the closeness of the four age groups studied and the gradual nature of the changes from sixth to twelfth grade. The trend most likely reflects the effects of the "reality check" that older adolescents are experiencing and the consequent doubts it engenders. A slight disillusionment concerning the future is probably a universal and inevitable feature of growing up and might not signal anything particularly wrong with the current state of society.

The other major source of concern relates to the differences in expectations and opportunities that teenagers from disadvantaged families and communities are likely to encounter. This, too, is a stubborn fact: Never has there been a society above the level of a hunting-gathering economy where equality of opportunity was achieved. Yet the American dream of personal success, that sustaining faith of our culture, is based on the belief that equality of opportunity, if not of attainment, can be realized. The results of our study point to some of the obstacles that make the playing field uneven for American adolescents.

Teenagers from disadvantaged sociocultural groups and historically oppressed minorities anticipate that they will be less likely to advance educationally than their more fortunate peers. Even though they expect the same occupational success, it should be clear that with less formal education, their chances of entering professional careers are severely diminished. If there is going to be a dangerous split in our society based on social class, as there has been in countless other societies, it will start in differential access to the education that makes social mobility possible. Family and community also influence the exposure a young person will have to knowledge and experiences relevant to learning the skills of his or her intended occupation. Some families provide role models, stimulation, support, and practical contexts in which children can begin to engage, often playfully and tentatively, in the roles that correspond to their career choices. Other families, either because the adults have not achieved success in careers or because of too little time and too many financial pressures, do not provide these opportunities.

By mid-adolescence, the network of contacts available in the community becomes an important factor in increasing some students' opportunities and depressing the chances of others. If the extended family, friends, neighborhood acquaintances, libraries, museums, informal agencies, and businesses can offer teenagers opportunities to learn and practice many skills relevant to adult roles, the transition to a productive career will be much enhanced. On the other hand, if the community lives in fear and poverty, has no exciting schools, libraries, and museums, and is isolated from the vital centers of society, it will be difficult for teenagers to develop realistic ideas about the future and to learn skills that might open up avenues of social mobility in the future.

These differences continue into late adolescence. More advantaged youth—those from Caucasian backgrounds who live in affluent communities and whose parents are highly educated—will know how to find internships, specialized training, summer employment, and other opportunities to begin practicing the skills of the occupations to which they aspire. They will be helped by the network of knowledge and contacts that constitutes the "cultural capital" of their family and social class. In contrast, youth from disadvantaged backgrounds are isolated from such networks, and without extensive remedial help they will continue to lack the choices so readily available to the others.

Surprisingly, however, these handicaps do not seem to have a negative effect on the attitudes about the future of disadvantaged youth. If anything, perhaps as a way of overcoming their disadvantages, these teenagers feel more powerful and confident when surveying the future than do their more advantaged peers. It may be said that the more affluent and educated youth have their own problems; they know that having started at the top, the most likely route of mobility is downward. Perhaps as a result, they are less optimistic about the future. In terms of openness to experience, the more advantaged students seem to have the edge, and this characteristic may be the most important in rapidly changing times. Probably the most important suggestions about improving teenagers' transition to a productive adulthood that have been raised by the findings of our study concern the support systems necessary for successful socialization into adult work roles. Much could be done to improve the learning and practice of adult roles for a wider range of youth.

{ **Part Two** }

LEARNING TO WORK

{ 4 }

IMAGES OF WORK AND PLAY

Jennifer Schmidt and Grant Rich,
with the assistance of Eleni Makris

T HROUGHOUT LIFE, most people move through a sequence of socially ordered transitions: from home to school, perhaps to college,
and then to a job. The choice of a career is one step in this process. More
and more this choice is heavily influenced by other decisions and is open
to change. According to Super (1957, 1976), one's concept of vocation typically undergoes at least four major realignments, and it has become clear
that radical career shifts are increasingly frequent (Havighurst 1982;
Jepsen 1984; Osipow 1986). An adolescent's career expectations are therefore no longer a very good indication of what work he or she will actually
do. The results presented in Chapter 3, while interesting, may have little
diagnostic value. They provide excellent insights into what careers
teenagers expect to pursue, but whether these expectations will be fulfilled is doubtful. Perhaps a more important question is: What general attitudes do today's adolescents have about work? Do they show any trace
of that work ethic that supposedly motivated previous adult generations?
If an adolescent's job expectations are no longer likely to predict future

reality, perhaps a more extensive assessment of how children feel about work will provide a more useful barometer of occupational socialization.

A young person's attitude toward a future career begins to take shape as he or she learns to associate the concept of work with specific activities and with certain experiential states, either positive or negative. If the concept of work becomes associated in the child's mind with negative experiences such as boredom or sadness, the child is likely to grow up taking for granted that work is something to be avoided. Whether or not teenagers develop a positive work ethic depends to a large extent on how they learn to think of work—what they mean by the term and how they feel when what they do is thought of as working.

Little is known about how such fundamental attitudes toward work are established in children's minds. We do know that by adulthood most people in our society experience a significant disjunction between work and play or leisure. Many jobs are avoided because they are too much like work, while other jobs are preferred because they provide more leisure opportunities. The career theorist Edward Bordin recognized more than fifty years ago that the difficulty students encountered in making career decisions was partially a result of their reluctance to commit themselves to jobs that might lead to boring or constricting lives (Bordin 1943). This tendency has hardly decreased; if anything, in the years since Bordin made this observation we have come to see work in increasingly negative terms, whereas leisure is ever more cherished. Yet a society where work is seen as necessary but undesirable, and play as useless but enticing, is likely to have serious trouble maintaining a productive and positive quality of life (Bordin 1990; Csikszentmihalyi 1975; Savickas 1995; Savickas and Lent 1994).

One of the first things we want to know about the development of career attitudes is how young people learn to perceive work and play in their own lives. What kinds of activities do teenagers call work and what do they call play? What is the quality of experience in activities that are work-like versus play-like? How do adolescents feel when they identify what they do as work rather than play? Are there demographic and social class differences in the development of attitudes toward work and play?

And how do teenagers who see what they do as more work-like differ from their peers who have a more playful orientation?

What's Work, What's Play?

We start our analysis of time spent in work and play by reviewing the 28,193 responses to the Experience Sampling Method (ESM) that 866 focal teenagers gave during the week in which they participated in the study. Each time their watches signaled, students recorded the specific activity in which they were engaged and marked on their response sheets whether they felt that whatever they were doing was "more like work," "more like play," "like both work and play," or "like neither work nor play." Students who report activities as being like both work and play are hereafter described as having a balanced response to such activities. Students who identify activities as being like neither work nor play are characterized as having been in a disengaged state.

The overall response pattern shows that adolescents spend about equal amounts of time in activities they perceive to be work-like (29 percent) and play-like (28 percent) (see Table 4.1). They spend slightly more time in activities that they feel are neither like work nor like play (34 percent). Adolescents describe only a small but, as we shall see later, important portion of their daily activities as being like both work and play (9 percent). Generally speaking, we can say that teenagers spend roughly equal amounts of time in activities they perceive as work, as play, and as neither of those.

Age differences in the percentage of time spent in these four activity types, although statistically significant, are not surprising. As students move through school they are increasingly likely to see activities as being like work and are less likely to identify them as being like neither work nor play. Gender differences are slight: In comparison with boys, girls say about 3 percent less often than boys that what they do is like play,[1] and 3 percent more often that they feel disengaged from the activity (that is, that they feel it is like neither work nor play).[2]

Differences according to ethnic backgrounds are slightly greater. Caucasians say that what they do is like play 31 percent of the time, Asians 27
percent, Hispanics 24 percent, and African-Americans 23 percent.[3]
Larger differences emerge when we examined time spent in the disengaged state. Hispanics and African-Americans report being disengaged
about 40 percent of the time, whereas this percentage for Asians and
Caucasians is just a little over 30 percent.[4]

Socioeconomic class, indexed by parent education, shows a trend that
is not surprising in light of the findings reported in Chapter 3. Children

TABLE 4.1   PERCENTAGE OF TIME SPENT IN WORK, PLAY, BOTH, AND NEITHER

	N	% Work	% Play	% Both	% Neither
Total	863	28.52	28.00	9.01	34.47
Gender					
Male	356	29.44	29.62	8.21	32.73
Female	507	27.87	26.87	9.57	35.70
Race/ethnicity					
Asian	55	31.40	26.77	11.17	31.53
Hispanic	134	29.14	23.91	7.50	40.64
African-American	162	29.31	22.82	10.96	38.41
Caucasian	503	27.85	30.86	10.05	31.86
Native American[a]	9	23.93	29.92	10.79	35.35
Grade in school					
Sixth	246	28.27	28.08	8.80	34.85
Eighth	243	25.72	27.15	8.68	38.45
Tenth	206	30.71	27.06	8.78	33.44
Twelfth	168	30.22	30.28	10.07	29.43
Parent education					
< High school	68	27.44	30.38	8.68	33.50
High school graduate	196	28.17	26.70	8.70	36.43
College graduate	128	29.70	28.57	9.65	32.09
Master's	93	26.34	34.63	9.51	29.52
Ph.D.	77	27.64	35.86	9.82	26.68

[a] Although represented in the table, data from the Native Americans in the sample
were not used for statistical comparisons by ethnicity because of small cell sizes.

of parents who have earned master's or doctoral degrees see what they do as being like play about 35 percent of the time, while children of parents whose highest degree is a B.A. or less see what they do as being like play only 26 percent of the time.[5] The reverse pattern holds for the state of disengagement. Parental education is not, however, associated with differences in the amount of time spent doing work-like activities or activities experienced as a balance of work and play.

To summarize these trends, it seems that Caucasian boys from better-educated families see their lives as being more playful, while minority girls from lower socioeconomic classes tend to see what they do as being neither work-like nor play-like. One might expect that social-class differences would affect the perception of life as being work-like, with less-privileged children seeing what they do as less voluntary and more like a job. We find instead a complementary pattern: The more economically privileged children see what they do as more like play. Apparently, favorable social conditions do not reduce the sense that one must work, but they do increase the likelihood that one will feel as if one were playing. The typical condition of the less economically privileged is not work but the indeterminate condition that is neither work nor play. Being in a socially disadvantaged position does not make a teenager look at the world as being work-like, but it seems to produce the somewhat disengaged, perhaps alienated stance in which activity is neither productive nor enjoyable.

Work-like and Play-like Activities

What kinds of things do teenagers do when they say that they are working? The types of activity that respondents identified as work-like demonstrate that these young people have developed highly stereotyped understandings of what is meant by work. School and jobs are almost always perceived as being like work, whereas leisure activities, especially passive ones such as watching television and listening to music, are seen to be like play and very rarely like work. The state of disengagement is reported most often for maintenance activities, such as relaxing, eating, bathing, and other forms of personal care, which are neither particularly productive nor fun; they fill time. If this is true, a person who feels that much of his or her time is spent in this disengaged state may feel more alienated from peers and society than someone who experiences most of life as work.

Perhaps the most interesting activities to adolescents are those that are perceived almost equally as being like work and like play.[6] Extracurricular school activities such as orchestra, debate, or athletics and the independent pursuit of art, games, or hobbies produce such balanced responses in many students. That which is seen to be both work-like and play-like may be experienced as both useful and enjoyable. With enough experiences of this kind, a young person can seek a career with a better-integrated and more optimistic attitude.

How Does It Feel to Work and to Play?

The quality of experience while doing work-like activities—how one feels—will determine whether a teenager will look forward to a future occupation with anticipation or with dread. Figure 4.1 shows how four central dimensions of experience—self-esteem, salience, positive affect, and enjoyment—vary depending on whether adolescents perceive what they are doing as work or play.

Self-esteem is defined as feeling good about oneself, feeling in control of the situation, being successful at what one is doing, living up to one's expectations, and living up to the expectations of others. *Salience* consists of three items: challenge, importance to self, and importance to the future.[7] *Positive affect* measures teenagers' sense of feeling happy, sociable, proud, and relaxed.[8] Finally, *enjoyment* was measured by a single item.[9]

The results suggest that adolescents not only define work in a rather stereotyped way but also experience work according to a standard societal view: as arduous labor that is important for the future but provides little pleasure. Nor does such work appear to be particularly relevant to students' self-esteem. The opposite is true when activity is seen as being like play: It is pleasurable but unimportant. When activity is seen as like both work and play, the experience tends to be positive on all counts; self-esteem is highest in such activities.[10] When an activity is identified as being

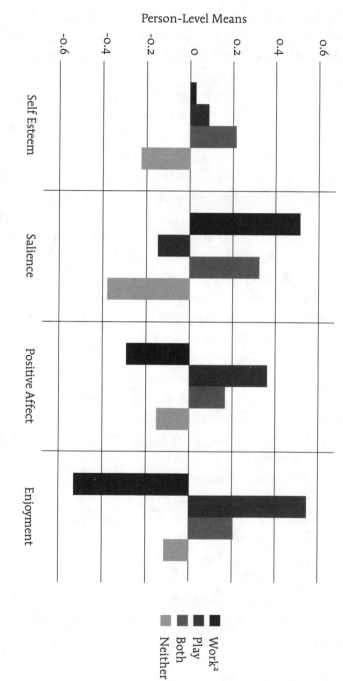

FIGURE 4.1 OVERALL QUALITY OF EXPERIENCE IN WORK AND PLAY

a. The raw scores on these four factors were then transformed into standardized scores at the person level (with each student's mean score being set to 0, with a standard deviation of 1) so as to compensate for individual differences in scale use and response style.

like neither work nor play, the quality of the experience is always significantly more negative than in any of the other three conditions.

A somewhat discouraging pattern emerges when the quality of work experience is analyzed by age. The older teenagers grow, the less positive they feel when what they do is work-like. When engaged in work-like activities, twelfth graders enjoy the activity less than sixth graders.[11] Affective dislike of work appears to be firmly established by sixth grade, and this dislike increases through the end of twelfth grade.

No gender differences were found in how it feels to work. Despite the fact that adult men and women tend to enter different occupations, the evidence suggests that girls aspire to similar or even more prestigious careers than those to which boys typically aspire (Garrison 1979; Dunne, Elliot, and Carlsen 1981; Herr and Enderlein 1976). The data presented here further suggest that the emotional coding of what work means to the individual student is similar for both genders. If there are differences in the experience of work, presumably they develop after high school, perhaps when young women must navigate between career and family and fight gender discrimination in the workplace. Although no gender differences appear in the perception of work, they do show up in the perception of other categories: play, activities that are like both work and play, and activities that are like neither work nor play. In play, for example, girls report significantly less concentration, less competitiveness, and less challenge than boys.[12] This pattern suggests that boys take play-like activities more seriously than girls do.

In activities perceived as neither like work nor like play, girls report significantly lower affect, greater concentration, less cooperation, and greater (but still low) challenge than boys.[13] Apparently, when the external structure that characterizes work-like and play-like activities is lacking, girls feel that they must make a greater psychic effort than do boys. In an activity perceived as like both work and play, girls report significantly less often than boys that they wish to be doing that activity,[14] an important finding if, as we suggest, it is in such balanced experiences of activity that teenagers might reconcile the split between productive and leisure activities.

Ethnic background and socioeconomic status account for surprisingly strong differences in the quality of work experience. Contrary to what one would expect, the less-privileged minorities (Hispanics, African-Americans) and those from less-educated families report more positive experiences in situations they define as work. For instance, the average score on self-esteem for Caucasians in work was -.05; for Asians it was .13, for Hispanics, .15, and for African-Americans, .17.[15] Respondents who ranked lowest in socioeconomic status in terms of parental education had the highest levels of self-esteem (.18), while those from the most educated families had the lowest self-esteem (-.19).[16]

These differences cannot be attributed to some students' inflating their reports because the analyses are based on z-scores, that is, deviation from the individual's own average self-esteem ratings for the week. So when Caucasians do something they identify as work, they rate their self-esteem below their own mean for the week; when African-Americans do the same, they report higher levels of self-esteem than they usually do. The experience of play is to a certain degree the mirror image of this pattern. Caucasian teenagers not only report that what they do is like play more often, but they enjoy themselves more and are happier when they report that what they are doing is like play.[17]

What Activities Are Perceived As Like Both Work and Play?

Adolescents spend nearly equal amounts of time in activities perceived as work-like, play-like, and like neither work nor play. A small yet significant portion of their time (9 percent) is spent in activities perceived as both work-like and play-like. When a work-like activity is accompanied by the perception that it is also play-like, the activity may increase a teenager's self-esteem, positive affect, salience, and enjoyment, thereby providing a needed bridge between things that must be done and things that one would like to do. In this sense, activities that invite such balanced responses might provide the most important training for the merging of personal commitment with social needs advocated by most theories of vocational development (e.g., Bordin 1990).

Activities that are described as being like both work and play comprised in equal measure schoolwork (25 percent)—usually of an active sort such as participating in discussion, taking notes, doing homework or lab work—and extracurricular activities such as arts, hobbies, games, and sports (24 percent). Almost equal amounts of such time are spent in maintenance activities (15 percent) and socializing activities (13 percent). Again, maintenance activities include eating a meal and relaxing, while socializing activities include talking with friends and family, going to the mall, chatting on the phone, or attending a party. In addition, 8 percent of activities producing this balanced response involve paid work. These activities seem to be fairly structured and more goal-oriented, having clear beginning and end points. Most of such work-and-play activities take place in school (46 percent) and in the home (34 percent). If work-and-play activities require more discipline and interaction, then it makes sense that they are performed in the more structured and social contexts of school and home rather than in the streets or the malls.

There are no statistically significant differences in the time spent in such activities by gender, race and ethnicity, grade, or socioeconomic status. All adolescents, then, seem to perceive similar proportions of their everyday activities as being like both work and play. Although teenagers spend only about 9 percent of their time in activities they report as being like a balance of work and play, these activities are unusually productive, self-affirming, and skill-building and hence merit close examination. What little time these students spend experiencing activities as a balance of work and play is uniformly characterized by high levels of self-esteem, positive affect, salience, and enjoyment (see Figure 4.1). In fact, all but one of the variables examined were positive and above the weekly mean for this condition. The only variable that was found to be below the weekly average was "easy to concentrate" (-.22). One explanation for the apparent paradox of adolescents' infrequent engagement in such positive experiences may be that such activities require concentration.[18] Preparing a violin piece for a recital or training for a cross-country meet calls for discipline and effort.

It is precisely the activities that are difficult but fun that provide the best training for a productive and personally fulfilling career. One implication for educators is that teenagers must be encouraged to see that starting any activity presents difficulties and that overcoming these will yield great dividends in experience and the development of new skills. Parents and teachers must also help ease teenagers' transitions during the discouraging period in which the activity seems too difficult to be worth a try and before intrinsic rewards make the activity self-sustaining.

Activities That Are Neither Work Nor Play

The adolescents in our sample report spending about one-third of their time doing activities that they perceive as being neither like work nor like play. Activities that students identify as producing this state of disengagement generally include maintenance activities (41.3 percent) such as eating, sleeping, and personal care and leisure activities (39.9 percent) such as hanging out with friends, watching television, or listening to the radio. Activities commonly perceived as being neither like work nor like play seem to be less structured, less goal-oriented, and for the most part less interactive than those activities commonly perceived as work, play, or both. Most of these activities take place in the home rather than in the structured environment of school or in the community. One neglected difference between adolescent social contexts may be the number of opportunities for action that each provides. Children who at home have nothing to engage their interest and attention are more likely to experience their days as neither work-like nor play-like. To the extent that such disengagement is neither enjoyable nor developmentally useful in the transition to productive adulthood, the frequency of disengagement can be seen as a dismaying indicator of things to come.

Who Spends More Time in Disengagement?

Time spent in an unfocused state varies by gender, race and ethnicity, grade, and socioeconomic status (see Table 4.1). Girls spend slightly more time than boys in activities identified as being like neither work nor play

(35.7 percent versus 32.7 percent).[19] Ethnic differences are greater: Hispanic teens spend the most time in such states (40.6 percent), followed by African-Americans (38.4 percent), Caucasians (31.9 percent), and Asians (31.5 percent).[20] Similarly, teenagers from less-privileged communities spend significantly more time in disengaged states than their more financially advantaged peers do. It is reasonable to suppose that children from higher-status communities would have more opportunities to engage in structured activities, be they work or play. Our findings also suggest that as students grow older, they spend less and less time in activities they perceive to have no purpose. It is unclear, however, whether the reduction of time spent in this category reflects a change in activity participation or a shift in judgment about which activities lack the traits of both work and play.

The Quality of Disengaged Experience

Despite the fact that adolescents spend vast amounts of time doing things that are neither work nor play, these activities are not perceived to be enjoyable or pleasurable. Activities accompanied by student disengagement are most often characterized by negative affect, low self-esteem, and little salience, challenge, or enjoyment. Girls appear to associate greater negative affect with such experiences than boys do,[21] whereas boys report lower levels of concentration and challenge. The experience is not particularly enjoyable for any of the racial or ethnic groups, but it is perceived as most enjoyable by African-Americans, followed by Caucasians, Hispanics, and Asians. Age differences are also complicated: Compared with the other age groups, eighth graders perceive such activities as having greater salience, positive affect, and enjoyment.

Such activities, in which adolescents feel disengaged from active work or play, also involve a degree of social disengagement. Students are most likely to be pursuing activities they identify as like neither work nor play when they are alone. Only 16.5 percent of adolescents' total working hours is spent alone, compared to 20.7 percent of playing hours and 18.2

percent of the hours spent in activities that are like both work and play. When teenagers report this feeling of disengagement from activity, time spent alone climbs to more than 30 percent.

Such "downtime," during which one can disengage from the stresses of daily life and prepare for the next spurt of activity, may be an occasional necessity in daily life that enables us to be more effective at work, in school, and in our dealings with others. Still, what is alarming about these results is the amount of time adolescents spend in this amorphous state, which they experience as decidedly negative. In more ways than one, the category of disengagement from both work and play seems to represent the opposite of balanced experiences of work-and-play activities. If an activity that combines the elements of both work and play provides a ladder to a purposeful and satisfying future career, the activity that lacks elements of either might well constitute a chute to an alienated occupational future. It seems all the more important that the opportunity to engage in activities that combine discipline and enjoyment be available to every teenager.

Clearly such opportunities are unevenly distributed. Underprivileged minorities spend 25 percent more time—ten hours more each week on the average—in this purposeless state than do Caucasians and Asian-Americans. One aspect of the cultural capital of affluent groups is that they are able to provide their children with a stimulating environment in which they can engage in structured activities that are enjoyable and useful. It is clear that when involved in such activities a young person feels stimulated, alive, and purposeful. It is likely that such early experiences in the family are a powerful means for the socialization of adolescents toward a productive adulthood.

But the amount of time children are involved in such activities is not determined entirely by the socially constructed opportunities in their milieus. Personal agency makes a great difference within each environment. Although adolescents in general spend a substantial amount of time in activities they characterize as like neither work nor play, there are many who spend minimal time in a state of disengagement and who by choice or circumstance devote unusually large amounts of time to work-like or play-like activities.

"Workers" and "Players"

One pattern that emerged clearly from the data was that while some adolescents consistently saw what they were doing as work, others rarely did so. Apparently, the perception that one's life is work-like or play-like is an individual trait that might be firmly established in the teenage years. To explore what this difference may mean, we decided to look at the extremes, groups we will refer to as "workers" and "players." Workers are those students who spend unusually large amounts of time doing work-like activities. Similarly, players were identified as those students who spend unusually large amounts of time in play-like activities.[22] Our data yielded 111 workers, who averaged 52 percent of their time in work. The number of players was 130, with the average amount of time spent in play being 56 percent. By this criterion, only two students qualified as both workers and players, and they were not included in these analyses.

Are workers and players more likely to be members of certain sociodemographic groups? It appears that age and gender do not make much difference, although workers are slightly over-represented among the tenth graders. But again, ethnic background and a more privileged social status appear to be implicated. Consistent with what we saw earlier, Caucasians are over-represented in the player group (72 percent as compared to 55 percent in the entire sample), as are children of highly educated parents. Clearly, it is easier to be a player if one is more affluent.

Do workers and players experience their lives differently? In some respects, the two groups are quite similar. For example, Figure 4.2 shows how the two groups experience those activities that each defines as work-like. Although the amount of time spent in work-like activities varies greatly among workers and players, both groups perceive work as highly challenging. Levels of perceived challenge among both workers and players during play-like activities were much lower (see Figure 4.3).

Yet there are some striking differences between the two groups. Workers perceive work-like activities as a much more positive experience than do players. While work activities tend to be relatively unenjoyable for both groups, they are considerably more unpleasant for players than for workers. Workers report higher levels of potency than players when doing

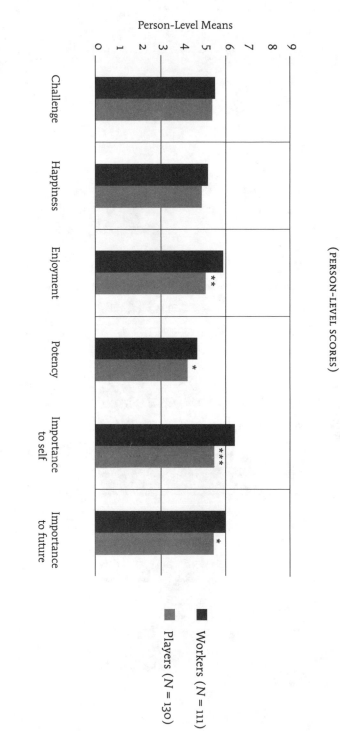

FIGURE 4.2 QUALITY OF EXPERIENCE DOING WORK-LIKE ACTIVITIES (PERSON-LEVEL SCORES)

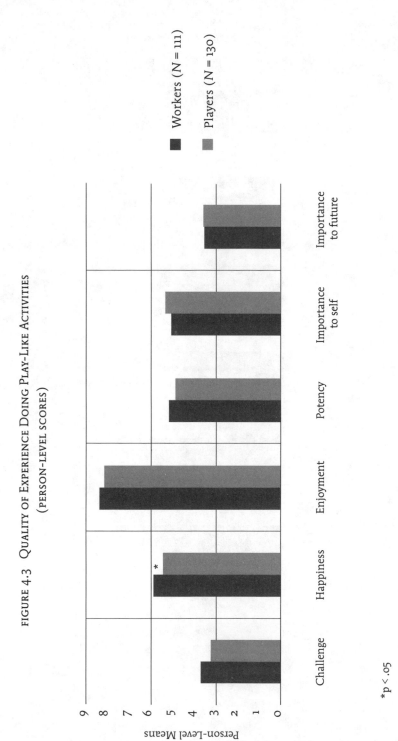

FIGURE 4.3 QUALITY OF EXPERIENCE DOING PLAY-LIKE ACTIVITIES
(PERSON-LEVEL SCORES)

*p < .05

work-like activities. Workers rate "importance to self" and "importance to future" higher than players when they work. All these differences suggest that players experience work as a challenging enterprise but for some reason are unable to translate this into importance to them personally or into any semblance of enjoyment.

Workers, not surprisingly, like work more than players do. But we were intrigued to find that workers also report a more positive quality of experience when they are engaged in activities they define as play (see Figure 4.3). Although workers and players experience play activities very similarly in terms of importance and potency, workers report higher levels of happiness than do players. So, being a worker need not mean that a person is a drudge. These teenagers are happy and enjoy their lives despite the fact that they see much of life as being like work, and work in general is a negative experience at this age. It appears, then, that workers enjoy the best of both worlds in that they are happier than players in both work and play activities.

Why Workers Work

Do workers spend so much time working by choice? Perhaps they feel forced to work as a result of family, peer, or other pressures, and would prefer a different lifestyle. On the ESM, students were asked to record whether they were doing a given activity because they wanted to, because they had to, or because they had nothing else to do. Any combination of these reasons was also accepted as valid, and each reason was coded as a separate answer—for example, "I was doing this activity because I wanted to *and* because I had to."

Workers reported doing work-like activities strictly because they wanted to twice as often as players did (22.2 percent versus 11.6 percent). If we add all of the cases in which wanting to do the activity was only part of the reason for doing it, the results are even more impressive: For workers there was some element of wanting to work in 30 percent of situations in which they were working, whereas players expressed some element of wanting to work in only 17 percent of such cases. These results suggest that workers are not being forced to work by outside influences any more than players are, and that in fact they feel somewhat freer in work-like activities. Interestingly, we do not see any large differences between workers and players in their reasons for engaging in play activities, which both groups experience most often as freely chosen.

How Workers and Players Describe Work and Play

The interviews we conducted with students suggest that there are consistent differences in the way workers and players talk about the role of work and play in their lives. There are notable variations in the importance these two groups place on work-like and play-like activities, in the degree to which they are motivated by work and play, and in their focus on specific future goals. Moreover, the trends appear to be consistent with the conclusions about workers and players based on the ESM data. We find that workers recognize their commitment to and enjoyment of work activities and future goals, while players are clearly more focused on less goal-directed, more playful activities.

The following excerpts from interviews with students identified as workers provide a good general picture of the worker that is emerging from our data. For example, a twelfth-grade male who aspires to be a biomedical engineer refers to himself as "problem oriented" and remarks that his work ethic and maturity have separated him from his peers throughout his development:

> I've always been, I wouldn't say mature but, I don't know, maybe it is mature. Just ever since I was a little kid even my parents said that I didn't fit in a lot when I was young, because I just seemed like I was older than the (other) kids. . . . I've just been driven and, uh, kind of independent.

Later he speaks of his deep commitment to and love for his math and science courses. He remarks that his love for these subjects has endured despite poor teachers. It is clear that his commitment to his studies is internally driven. He notes that his parents have never pushed him: "The approach they've taken is pretty much, I mean, I've always, you know, pushed myself, and they don't really push me. In fact, they told me to work less."

Another tenth-grade boy expresses a similar internal drive to be occupied by productive, work-like activity. Even though he holds a part-time job in a library, he notes that he is not driven to work by a desire for money:

> Actually, [money is] not one of the main reasons. The main reason is just to keep me occupied when I don't have much else to do. Last summer.... I went to Northwestern [University]. I took a summer course. It's just something to do to pass time, and you know, you get extra money while you're doing it.

Clearly this young man has found ways to spend as little time as possible disengaged. This affinity for working for work's sake came out in our interviews with younger workers as well. A sixth-grade girl describes how she often chooses to help her grandmother, an office cleaner, with her work: "I clean the office from top to bottom. I don't get lazy when I'm at the last room. I finish it up.... But I don't want the money, I just do it because I want to do it." She describes herself as an "explorer" and talks at length about her desire for knowledge: "I like to just, like, explore stuff— refrigerator or stove, washing machine. How (does) the water get in, about pipes, a lot of pipes bring the water. Where (does) the water come from?" She tells the story of how she once destroyed her grandfather's dentures. She "took them apart" with a hammer to see how they worked and to see whether she could reassemble them. Unfortunately for her grandfather, she could not. She says that in addition to her hands-on explorations, her curiosity often takes her to the library to research topics of interest.

The intrinsic rewards and satisfied curiosity that infuse workers' experiences are not apparent in players' comments. Whereas workers express enjoyment in work activities and have an appreciation for and commitment to the process of work, players tend to minimize work in favor of maximizing fun. Players' comments suggest that they are committed to avoiding activities that they perceive as work and are motivated by activities they perceive as fun and play. A twelfth grader who works in her mother's store says she does it only because it is "fun." She does not think that any of her work experience could be useful in the future and is uncertain what she wants to do upon graduation. Although she has considered many occupations, she wants to be either a doctor or a nurse "because it's a monetary factor and I guess it's kind of fun. Well, I really don't know very much about either one of them. They just sound fun."

Unlike workers, players have vague ideas of the future. They appear unguided and know very little about what they want to do or become or how to get there. Most just want to have fun and avoid situations they perceive to be work-like. Another graduating senior who expresses the wish to be a lawyer, but has not yet taken steps to apply to college, observes:

> None of my other friends really know what they want to do. I mean they know they want to go to college and they know they're probably going to need to go to graduate school, but no one's really sure exactly where they're going to be and what they're going to be doing. They just talk about how they want to, you know, be friends and have barbecues.

These students have no clear plans for the future yet seem unconcerned. Another graduating senior does not quite know what to do after high school, but he definitely knows what he does not want:

> The main point, my main goal in personal career is not to have a nine-to-five job where I sit in an office and write or sit in an office and type or whatever. It's this, I get ill almost thinking about that. I want to get out and do things and meet people.

Players express a resentment of the conventional lifestyle. They believe that work will hamper their opportunities for a carefree life and will keep them from being happy. Another senior male who does not have a job and does not think he will go to college says: "I don't think I'm going to be a...I don't think I'm gonna have a typical lifestyle when I grow up. I hope not." Players strive to avoid routine and hope to find fun outside of typical productive roles. In general, they do not expect work to be personally fulfilling and have very hazy ideas of what jobs they might seek once out of school. Workers, on the other hand, strive to avoid wasting time and enjoy being occupied, doing a good job, being productive and independent. They expect to be fulfilled through their jobs and therefore have much clearer vocational aspirations.

Because our data are cross-sectional, it is impossible to tell how these two groups developed their distinctive orientations toward work or to identify the long-term effect these orientations will have on their working lives as adults. Clearly, surroundings that provide ample human, cultural, and physical resources affect young people's development, but our results suggest that personal agency also has a great deal to do with the picture. A house cleaner's child, as well as the child of a wealthy surgeon, can learn to see work as an opportunity to enjoy doing his or her best in an activity that will be important to his or her future.

Teenagers' Experience in Paid Employment

Much recent research on adolescent work has focused on the structural, social, or psychological aspects of teenagers' experience of paid employment (c.f. Greenberger and Steinberg 1981, 1986; Mortimer and Borman 1988; Mortimer et al. 1990; National Research Council 1998; Steinberg, Fegley, and Dornbusch 1993). Researchers have presented strong arguments for both the costs and benefits of adolescent employment in terms of its effects on academic achievement, physical and psychological well-being, and long-term earnings and career attainment. The effects of adolescent employment on immediate and long-term outcomes are complex and not yet fully understood.

Our aim is not to take a position on whether adolescent employment is good or bad. We focus instead on the types of jobs students in our sample hold, how much time they spend working for pay, and how they feel when they are at their jobs. This account of paid work is thus more descriptive—it is intended to give a general picture of students' paid work experiences rather than highlighting particular effects of work experience. Few sixth and eighth graders are formally employed, so the results reported below are for the approximately 2,400 students from the full sample who were in high school at the time of data collection.

Working Patterns of High School Students

Among the high school students in our full sample, just under 70 percent have held paid employment at some time in their lives. Although only 38 percent were working at the time we collected data, a considerable number of students not then employed (about 30 percent) reported that they had worked at some point in previous school years or during summers. The high percentage of teens with work experience found in our sample is consistent with reports from other national data sets, which indicate that the number of students who work is significant and has risen over the past twenty years (U.S. Department of Labor 1993; U.S. Department of Commerce 1993; U.S. Department of Education 1991). Grade differences in employment patterns are as expected. Far fewer tenth graders than twelfth graders have work experience. By tenth grade about 57 percent of students report that they have worked at some time in their lives; this percentage reaches 86 percent for twelfth graders. These findings are consistent with other surveys: It appears that about 80 percent of American adolescents are employed while in secondary school (Bachman and Schulenberg 1992).

There are also differences in labor force participation by social class. Using our five-point measure of community social class, we find the greatest percentage of work experience among teenagers from upper class backgrounds (about 76 percent), although work for this group more often takes place during summers than during the school year. It appears that for upper-class children and their families, work experience is perceived as valuable and worthwhile, so long as it does not interfere with studies. Students who tend to work through the school year were most often from working class or middle class backgrounds. Interestingly, students from the poorest communities had the least work experience: Only about 64 percent said they had ever worked, and less than one-half of this group was working at the time of the study. This pattern likely reflects the lack of employment opportunities that exists in poorer communities.

What Kinds of Jobs Do Working Teenagers Hold?

A large proportion of working teenagers hold jobs that are not easily classifiable (see Table 4.2). About 15 percent of the working students in our sample reported that they were doing "other" jobs. That those jobs were often informal illustrates the transient nature of adolescent work experience. Some of the more traditional jobs held by teens include work as a store clerk or salesperson, work in the fast-food industry, and babysitting.

Again, there are considerable differences in the type of job held along demographic lines. By adolescence, gender stereotypes in work roles have

TABLE 4.2   TYPES OF JOBS HELD BY HIGH SCHOOL STUDENTS WHO WORK

Job Type	% of Working Students
N = 310	
Clerk/salesperson	17.8
Fast food	14.7
Babysitter	13.3
Office/clerical	10.9
Lawn work/odd job	5.8
Manual laborer	4.4
Camp counselor/lifeguard	4.1
Waiter/waitress	4.0
Hospital/health	2.8
construction	1.5
Paper route	1.5
Farm worker	1.5
Housecleaner	1.4
Factory worker	1.1
Other	15.3

already emerged, with more boys doing lawn work, odd jobs, newspaper delivery, and manual labor. Girls, on the other hand, more often earn money as babysitters, sales clerks, and house cleaners. Differences by race and ethnicity are less striking. Compared to other groups, more Caucasian adolescents do lawn work, odd jobs, and babysitting, while more Asian teenagers work in office buildings. Grade differences in employment are again predictable: Tenth graders earn money doing less formal jobs like lawn work, odd jobs, newspaper delivery, and babysitting, while more twelfth graders work in retail sales and offices. Class differences in employment are also apparent. Teenagers from the most affluent backgrounds tend to hold jobs that are seasonal, primarily summer jobs such as lawn work, camp counseling, and lifeguarding. Teenagers from upper-middle-class backgrounds more often earn money in the "white-collar world," working as file clerks and receptionists in office buildings. Working-class and middle-class adolescents are more likely to earn money working in fast-food restaurants. More than any other group, adolescents from the poorest neighborhoods say that they earn money doing "other" activities that are not easily categorized.

Time Spent in Paid Work

Among the teenagers in our sample who worked, about one-third spent fewer than fifteen hours per week on the job. Another third spent about sixteen to thirty hours working. Our findings are consistent with those of other national studies of adolescent work patterns. The U.S. General Accounting Office (1991), for example, found that high schoolers work about twenty hours per week on average. Adolescent boys and girls invest similar amounts of time in paid work. Although there are substantial gender differences in the type of jobs adolescents hold, there are no real differences by gender in the number of hours worked. As might be expected, twelfth graders spend a greater number of hours working than tenth graders. The greatest number of tenth graders work under fifteen hours per week, while the most frequent number of hours worked for twelfth graders is sixteen to thirty hours.[23] There are only marginally significant differences in the number of hours worked by race and ethnicity, with Asians working the fewest hours, followed by Caucasians, African-Americans, and Hispanics.[24] We find considerable differences in the number of hours worked by social class. Adolescents from more economically privileged families work fewer hours than those from families that are less advantaged financially.[25]

Quality of Experience in Paid Work

To explore how teenagers feel at work, we again turn to our data from the subset of the full sample who completed the ESM. Because our focus is on paid work, we use data from high school students only, of which 159 held jobs. Paid work seems to be generally regarded as an activity that is important and engaging and promotes feelings of positive self-regard; it is characterized by above-average levels of salience (average z-score = .34), concentration (.36), and self-esteem (.37). Affectively, however, paid employment appears to be a neutral or even slightly negative experience. Jobs are associated with average levels of affect (.03) and below-average levels of enjoyment (-.17) and happiness (-.10).

There are no differences in the quality of experience in paid work by race or social class, and there are only a few marginally significant differences by gender and age. Boys tend to concentrate more than girls in paid work (boys = .55, girls = .25),[26] and tenth graders tend to enjoy work more than their twelfth-grade peers (tenth grade = .10, twelfth grade = -.29).[27] On the whole, however, paid work seems to be experienced similarly by all students.

We compared how students feel in paid work to the way they feel when doing schoolwork, socializing, watching television, and engaging in maintenance activities such as personal care. Not surprisingly, there are vast differences in the quality of experience among these various activities. Paid work is clearly the most positive of the five activities in terms of self-esteem (see Table 4.3). Concentration is very high in paid work, as it is in schoolwork, both of which have significantly higher concentration levels than watching television, socializing, or engaging in maintenance activities. Salience, a measure of importance, is significantly higher in paid work than it is for socializing or watching television, but significantly lower than when students pursue school activities. Affect in paid work is not very different from that associated with schoolwork, television watching, or maintenance, but it is significantly lower than socializing. Paid work is also a relatively unenjoyable and unhappy experience—about on a par with doing schoolwork—and is less enjoyable than watching television or socializing.

Adolescents' feelings during paid work are thus not so very different from the way they feel when doing work-like activities. Although self-esteem is generally higher in paid work than in work-like activities in general, both are characterized by high importance and concentration but low levels of enjoyment. The fact that adolescents fail to take pleasure in their early employment experiences may be problematic in that students' current experiences may affect their expectations of future career fulfillment.

The Conundrum of Work in Adolescence

The way in which images of work develop in adolescence is by no means simple and obvious. Yet these images will be decisive in helping young

TABLE 4.3   MEAN QUALITY OF EXPERIENCE SCORES IN PAID WORK VERSUS OTHER ACTIVITY TYPES FOR TEENS WHO HAVE JOBS

	1 Job	2 School	3 Social	4 TV	5 Maintenance
N = 159					
Self-Esteem	0.37[a]	-0.01	0.02	-0.25	-0.07
Salience	0.34	0.59	-0.08	-0.78	-0.37
Positive Affect	0.03	-0.15	0.32	-0.09	-0.04
Enjoyment	-0.17	-0.32	0.27	0.30	-0.02
Happiness	-0.10	-0.17	0.28	0.01	-0.01
Concentration	0.36	0.37	-0.09	-0.30	-0.38

[a] Quality of experience values are calculated as z-scores.

people frame career decisions that will determine the shape of their productive lives. In the first place, there is a general agreement among young
people as to what kind of activities qualify as work and as play. The cultural stereotypes are learned early: Productive, academic activities are assimilated to the concept of work and leisure activities to the concept of
play. There is also agreement as to what it means to work: It is important
to one's future but not something one likes doing.

Strong and counterintuitive differences appear among ethnic and social class subgroups in their attitudes toward work. As children become
older, they tend to see what they do as more work-like, but it is regrettable
that with age, the quality of experience during work also deteriorates. The
results of ethnic and social-class analyses are particularly puzzling. Why
do privileged Caucasian children from educated families dislike work
more than less-advantaged minorities? Why do they see what they do as
more like play, and why do they have such a positive experience in play?

These patterns suggest a rather ominous scenario for the future of
work in America. Young people in general are developing rather negative
images of work. Even though everyone agrees that work is important to
one's future, it is still, by and large, felt to be depressing and dull. Contrary to received wisdom, it is not the more affluent white, middle-class
children who support the work ethic. Work appears to be a more integral
part of the self-concept of minority children. Hispanics and African-
Americans from families of lower socioeconomic status experience work
as more intrinsically rewarding. Of course, this initial attraction to work
by the underprivileged may later change into bitterness when underem-
ployment and unemployment take their toll.

Economically disadvantaged teenagers spend greater amounts of time
than their more advantaged peers in a state of disengagement—that is,
one that is neither like work nor play. Disengagement is characterized by
teenagers as being neither productive nor enjoyable, and is commonly accompanied by feelings of low self-esteem. Spending large amounts of
time in this unpleasant, unfocused state is unlikely to promote positive
development. While the primary focus of this chapter has been work and
play, it is important to keep in mind that the amount of time spent in

disengagement could have implications even more serious than the amount of time spent in work or play.

Is this trend evidence of a sea change, an indication that our society is raising a generation of relatively affluent youth uninterested in work and of less-affluent youth who look forward to working but may not get good jobs when they enter the labor market? These grave and important issues cannot be resolved with certainty on the basis of the present data. In a few years, when the longitudinal results of this study become available, we may be able to be more confident about the implications of the findings.

A more encouraging result of the analyses in this chapter concerns those youngsters who stand out from the crowd because they, more than their peers, are able to see what they do as being work-like. Given the general dislike for work, one would expect these young workers to be generally more troubled and unhappy than their more playful peers. Yet the opposite is true. Young people who are able to ignore the cultural stereotypes against work apparently learn to appreciate the exciting challenges that work also provides. This important finding falsifies the hypothesis, so deeply ingrained in our culture, that work is necessarily bad for one's psyche.

We see that it is possible, even for notoriously skeptical teenagers, to develop positive attitudes toward the productive side of their lives. What is more, those who do so apparently also enjoy their lives more and are happier. They have a more purposeful view of the years ahead, and they seem to find personal fulfillment in their work. The youngsters who have developed this positive work ethic are not primarily the offspring of rich and educated parents; on the contrary, poor and socially marginal youth are over-represented in this group. At the other extreme are young people who frequently feel that what they do is neither like work nor like play. These teenagers are also likely to come from disadvantaged families, yet their attitude toward work is one of disengaged and passive resignation. Of course, the question remains: What proportion of the coming generation will develop the worker's identity? How stable and enduring is this point of view? How useful will it be in the years ahead? What may be done to expand this positive identity among young people?

LEARNING TO LIKE CHALLENGES

Joel Hektner and Kiyoshi Asakawa,
with the assistance of Shaunti Knauth and
Desiree Henshaw

BY EARLY ADOLESCENCE, work acquires a host of negative connotations that persist throughout high school. At the same time, those teenagers who define more of what they do as being like work seem to have a better overall quality of experience than their peers who see what they do as being more like play. How can these contradictory results be reconciled? One explanation is that the "workers" have been successfully socialized to accept work as a necessary but onerous task. Because they have identified themselves as future workers, they feel that their self-image is consistent with the norms and traditions of their communities. From their compliance with these norms and traditions and their sense that significant figures in their lives approve of what they do, they feel better about themselves, even though their work-like activities may not be especially appealing.

But there is a more optimistic explanation for these results. It is possible that young workers have actually learned to derive enjoyment from productive activities. After all, there is a strong tradition, running from

Marx to Freud, that holds work to be a person's principal means of self-expression and the source of deepest satisfaction (Fraser 1962; Furnham 1991). This possibility is supported by several studies of adults that show that work offers the most positive experiences in daily life. Despite strong cultural stereotypes against work, it appears that, compared with what else life has to offer, work is actually not so bad. In a survey conducted by Yankelovich (1981), 84 percent of American men and 77 percent of American women said that they would continue working even if they were to inherit enough money to no longer need a job. Other studies show that adult workers tend to feel more active and creative and have better concentration on the job compared with how they feel in their free time at home. Their self-esteem is higher, and they feel a deeper sense of satisfaction about their actions (Csikszentmihalyi and LeFevre 1989; Wells 1988). On the other hand, Larson and Richards (1994) report that although workers feel more attentive, skilled, alert, strong, and in control on the job, they feel happier, more cheerful, and less frustrated at home.

It is true that many of life's best moments come not from work but from leisure activities such as skiing, surfing, watching a good movie, or having a satisfying romantic relationship (Brandstätter 1991; Csikszent-mihalyi 1990). Opportunities for such experiences, however, are relatively few and jobs take up a much larger part of our lives. It would follow that those who learn to enjoy work should have a better quality of life overall than those who have to wait for rare leisure activities before they can feel that their lives are enjoyable. Fortunately, work and enjoyment are not antithetical, as is often supposed. To better see how this might be so, let us consider a theoretical model that helps to connect the two concepts.

The Relationship Between Enjoyment and Challenges: The Flow Model

In studies in many different cultural settings, it has been found that people most enjoy what they are doing when their abilities match the opportunities for action in the situation. A balance between high levels of challenge and high levels of skill is consistently reported when activities are enjoyed. Activities in which a balance of challenge and skill is reported include rock climbing, chess, and surgery (Csikszentmihalyi 1975); the leisure activities of older adults (Hahn 1988; Mannell, Zuzanek, and Larson 1988); interaction with computers (Trevino and Webster 1992; Webster and Martocchio 1993; Webster, Trevino, and Ryan 1993); work on the assembly line and in clerical and managerial occupations (Csikszentmihalyi and LeFevre 1989); recreational sports (Stein et al. 1995); teaching (Coleman 1994); figure skating (Jackson 1992); psychiatric rehabilitation (Massimini, Csikszentmihalyi, and Carli 1987; Delle Fave and Massimini 1992); motorcycling in Japan (Sato 1988) and in Germany (Rheinberg 1995); and studying various subjects in high school (Csikszentmihalyi, Rathunde, and Whalen 1993).

Enjoyable experiences are usually described as having a cluster of related subjective dimensions. Aside from the balance of challenges and skills, enjoyable experiences provide clarity of goals: knowing what must be done from one moment to the next. Another dimension is immediacy of feedback: A person always knows how well he or she is doing. For instance, if a young boy enjoys fixing a bicycle, it is likely that he will say that he knows exactly what he has to do—the chain must be tightened just so—and that he can test as he goes along whether the chain is working as it should. He is also likely to feel that, although the task is difficult, he can succeed at it. In any activity with these characteristics, the boy will likely become absorbed and temporarily forget anything irrelevant to his task. Problems with school, friends, and family will disappear for a while. He will lose his self-consciousness, or the "me" aspect of the self described by George Herbert Mead ([1934] 1974). Time will seem to pass quickly. When all these aspects of the experience are present, any task will be worth doing for its own sake.

This cluster of phenomenological dimensions has been called *flow*, a term that recurs in people's descriptions of optimal experience (Csikszentmihalyi 1990). Flow describes the spontaneous, seemingly effortless aspect of such experiences. Yet this apparent effortlessness is the result of the close match between high levels of challenge and the skills that are appropriate to the task at hand. Our bike mechanic might operate automatically, apparently without thinking, his fingers following the right sequence as if they moved by themselves, but this effortless spontaneity can only be achieved by someone who knows what needs to be done and has learned to do it well.

Clearly it would be wrong to claim that achieving flow is our only motivation to act. In fact the contrary is true: Most of the time we prefer to do things that are relaxing and comfortable, things that require little skill or expenditure of energy. After all, watching television takes up the largest part of our free time (Kubey and Csikszentmihalyi 1990). Nevertheless, when people think back on those times when they felt most alive, when what they did was most enjoyable and meaningful, chances are that it was when they had occasion to confront a task they were only just able to master. These occasions can become milestones in memory, events that one wishes to experience again and again.

Why should meeting high challenges with high skills be something we enjoy doing for its own sake, even without extrinsic rewards? The reason does not seem to be that we are brainwashed as children or socialized into enjoying difficult things. It is more likely that we are born with a preference for acting at our fullest potential. Perhaps enjoying mastery and competence is evolutionarily adaptive, just as it is adaptive to find pleasure in food and sex (Csikszentmihalyi 1993; Inghilleri 1999; Konner 1990; Ryan 1992; White 1959). In the development of the human nervous system a connection must have been established between hard work and a sense of pleasure even when the work was not strictly necessary. It is this connection that makes creativity and progress possible. Whatever the reason, people from a wide range of cultures are attracted to activities and situations that demand high levels of skill.

Although we all may have the ability to experience flow, there seem to be systematic differences among people in the frequency and intensity of such experiences. Surveys in the United States and Germany have found that about 15 percent of the population claims never to have experienced this state, and a similar proportion says that they experience it several times each day. The remaining 70 percent report it with different degrees of frequency, on average once every few weeks (Csikszentmihalyi 1997). Those capable of flow could often be described as having an autotelic personality—that is, a tendency to become involved in activities for their own sake (Csikszentmihalyi 1975). Talented students who reported higher challenges matched with higher skills—and thus had an autotelic personality—tended to have a more positive view of their lives, especially during productive activities such as studying, doing homework, or working (Adlai-Gail 1994; Csikszentmihalyi, Rathunde, and Whalen 1993; Hektner 1996).

Virtually everyone has the potential to develop an autotelic personality; however, early experiences and the social environment may restrict many young people's ability to find enjoyment, except perhaps in such leisure activities as sports and entertainment. Yet an adult who can only enjoy leisure is not prepared for a fulfilling life. Individual well-being, as much as societal well-being, depends to a large extent on whether children will also learn to experience flow in productive activities. Children who grow up in the inner city may learn that to survive all their psychic energies must be focused on self-protection. For many, enjoyment can become narrowly defined as the ability to prove oneself, show off, and intimidate others. Such persons are rarely able to develop skills that are less geared to survival. The reverse is true of many suburban children who, rather than being overwhelmed by challenges, live in a protective cocoon that produces more boredom than flow. These children run the risk of growing into listless, conforming, dissatisfied adults. Thus, one way to conceptualize the transition into productive adulthood is to ask: Are adolescents who spend more time in high challenge and high skill situations more motivated and better prepared for the future? Are they better equipped than others to be active agents in their own career-forming experiences?

Flow and the Quality of Experience

The Experience Sampling Method (ESM) was used to capture moments of flow as they occurred in everyday life. In previous ESM studies, flow has been measured using ten-point scales of challenge and skill that respondents applied to their current activity at a given signal. This made it possible to measure flow independently of the positive cognitive and affective states that are expected to accompany it. Initial formulations of the theory predicted that the full positive state of experience associated with flow (high concentration, involvement, happiness, satisfaction, and so forth) would most likely occur when challenges and skills were in balance. The empirical results, however, led to a reformulation of the theory (see, e.g., Massimini and Carli 1988): The full effects of flow only appear when challenges and skills are not only in balance but are also relatively high. In practice, flow has been identified in previous studies as *any event in which a person rates levels of both challenge and skill above his or her weekly average.*[1] We define flow in this way in our analyses, and we contrast flow with three other states defined by the ratio of challenge to skills: *anxiety*, in which the challenge of the activity is higher than average but the required skill is lower; *relaxation*, in which skill is reported as higher than average but challenge is lower; and *apathy*, in which both challenge and skill are below the person's weekly average. Seven variables are used to measure the quality of experience adolescents report while in these states: level of concentration, enjoyment in the activity, feelings of happiness, feelings of strength, the extent to which the person wishes to be doing the present activity, level of self-esteem, and the extent to which the person sees the activity as important in relation to future goals.

When the adolescents in our focal sample are in flow, they report levels above their own averages for concentration, enjoyment, happiness, strength, motivation, and self-esteem, as well as the feeling that the activities in which they are engaged are important to their futures (see Table 5.1). It is clear that flow offers a highly positive experience for teenagers. Adolescents who are in flow are the most likely to feel that what they are doing is important to their future goals. Pleasure that is rooted in the activity at hand is also experienced as being related to life's broader framework and thus to future development.

A richer picture emerges when the flow experience is contrasted with other combinations of challenge and skill. In the state of anxiety (defined as high challenge and low skill), concentration and future importance are above the weekly average. All the other measured dimensions of experience are negative: Enjoyment, happiness, strength, motivation, and self-esteem are all below average levels. Anxiety is the state in which teenagers report the most negative motivation—that is, a strong desire to be doing something else.

Relaxation (defined as high skill and low challenge) shows a pattern that is almost the reverse of anxiety. Relaxation is not an unpleasant state for teenagers. Concentration and future importance are below average, but teens experience enjoyment, happiness, motivation, and self-esteem. If relaxation is the mirror image of anxiety, apathy is the mirror image of flow. In apathy (defined as low challenge and low skill), teenagers report the lowest quality of experience overall. Concentration, enjoyment, happiness, strength, motivation, and self-esteem are all significantly lower than average. Activities that bring on apathy are unlikely to be goal related. They include the routines of everyday life such as cleaning up, dressing, eating, resting, or riding a bus to school, as well as passive leisure activities like staring out the window or watching television. Why don't adolescents try harder to avoid apathy if it provides neither

TABLE 5.1   QUALITY OF EXPERIENCE WHILE IN FLOW, ANXIETY, RELAXATION, AND APATHY

Quality of Experience (Person-level z-scores)	States of Experience			
	Flow	Anxiety	Relaxation	Apathy
N = 824				
Concentration[a]	.48***	.26***	-.17***	-.39***
Enjoyment	.13***	-.30***	.18***	-.20***
Happiness	.09***	-.22***	.12***	-.13***
Strength	.20***	-.06**	.02	-.15***
Wish to be doing activity	.04*	-.27***	.12***	-.08***
Self-Esteem	.38***	-.28***	.14***	-.40***
Importance to future goals	.43***	.27***	-.17***	-.32***

$* = p < .05$

$** = p < .01$

$*** = p < .001$

[a] Each category is compared to the other three categories combined, with t-tests.

immediate gratification nor the promise of future rewards? Apparently, the ease of such mental routines makes apathy acceptable despite the fact that it offers little in return.

Comparing the four states highlights the importance of the flow experience for teenagers. Flow is the only condition in which high challenges are linked to feelings of enjoyment, self-worth, and ongoing development. This is not to suggest that all other states should be avoided, even if they could be. The anxiety of tackling a challenge without having the skills necessary to surmount it is part of the process of learning. It prompts us to develop higher skills in order to return to flow. Alternating anxiety with the satisfaction of a flow experience helps adolescents to understand that learning is indeed a process and that their skills will grow. The state of relaxation is also integral to the adolescent experience—the "downtime" that many teenagers love and need. But enjoying downtime does not lead to further growth. It is only in flow that teenagers learn to enjoy the challenges necessary for reaching their goals.

Flow in Different Activities

Where do these moments of high challenge and skill come from? Table 5.2 lists the most frequent activities that the focal sample of teenagers engaged in during a typical week. For each activity we report how often it is experienced as flow-like, relaxed, apathetic, or anxious. The strongest sources of flow in the lives of teenagers are productive activities. Classwork, homework, and jobs all provide more flow experiences than the average (26 percent) across all daily events. Participation in games, sports, and hobbies also results in higher frequencies of flow. Every other activity, however, is lower than average in producing flow. The lowest incidence of flow is reported when teens are resting, eating, or watching television or movies.[2]

Relaxation is highest when teenagers are resting, eating, watching television or movies, or listening to music and lowest in high-flow activities, such as work and active leisure. A similar pattern holds for apathy: The highest levels of apathy are reported when watching television and the lowest when doing homework. Students experience higher-than-average levels of anxiety when engaged in homework, classwork, games and sports, and working on the job. Anxiety is almost unknown when students rest, watch television, eat, or listen to music.

These patterns begin to explain why teenagers spend time doing the kinds of things that fill their daily lives. Productive activities and active

TABLE 5.2 PERCENTAGE OF TIME IN FLOW AND NONFLOW STATES
IN VARIOUS ACTIVITIES

Activity Categories	N	Flow	Anxiety	Relaxation	Apathy
All activities[a]	824	26%	17%	31%	25%
Productive					
Classwork	824	38.31***	29.12***	16.79***	15.78***
Homework	460	44.47***	30.85***	12.70***	11.98***
Job	189	41.87***	20.68**	23.55**	13.90***
Leisure					
Socializing	761	19.73***	12.32***	38.27***	29.68***
Games and sports	512	44.33***	23.58***	16.52***	15.56***
Television	726	12.83***	6.13***	43.05***	37.98**
Watching movies or listening to music	311	15.05***	6.62***	43.54***	34.80***
Hobbies	625	33.85***	18.52	29.84	17.80***
Thinking about...	457	19.24***	14.83	31.45	34.48***
Maintenance					
Chores	389	26.46	18.09	31.18	24.27
Eating	642	12.80***	6.13***	50.14***	30.93***
Grooming/ personal care	623	17.81***	11.34***	39.72***	31.14***
Resting	462	11.29***	4.11***	49.50***	35.10***
In transit	707	17.35***	10.43***	40.18***	32.05***
Other	449	22.47*	15.04	30.68	31.81**

* = p < .05

** = p < .01

*** = p < .001

[a] Each activity is contrasted with the total for all other activities, with person-level t-tests.

leisure are enjoyable—they produce flow—but they can also make one feel anxious. By spending their free time in passive leisure activities, teenagers can avoid anxiety. Although these activities fail to produce enjoyable flow experiences and may result in apathy, they are relaxing and anxiety-free.

Do particular activities induce more intense flow? We explored six broad categories of activities: productive, social, active leisure, passive leisure, maintenance, and other (see Table 5.3). The highest level of flow is reported when teenagers are engaged in productive activities, including all classroom activities, homework, and extracurricular activities, as well as time spent on a job. Active leisure, such as pursuing a hobby or playing sports, shows an almost equally high level of flow. There is a marked drop in the level of flow reported while socializing with family or friends. Passive leisure, such as listening to music or watching videos, appears even less conducive to flow than engaging in maintenance activities such as eating or grooming.

How do these teenagers actually spend their time with respect to flow? We compared those students who are most and least likely to report being in flow overall, the upper quartile (high-flow) and lower quartile (low-flow) groups on the continuous measure of flow. Those teenagers who most often report being in flow spend much more time—seven hours more per week—in productive activities and about three hours

TABLE 5.3   AVERAGE INTENSITY LEVEL OF FLOW IN DIFFERENT ACTIVITIES
            (RESULTS AT PERSON-LEVEL)

Activity Categories	Number of Responses	Mean Flow Scores
Productive	806	5.38
Social	735	4.04
Active leisure	705	5.20
Passive leisure	773	3.65
Maintenance	799	3.72
Other	588	4.32

$F = 159.94$

$p < .0000$

more in active leisure. These same students spend significantly less time—about two to three fewer hours per week—in socializing, passive leisure, and maintenance activities. Yet despite these differences in how the two groups spend their days, the similarity in the overall distribution of their time is striking. Both groups spend the greatest amount of their time in productive activities, the second greatest amount of time in maintenance activities, the next greatest in passive leisure, and the least time in active leisure pursuits and "other" activities.[3]

A closer look within the broad categories reveals further differences in how the two groups spend their time. High-flow students spend more time engaged in schoolwork and homework, more time on the job, and less time watching television. All these differences are statistically significicant. There is no significant difference, however, in time spent in extracurricular activities and sports, which seem likely to offer the combination of challenge and skill that promotes flow.

This comparison of low- and high-flow students suggests several ways in which teenagers' daily activities influence their opportunities to enjoy challenges. First, teenagers are relatively constrained in the range of activities they engage in. Required school attendance means that teenagers spend most of the day involved in school-related tasks. Most teenagers, it appears, also spend a good deal of their time in passive leisure. Although this may seem an active choice rather than a response to a constraint, challenging activities are not always available. Teenagers often depend on adults to provide transportation, coaching, and club sponsorship—not to mention encouragement—for many productive and active leisure activities. Unfortunately, such logistical and emotional support from adults cannot be taken for granted.

Yet, despite an overall similarity in how their time is spent, teenagers have markedly different experiences in relation to flow. Small differences in the amount of time spent on schoolwork seem to have important developmental consequences. Education research argues that a certain set of school and classroom conditions, including time spent on instruction, must be present before students actually can be said to have the "opportunity to learn" (Hallinan and Sorensen, 1986). It appears that teenagers need opportunities to engage in flow; that is, they require repeated encounters with the types of activities most likely to develop and challenge their skills. Modest differences in the level of such opportunities may lead to profound differences in the quality of students' daily experience and even greater differences in their future use of time.

Flow and the Presence of Others

Prior ESM research with teenagers has shown that the experience of an activity varies according to the presence of others. Eating a meal or shopping is more likely to be seen as play when teens are with their peers and as work when young people are with their families. How does the company of others relate to teenagers' likelihood of experiencing flow? The answer is that students in the high-flow group spend significantly less time alone and more time with others (three percentage points in either direction) than students in the low-flow group do. These "others" tend to be other family members: The high-flow group spends 4 percent more time with the family. There is no significant difference in the amount of time spent with friends. The overall distribution of time spent with others is similar for low- and high-flow teens: Both groups spend the majority of their time with others. Flow does not appear to be a solitary activity. These findings also suggest the advantage of what has been called "social neoteny" (Csikszentmihalyi, Rathunde, and Whalen 1993), or the continued dependence of teenagers on family support as they are developing the skills that will allow them to become independent.

Flow and Personal Growth

Overall Quality of Experience.   Flow appears to be closely related to the immediate quality of experience. But does it make a difference with respect to longer-term outcomes? Given the tendency of flow to provide enjoyment that motivates productive activities and drives skill development, we might expect that students who are often in flow would be better prepared for the future both affectively and cognitively.

We have found that certain types of activities and companions are more likely to promote the experience of flow for all adolescents. We now examine whether the quality of teenagers' individual experiences is related to the frequency with which they are in flow. Again, we look to whether teenagers report high levels of concentration and self-esteem, tend to enjoy the activity at hand, are happy, feel strong, wish to be doing the activity, and feel that the activity is connected to their future goals. The question is whether these qualities of experience are associated with high challenges and skills just at the moment or whether they are usually higher for those who report higher challenges and skills more frequently throughout the week. Can we distinguish between flow as a state and flow as a trait?

We found that when students in the high-flow group are engaged in productive activities, they report higher levels of concentration, higher self-esteem, and a stronger sense that what they are doing is relevant to future goals (see Table 5.4). They are not different from the low-flow group in terms of how much they enjoy the activity, how happy they are, how strong they feel, or how motivated they are when engaged in productive activities. The pattern when students are involved in active leisure pursuits is almost the same as the one for productive activities, but here the high-flow group also differs from the low-flow group in that they report enjoying leisure activities more.[4]

These results suggest that being able to respond to high-challenge activities with appropriate skills is an integral part of a young person's immediate and long-range well-being. But is there evidence that this ability is also related to attitudes associated with adult success? To answer this question, we selected a number of variables from the Career Orientation Scale (COS) as well as the ESM. The first set of dependent variables from the COS measured *future orientation*. Did students who were more often in flow feel more optimistic about the future, more open to experience, and less pessimistic? The second set of variables related to *motivation*. Did frequency of flow relate to the strength of intrinsic, extrinsic, and social motivation? The third set included the *career literacy* scores derived from the COS. Did students with more flow experiences have a better knowledge of the workplace? Finally, from the ESM, we tested the relationship between flow and *perceptions of activities as being like work or like play*. Did flow correlate best with a perception of one's actions as being more like work or more like play?

Future Orientation.   In one part of the COS, students were asked to rate nine adjectives describing attitudes about the future. These attitudes can be grouped into three clusters measuring a sense of optimism based on feelings of confidence and personal power, curiosity and openness to experience, and a sense of doubt and pessimism about the future.[5] We found that when students experienced flow, they tended to feel opti-

TABLE 5.4   QUALITY OF EXPERIENCE FOR HIGH-FLOW AND LOW-FLOW
GROUPS (RESULTS OF T-TESTS AT PERSON LEVEL)

	High-Flow Group	Low-Flow Group
N	202	202
A. While in productive activities		
Concentration	7.02**	6.52**
Enjoyment	5.25	4.89
Happiness	4.86	4.82
Strength	4.55	4.62
Wish to be doing activity	3.88	3.87
Self-Esteem	6.35**	5.86**
Importance to future goals	5.06**	4.41**
B. While in active leisure activities		
Concentration	6.82**	5.99**
Enjoyment	7.77*	7.30*
Happiness	5.39	5.44
Strength	4.90	4.88
Wish to be doing activity	6.13	6.01
Self-Esteem	6.38**	5.86**
Importance to future goals	3.65***	2.86***

* = p < .05

** = p < .01

*** = p < .001

mistic about the future. This result confirms theoretical expectations that confidence and power would be difficult to experience if levels of challenge and skill were low, or if the two were not in balance. Adolescents who spend more time in states of apathy, anxiety, or relaxation would be expected to feel neither confident nor powerful about the future. We also expected flow to have a positive association with openness to experience and a negative association with pessimism. The direction of these relationships is confirmed by the results in Table 5.5.

TABLE 5.5 ASSOCIATIONS BETWEEN MEAN FLOW SCORES AND OTHER OUTCOME MEASURES

Dependent Variables	Beta[a]
N = 310	
Future orientation	
Optimism	.15**
Openness to experience	.03
Pessimism	-.08
Sources of motivation	
Intrinsic	.09
Extrinsic	.13*
Social	.15**
Career literacy	
Job knowledge	-.04
Fitscore	-.10*
"Learn-do"	.09
Perceptions of work and play	
% Activities like work	.23***
% Activities like play	.13*
% Activities like both	.16**
% Activities like neither	-.32***

* = p < .05

** = p < .01

*** = p < .001

[a] Standardized coefficients of flow in separate regression models predicting each dependent variable, while controlling for gender, grade, race, parent education, school grades, and social class of community.

Sources of Motivation.   Students rated the importance of three major types of rewards or sources of motivation.[6] We expected that intrinsic motivation, characterized by "being interested in what you are doing" and "enjoying what you are doing," would be positively related to flow. It was, but the correlation was not as strong as for the other two sources of motivation, extrinsic and social (see Table 5.5). The more flow students report, the more they value such things as "preparing yourself for a secure job" and "living up to your parents' expectations." While unexpected, this finding does not contradict our basic premises. Undoubtedly, students who are often in flow cannot sustain their efforts in most activities through intrinsic motivation alone but also need extrinsic rewards and social recognition for their accomplishments. When working on a difficult task, these students perceive a broader range of potential rewards for their efforts. They believe that if they work hard, they will gain material benefits and social recognition as well as the rewards of a job well done. As several researchers have realized (Amabile 1983; Csikszentmihalyi, Rathunde, and Whalen 1993; Deci and Ryan 1985), intrinsic and extrinsic rewards are not mutually exclusive. Adolescents who are often in flow might have an advantage in that they have learned to anticipate more rewards than their peers do. Because they are able to envision more potential rewards for their efforts, they can sustain their motivation even when the task becomes daunting.

Career Literacy.   The three variables in this set were designed to measure how much students know about occupational roles and job practices (Knowledge, Fitscore) and whether they had any experience relevant to occupations of interest to them (learn-do scores).[7] It was expected that students who were more often in flow would score higher on all three measures of career literacy (see Table 5.5). However, this expectation was not borne out by the data. Instead, the only significant association was a *negative* one between flow and Fitscore, which tested the respondent's ability to recognize which one of three jobs was dissimilar to the other two. For example, in the triad "economist," "bank teller," and "sales clerk," the first one—a professional position—does not fit with the other two. Although this test has solid psychometric properties, it may also measure reasoning ability and content knowledge. In any case, there is no good explanation of why students who measure high on flow would score lower on this measure.

Perceptions of Work and Play.   We tested whether students who experience frequent flow are more likely to see activities as being like both work and play and are less likely to see them as being like neither work nor play. Indeed, our results show that students who often experience flow tend to see their activities as being like work, play, or both (see Table 5.5). Compared with their peers who experience less flow, high-flow students are less likely to say that their activities are like neither work nor play. This finding has important implications for understanding young people's transition to a satisfying adulthood. It suggests that teenagers who perceive high challenges in their lives and feel they have the skills to cope with them are developing a sense that their daily activities involve elements of work and play. Those who lack challenges and skills, or feel that these are not in balance, evaluate what they do as being neither productive nor playful. Such a stance toward one's experience may foreshadow an unfortunate alienation from life's activities and an adulthood lacking in either accomplishment or pleasure.

The Variety of Challenges in Adolescence

Experiencing high levels of challenge and skill is part of an important dynamic in the transition from adolescence to adulthood. Whenever teenagers report being in high challenge, high skill situations, the quality of their experience is positive. This kind of experience tends to be most pronounced when teenagers are involved in productive activities such as study and when they are in active leisure pursuits. Furthermore, adolescents who are more likely to experience high levels of challenge and skill have a better overall quality of experience, are more often involved in productive activities, are more motivated and optimistic, and have higher self-esteem than their peers who experience flow less often. These trends persist even when social class, grades, ethnicity, and other potentially confounding variables are held constant, and despite the fact that productive, work-like activities tend to have negative connotations.

But what exactly are these challenges that adolescents in our study report when the pager signals at random moments in their lives? The very concept of challenge immediately becomes more complex and ambiguous when we begin to look at different individuals' perceptions of what challenge means. One girl finds tennis challenging: "I just like taking all my strength and hitting the ball....If anything bad is on my mind, I can pretend the ball is that person...and just whack it." Another enjoys singing in the choir and solving math problems. For some it is a challenge to resolve family problems; for others challenge means preparing for a career in the law or learning to drive.

Everyday life also presents an array of small problems—topical challenges that must be met, such as choosing the right gift for a sister or getting homework done on time. Teenagers, bear in mind, usually say that they don't *like* challenges, that they prefer things to be easy. Given a choice, they would usually prefer to be in the state of relaxation, where skills are higher than challenges. Yet the ESM shows that despite these preferences, it is when adolescents are challenged to get the most from their skills that they truly get the most from experiences.

{ 6 }

FAMILIES AND THE FORMING OF CHILDREN'S OCCUPATIONAL FUTURE

Kevin Rathunde, Mary Ellen Carroll,
and Molly Pei-lin Huang

D URING CHILDHOOD and youth, emerging occupational paths are strongly shaped by family characteristics and experiences. Until about two centuries ago, children learned adult work skills within the family. A farmer's son helped his father in the fields, the mason's son apprenticed to be a mason, and girls learned from their mothers the complex skills required to run a household. It was not until the Industrial Revolution in the mid-nineteenth century, and then only in the more industrialized nations, that most children had their first taste of work outside the family—and usually a bitter taste at that (Thompson 1963).

In today's economy, parents rarely teach children the work skills they will need as adults. Instead, the role of the family in socializing children to an occupational future consists of arranging for schooling and of exposing children to the values, motivations, attitudes, and expectations that they will need to find a satisfying, productive niche when they reach adulthood. As Parsons argued (1952), it is particularly in the family, with its face-to-face interactions and strong emotional bonds, that children can learn to accept discipline and internalize standards of conduct.

Family dynamics and their influence on the attitudes and actions of youths have often been overlooked in large data sets with nationally representative samples because of the difficulty of identifying, isolating, and measuring the most critical components of family interaction. Research has instead focused on the links between family characteristics and students' school success. Researchers have found that parents' level of education, family income, and parents' working status are strong predictors of school success. These predictors do not, however, provide the parent or school professional with many options for improving the situation. Moreover, these characteristics only generally describe the family environment, and as a result afford very limited explanations of how any particular child in a family is affected. For example, although a mother's financial resources may remain constant, her resources of energy and time may vary with the number of dependent children she has. Thus, the oldest and youngest children in a family might well describe their experiences quite differently. In examining the relationship between family dynamics and adolescents' performance in school, it is important to capture the family experience as each adolescent perceives it.

In adolescence, young people test their independence yet are reassured by the supportive net that the family provides. Teenagers typically say they feel pushed and pulled in many directions. These forces originate both in the individual and from such sources as friends, teachers, and family. As adolescents' needs and social participation broaden beyond the family, we can ask whether families continue to influence adolescent development. Do outside patterns of social interaction erode the family's effects on the individual? It might be argued that patterns established in childhood would be relatively fixed by the teenage years and the family's continuing influence would be minimal; in Vygotskian terms, the "intermental" would have already become the "intramental" (Vygotsky 1978). Adolescents have a wider social radius than young children and can fall under the sway of peer influence to a much greater degree (Harris 1998). They also have wider unsupervised exposure to symbolic media such as television, books, music, and film.

Despite these influences, research suggests that parental qualities such as love and discipline (referred to by various names in the parenting literature) are still important to adolescent development (Damon 1983; Irwin 1987; Maccoby and Martin 1983). For example, Reiss (1981) has argued that the family provides a "paradigm" that strongly affects the manner in which adolescents construct, and therefore experience, their worlds. It is not claimed that other influences at school (culture, teacher style, subject matter, presence or absence of friends, and so forth) have no effect, but that basic orientations formed within the family strongly influence how adolescents interpret their immediate circumstances and tasks.

Which aspects of family interaction are the most influential in providing an optimal developmental environment? Baumrind (1987, 1989) has associated the combination of *responsiveness* and *demandingness* (i.e., authoritative parenting) with optimal competence in adolescence. Cooper and her colleagues (1983) found that the combination of *connection* and *individuality* in family interaction (i.e., listening and coordinating views and expressing individual opinions) was related to adolescents' identity development and role-taking skills. Both of these outcomes demonstrate effective differentiating and integrating processes: Creating an identity requires a period of *crisis* (the exploration of alternatives) followed by *commitment* (making firm decisions) (Marcia 1980), and role-taking requires considering the perspectives of others in formulating one's own (Cooper et al. 1983). Finally, Hauser's (1991) research has revealed how supportive (*affective enabling*) and challenging (*cognitive enabling*) "moves" in family conversations were related to better adolescent ego-development; it also appears that higher stages of ego-development are increasingly dialectical in nature (Kegan 1982; Loevinger 1982).

Family support refers specifically to the parents' responsiveness to the child, but more broadly includes the responsiveness of the entire family unit. In a responsive family, the child is comfortable in the home, spends time with other family members, and feels loved and cared for. Challenge refers to the stimulation, discipline, or training that parents and other family members direct towards the child. Its aim is to foster autonomy and self-direction. Challenge also includes the expectations the child perceives family members to have of him or her and the child's desire to fulfill those expectations. A family environment is challenging when parents expect adolescents to take on greater responsibilities, learn new skills, and take risks that lead toward greater individuation. Teenagers practice reorganizing their attention, being more objective, and formulating plans of action that accommodate new expectations and goals. In a family environment that is both challenging and supportive, a parent listens in a nonjudgmental manner while allowing the child to explore special interests in a secure and relatively distraction-free environment. In such an atmosphere, an adolescent can engage the world less self-consciously, feel less constrained by demands, and thus more attuned to his or her own subjective experiences. Family support seems to be linked specifically to a child's playful, spontaneous, and affectively charged experiences, while family challenge figures in purposeful, self-conscious, goal-directed activities. When both these conditions are present, children are more likely to confront their adult responsibilities with enthusiasm as well as competence (see Csikszentmihalyi and Rathunde 1993; Csikszentmihalyi, Rathunde, and Whalen 1993; and Rathunde 1996).[1]

Although the dynamics of each family vary, we looked for patterns of similarity that would enable us to speak more generally about adolescents' family experiences. We wanted to develop a way of categorizing family contexts that recognized the different degrees to which adolescents perceived support and challenge to be present in their homes. The result is a typology of four family contexts that offers a new way to understand and measure the varying effects of family dynamics on adolescents' lives. Do families perceived as combining support with challenge raise children who are more optimistic and motivated and who have better work habits than those from families where support and challenge are less forthcoming? Do these differences relate to a child's success in school?

Measuring Support and Challenge

To measure the supportive and challenging aspects of an adolescent's family environment, we administered the Support/Challenge Questionnaire (SCQ). The SCQ was designed by Kevin Rathunde and colleagues for use in the study of talented teenagers by Csikszentmihalyi, Rathunde, and Whalen (1993). In our study the SCQ was expanded and included within the larger Teenage Life Questionnaire. The thirty-two items that make up the SCQ measure support and challenge separately on an "agree" or "disagree" scale. For instance, with regard to support, adolescents either agreed or disagreed with statements such as: "In my family I feel appreciated for who I am" or "We enjoy having dinner together and talking." With regard to challenge, they responded to such statements as: "In my family I am expected to do my best," or "We express our opinions about current events, even when they differ." Items were worded both positively and negatively, and they were phrased to address family dynamics as a whole. (See Appendix C for a full list.)[2]

To create the family typology, the support and challenge indices were each split at the mean. This yielded four family types, with the following distribution of students within each type: high support/high challenge (HS/HC, 45 percent); high support/low challenge (HS/LC, 11 percent); low support/high challenge (LS/HC, 14 percent); and low support/low challenge (LS/LC, 30 percent).

We predicted that adolescents from high-support/low-challenge families (HS/LC) would spend the most time with family members and that adolescents from low-support/high-challenge families (LS/HC) would spend the most time alone. To test this hypothesis, responses from the Experience Sampling Method (ESM) were aggregated to create estimates of time spent with family members and time spent alone. As expected, students from HS/LC families spent the equivalent of four more hours a week with their families than did LS/HC students.[3] The opposite was true for time spent alone, with adolescents from HS/LC families spending roughly four fewer hours a week alone than LS/HC adolescents.[4] Thus, even though the support and challenge indices are strongly correlated, they appear to be measuring different family characteristics.

The Relation of Family Context to Adolescent Attitudes and Experiences

The first set of analyses using the four family types examined whether students who perceived their families to be high challenge or high support

were more optimistic, better motivated, and had a better quality of experience. As expected, all these relationships were borne out (see Table 6.1).[5]

Respondents who saw their families as both challenging and supportive tended to have significantly higher self-esteem than their peers. They
also saw whatever they were doing as more important to present as well
as future goals. In addition, they tended to see whatever they were doing
as being like work more often than like play or like neither work nor play.

The family's principal contribution during the adolescent years appears to be to deepen and make more specific these students' motives, increasing levels of orientation to the future (salience), optimism,
self-esteem, and responsiveness to various motivating stimuli. By itself,
high family support is associated marginally with time spent in flow during the ESM week. More notably, teenagers who feel supported by their

TABLE 6.1   SELECTED VARIABLES SIGNIFICANTLY RELATED TO FAMILY TYPE

When adolescents perceive their families as providing:

both high challenge and high support, they are likely to . . .

    report being engaged in work-like activities*a

    report higher self-esteem****

    report higher salience in their main activities***

high support only, they are likely to . . .

    report a higher percentage of time spent in flow*

    be more optimistic***

    be more open to new experiences***

    be more intrinsically motivated****

    be more extrinsically motivated**

    be more socially motivated***

high challenge only, they are likely to . . .

    report more time in activities that are like both work and play*

    report less time in activities that are neither work nor play**

    be in a better mood, on average, during the week****

    be less pessimistic***

Significance of F value: *$p < .1$ **$p < .05$ ***$p < .01$ ****$p < .001$

    a MANCOVA, gender, grade level, race, school grades, and parental education controlled.

families tend to be optimistic and motivated; those who feel challenged by their families tend toward experiences of high quality and a sense of goal-directedness.

Thus, respondents from the high-support families, more than others, were optimistic and open to experience. The largest differences were in terms of motivation: These respondents felt stronger motivation, whether intrinsic, extrinsic, or social. Students from families perceived to be primarily challenging reported feeling in a significantly better mood than usual during the entire week of ESM testing. They also more often perceived activities as being like both work and play and reported less time in activities that were like neither work nor play. These high-challenge students also tended to be significantly less pessimistic. Finally, families perceived as both supportive and challenging were associated with the highest levels of self-esteem reported by our respondents and the strongest sense that activities engaged in during the ESM week were contributing to future goals. No relation was found between family types and students' knowledge about the world of work. The three variables measuring this construct (Knowledge, Fitscore, learn-do) did not differ according to family type. (See Appendix C for a description of these variables.)

We now turn to findings showing that attitudes and performance in school were very different for children in the four family types. These findings, in conjunction with the attitudinal and experiential results reported here, indicate that the dynamics of family interaction may have a strong effect on how well prepared an adolescent will be to face the future, and especially on his or her capacity for a successful transition to the working world.

Family Context and School Outcomes

To determine the relation between family contexts and school performance, three school outcomes are analyzed: attitudes about school, time spent on homework, and grades. These school outcomes were selected for two reasons. First, previous research has linked them to school achievement. For example, students with positive attitudes toward their schools, teachers, and classmates are more relaxed and open to experience at school and therefore better prepared to learn. Second, we expect family support and challenge to have a strong effect on these outcomes, given our findings regarding their broad motivational significance. The analyses were performed on the entire cohort sample, controlling for student's race or ethnicity, grade in school, gender, and parental education. The results suggest that the combined levels of support and challenge in the family are useful predictors of adolescents' school outcomes.

Student Attitudes Toward School

We expected to find that a highly supportive family environment would be associated with students' positive attitudes about school. Fifteen items on the Teenage Life Questionnaire probed students' attitudes about their schools, teachers, and fellow students. (See Appendix C for the questions.) Factor analysis of these questions yielded four attitudinal dimensions: positive attitude toward teachers, positive attitude toward students, feelings of security, and sense of school cohesiveness.[6] The results of this analysis provide some support for our original hypothesis (see Table 6.2). After controlling for the background variables, only family support was a significant predictor of positive attitudes toward other students, and it was a stronger predictor than challenge of attitudes toward teachers, feelings of security in school, and perceived school cohesiveness. Although high challenge also predicted positive attitudes toward teachers, feelings of security, and sense of school cohesiveness, support accounted for more of the variance in these measures.[7] The questionnaire measures also indicated that students from supportive homes were more "upbeat" and positive about their learning environments.[8]

Time Spent on Homework

Another important indicator of adolescents' school performance and preparation for the future is the amount of time spent on homework. Because completing homework is largely a matter of planning ahead and exercising self-discipline in postponing other activities, we expected that adolescents who perceive their families to be more challenging (i.e., adolescents who have presumably had more pressure and more practice in

TABLE 6.2 STUDENTS' ATTITUDE ABOUT SCHOOL BY FAMILY TYPE

	High Support High Challenge[a]	High Support Low Challenge	Low Support High Challenge	Low Support Low Challenge	F-test Statistics[1]
Positive attitude about teachers	$17.02,^a$ (3.1)[3]	16.5^b (3.0)	15.8^d (3.4)	15.0 (3.6)	$F_{support} = 92.2$*** $F_{challenge} = 19.2$*** $F_{support*challenge} = 1.1$
	N = 1246	N = 300	N = 398	N = 833	
Positive attitude about other students	7.2^b (1.8)	7.1^c (1.8)	6.8 (1.9)	7.0 (1.9)	$F_{support} = 9.9$** $F_{challenge} = 0.3$ $F_{support*challenge} = 2.2$
	N = 1276	N = 307	N = 408	N = 867	
Feelings of security	9.5^a (1.6)	9.2^b (1.7)	9.0^d (1.8)	8.7 (1.9)	$F_{support} = 47.2$*** $F_{challenge} = 11.1$** $F_{support*challenge} = 0.1$
	N = 1299	N = 306	N = 404	N = 864	
School cohesiveness	8.4^a (1.7)	8.2^d (1.7)	8.0^d (1.8)	7.8 (1.7)	$F_{support} = 26.5$*** $F_{challenge} = 8.2$** $F_{support*challenge} = 0.0$
	N = 1292	N = 309	N = 411	N = 874	

[1] F-test statistics are results of 2x2 MANCOVA (high/low support by high/low challenge), adjusting jointly for the covariates: gender, parental education, ethnicity, and grade.

*p < .05 **p < .01 ***p < .001

[2] Means are adjusted for the covariates.

Superscripts indicate significant differences (p < .05) between family types.

[a] Significantly different from HSLC, LSHC, and LSLC families

[b] Significantly different from LSHC and LSLC families

[c] Significantly different from LSHC family

[d] Significantly different from LSLC family

[3] Standard deviations are in parentheses.

accommodating expectations at home) would be doing more homework. The data provided an excellent opportunity to test this hypothesis because of the availability of two convergent measures, one deriving from the Teenage Life Questionnaire and one from the ESM.

Two items on the Teenage Life Questionnaire asked about homework: one about time invested in homework in school and one about time devoted to doing homework outside of school. Responses ranged from 1 to 8, and each response category indicated a different number of hours per week (e.g., 3 = two to three hours, 4 = four to six hours, 5 = seven to nine hours, and so forth). The ESM can be used to estimate time by counting the number of signals each student responded to while doing a particular activity such as homework. This count is then transformed into a percentage of the respondent's total number of signals for the week, thus providing an estimate of hours spent in that activity. Table 6.3 reports the time-use results of both the Teenage Life Questionnaire and the ESM.

Both homework estimates confirmed the perception that high challenge in the family is associated with more time invested in homework.[9] The comparisons of ESM and questionnaire results suggest a substantial effect for challenge and no effect for support or the interaction of support and challenge. The means from the questionnaire estimates indicate that the high-challenge families (HS/HC and LS/HC), in comparison to the low-challenge groups (HS/LC and LS/LC), were doing about two to three hours more homework per week outside of school. The ESM time estimates told a similar story: The high-challenge groups again reported doing more homework than the low-challenge groups and also spending about two hours more per week doing homework.[10]

Grades in School

Final analyses examined students' self-reported grades. Although self-reported grades have less face validity than actual grade point averages, the two are usually highly correlated. In addition, grades provide a relatively narrow look at positive school performance because they say little about personal or motivational qualities that can help students prepare for their futures. Nevertheless, self-reported grades were among the best school outcome measures available in the data set.

Two measures of grades were computed from questions on the Teenage Life Questionnaire. The first was based on student responses to

TABLE 6.3 NELS AND ESM ESTIMATES OF TIME DOING HOMEWORK BY FAMILY TYPE

	High Support High Challenge[a]	High Support Low Challenge	Low Support High Challenge	Low Support Low Challenge	F-test statistics[1]
NELS time estimates					
Time doing homework in school[4]	2.92,[a] (1.5)3	2.7 (1.3)	2.9 (1.6)	2.7 (1.5)	$F_{support} = 0.1$ $F_{challenge} = 6.1*$ $F_{support*challenge} = 0.7$
	N = 1090	N = 250	N = 316	N = 693	
Time doing homework outside school	3.9[a] (1.9)	3.2 (1.8)	3.7[a] (1.9)	3.3 (1.7)	$F_{support} = 0.0$ $F_{challenge} = 37.4***$ $F_{support*challenge} = 3.6$
	N = 1146	N = 252	N = 347	N = 746	
ESM time estimate					
Time doing homework	13.8[b] (8.7)	11.5 (7.1)	14.6[a] (10.3)	11.6 (8.3)	$F_{support} = 0.6$ $F_{challenge} = 8.8**$ $F_{support*challenge} = 0.2$
	N = 330	N = 49	N = 99	N = 155	

[1] F-test statistics are results of 2x2 MANCOVA (high/low support by high/low challenge), adjusting jointly for the covariates: gender, parental education, ethnicity, and grade.

*p < .05 **p < .01 ***p < .001

[2] Means are adjusted for the covariates.

Superscripts indicate significant differences (p < .05) between family types.

[a] Significantly different from HSLC and LSLC families

[b] Significantly different from LSLC family

[3] Standard deviations are in parentheses.

[4] Coding for time doing homework "in" and "outside" school: 1 = none, 2 = 1 hour or less, 3 = 2–3 hours, 4 = 4–6 hours, 5 = 7–9 hours, 6 = 10–12 hours, 7 = 13–15 hours, 8 = over 15 hours.

the question: "Which of the following statements best describes your grades on your last report card?" A second question directed students to "circle the statement that best describes your grades from the sixth grade up till now" in reference to English, math, science, and social studies. The responses to the latter question were summed and divided by the four subject areas to produce one composite grade point average since sixth grade for each student.

We expected grades to be related to family support and challenge. Challenge would presumably relate to grades through students' valuing achievement more highly and being better prepared to work hard. Support would be related to grades through students' being in a more positive frame of mind while doing schoolwork. Table 6.4 presents the results for both analyses. Both high support and high challenge were significantly related to recent and cumulative grades.[11] On the latter measure, family challenge was the stronger predictor. Teenagers who felt supported and challenged at home reported higher recent grades, and higher cumulative grades, than did students from the other three family groups. Students from HS/HC families on average reported grades in the A–B range.

The findings regarding these school outcomes and adolescents' family dynamics permit the following conclusions. Family support is strongly linked to the social-emotional variables that one might informally think of as revealing an optimistic frame of mind. It is also associated with seeing teachers as more empathetic and helpful, feeling psychologically and physically more secure at school, sensing that the school culture is more cohesive, and especially with seeing other students in a positive light.

Family challenge, on the other hand, was more strongly associated with what might be called a determined frame of mind. When students from high-challenge families sat down to do homework, they apparently approached the task more objectively, as a means to future growth and achievement. Not surprisingly, students who reported more challenge at home also did more homework: by all estimates, at least two hours more homework per week. Finally, higher student grades were associated with both support and challenge. Whether reporting their most recent grades or their cumulative grade point average across a variety of subjects, those students excelled more in school who felt the push to risk individuation while knowing they had a safety net of approval and acceptance below them if they fell.

The findings that link optimism to family support and determination to family challenge replicate in many ways the results summarized in Table 6.1 concerning students' general attitudes. In school or out, it looks as though the way teenagers experience family interaction is related to two fundamental dimensions of their lives: how much they enjoy the present and how ready they are to face the future.

TABLE 6.4 RECENT AND CUMULATIVE GRADES BY FAMILY TYPE

	High Support High Challenge[a]	High Support Low Challenge	Low Support High Challenge	Low Support Low Challenge	F-test statistics[1]
Recent grades[4] (last report card)	2.52[a] (1.5)3	3.0[c] (1.7)	3.0[c] (1.7)	3.3 (1.8)	$F_{support} = 23.1$*** $F_{challenge} = 27.0$*** $F_{support*challenge} = 2.31$
	N = 1215	N = 276	N = 377	N = 804	
Cumulative grades[5] (since 6th grade)	3.2[a] (0.6)	3.0 (0.6)	3.1[b] (0.7)	2.9 (0.7)	$F_{support} = 4.2$* $F_{challenge} = 36.4$*** $F_{support*challenge} = 1.6$
	N = 728	N = 186	N = 207	N = 450	

a

[1] F-test statistics are results of 2x2 MANCOVA (high/low support by high/low challenge), adjusting jointly for the covariates: gender, parental education, ethnicity, and grade.

*p < .05 **p < .01 ***p < .001

[2] Means are adjusted for the covariates.

Superscripts indicate significant differences (p < .05) between family types.

[a] Significantly different from HSLC, LSHC and LSLC families

[b] Significantly different from HSLC and LSLC families

[c] Significantly different from LSLC family

[3] Standard deviations are in parentheses.

[4] Coding for recent grades: 1: mostly As, 2: = about half As and half Bs, 3 = mostly Bs, 4: about half Bs and half Cs, 5 = mostly Cs, 6 = about half Cs and half Ds, 7 = mostly Ds, 8 = mostly below D.

[5] Coding for cumulative grades: 4 = A, 3 = B, 2 = C, 1 = D, 0 = below D or F.

Experience While Doing School-Related Activities

Two composite ESM variables were selected to represent the "present" and "future" aspects of engagement or undivided interest—namely, mood and salience. Mood is the sum of the individual items excited, relaxed, happy, strong, active, sociable, and proud.[12] Salience includes the items' importance to self and importance to future goals.[13] Thus, ESM reports of high mood and high salience would suggest that students felt positive affective states and energy (a variable hypothesized to be related to family support) and that they also felt they were applying themselves toward goals that were relevant to themselves and their futures (a variable presumably related to family challenge). Such a combination captures the meaning of the experiential mode that coordinates play-like and work-like orientations. Scores for these two variables were obtained by selecting all the ESM signals that occurred in school-related activities (signals that occurred in class or while the students were doing productive activities) and then aggregating those signals for each student.

Results for student experience were consistent with predictions. Family support was significantly associated with students' moods in school-work, whereas challenge was not, and there was no interaction between support and challenge.[14] Conversely, students' feelings of salience were significantly associated with family challenge but not with support, and there was no interaction.[15] Thus, students who described their families as supportive reported better moods in school; students who said that their families noticed accomplishments and expected them to do their best reported being more focused on career-relevant goals.[16] Figure 6.1 plots the adjusted means for mood and salience across the four family groups.

These findings replicate those reached earlier for talented teenagers by Csikszentmihalyi, Rathunde, and Whalen (1993). In that study, family support was related specifically to momentary moods and challenge to thoughts about goals. Because the present sample is approximately three times the size of the talented teen sample and contains a greater diversity of age, ethnicity, and socioeconomic status, our study's results expand the generalizability of the talented-teen findings.

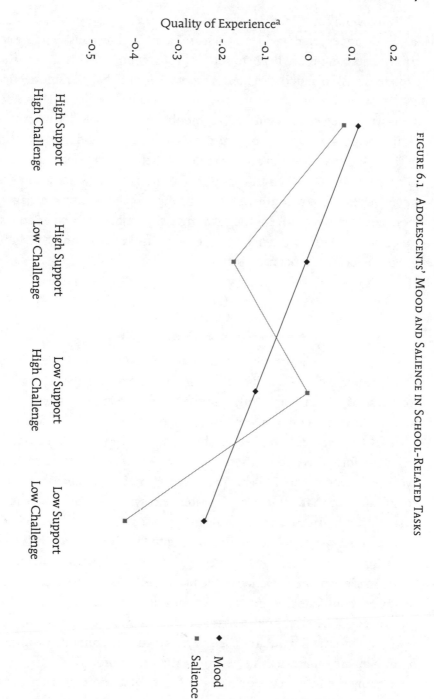

FIGURE 6.1 ADOLESCENTS' MOOD AND SALIENCE IN SCHOOL-RELATED TASKS

Quality of Experience[a]

0.2
0.1
0
-0.1
-.02
-0.3
-0.4
-0.5

High Support
High Challenge

High Support
Low Challenge

Low Support
High Challenge

Low Support
Low Challenge

◆ Mood
■ Salience

[a] Adjusted for age, gender, ethnic background, and parental education.

Thus, when actually in class or sitting down to do homework, the adolescents who reported having warm, consistent, and responsive home environments were more likely to report positive moods. This means that adolescents from supportive homes reported feeling happier, more energetic, and less on guard when they were productively engaged. Those students whose perceived home environments featured lively debate among family members, modeling of goal-directed behaviors, and high expectations for individuality and agency reported their school-related activities to be more salient to their futures than did their peers. We see again that a dynamic family environment fosters young people's ability to engage in productive activity as well as their willingness to relate such experience to their futures. Both are crucial to the successful negotiation of educational and occupational trajectories.

Narratives of Family Life

As expected, the quantitative data show the strong links between family structure and dynamics and adolescent outcomes. Despite the rumored weakness of the nuclear family and the array of institutions competing for influence over children, our results suggest that teenagers' family experiences are strongly related to their attitudes, motivations, habits, school performance, and self-esteem. Numbers and tables do not, however, give a good sense of exactly what transpires in families that differ in complexity. For that, we turn to the interviews with students and parents to see how they describe their family interactions. The parent and adolescent interview data were sorted according to family type and then were selected for review based on the presence of both parent and child interviews. Single interviews were included where ethnic, racial, or site representation could not be maintained through paired interviews. The interviews chosen were representative of the full sample. They are not analyzed systematically but are used as illustrations; conclusions drawn from them are intended as suggestions rather than proof.

Reading the interviews, one gets the sense of a strong consensus between children and parents about what they value and desire from life and from one another. Across all families, a number of common themes emerge. Almost all teenagers say that their parents expect them to be responsible, keep their rooms clean, do their best in school, and succeed in life. They report that their parents want them to do whatever will make them happy. Parents confirm their children's perceptions, saying they want above all for their children to be happy, to do what they want to do, to be successful at it, and to get as far ahead in life as possible. Although hopeful, parents' remarks are also usually qualified and cautious, recognizing that many hopes may not be fully realized.

These similarities, however, soon give way to strong differences clustered around issues of communication, family interaction, and clarity in parents' and children's beliefs and goals. The frequency, breadth, and substance of communication between parents and children varies greatly across families. For some families, communication patterns are influenced by the adolescent's degree of comfort with and access to a parent and more by how parents and children get along. In other families, the lines of communication may be open, yet little information of any substance seems to get through.

Another dimension of family life where large differences appear is the extent and kind of mutual involvement among family members, or family interaction. Some children talk about their parents as if their lives proceed along separate tracks; there might be communication but very little interaction, few joint activities, and little sense of shared interests or passions. In such families, the parent also looks at the child as if from a distance; approvingly perhaps, but with no indication that their lives directly influence each other's. In still other families, both teenagers and parents talk about their mutual relationships as an unfolding drama where each person's actions are interlocked with the other's, and where dreams and plans are shared—perhaps to excess.

Finally, families differ greatly in the extent to which parents purposely shape a child's development. There are families in which parents seem to have resigned any educational or socializing function, either because they feel they have failed or because they feel unsuited, for whatever reason, to advise and discipline their children. Parents in some families have a clear agenda that they are determined the child will follow. In those situations, teenagers sometimes complain that they are being pushed too hard and that they have few choices. In still other families, parents' and children's behaviors emerge primarily from their beliefs about the immediate and long-term relevance of their actions to future goals. With such diversity among families, we must ask whether these differences correspond to the varying intensity of support and challenge in each of the family types.

High-Challenge, High-Support Families

Parents and adolescents in these families speak of themselves and their actions as being highly intentional. Parents in these families express their own strong motivation and expect children to learn from their example. Family members speak frequently of being involved in and influenced by supportive and socializing networks outside the immediate family—especially in the church, extended family, or community groups. Parents and teenager appear deeply involved in each other's lives. For example, here is Tracy talking about her family life:

> [On Saturday] I go to Mass with my family. . . . And then my grand-mother's house is right next door. So we go over there and have supper. . . .
> My grandparents, my family and my uncle's family . . . my aunt and her family . . . and usually afterwards all the adults get together, they play euchre [a highly competitive card game]. . . . My dad is with me as far as sports go. . . . He's keeping the book for the softball team, so he's there with me. . . . They [parents] want me to do better than what they've done in their life as far as education goes. Being secure financially. . . . They have always told me: "Do your best." And if you're happy with your effort and what you've done, then that's good enough for them, too.

Following is what Tracy's father says. Note that while he tries to leave his daughter as free as possible, he has definite expectations for her future:

> What I would like to have for my children . . . just to have them see the need to reach their full potential and not lay back and just do enough to

get by. I'd like to see them...be happy with what they are doing....I know this might sound kind of corny but I really am trying to leave it up to her. Because it's her right and as long as she goes to college and she is going to a pretty reputable school, and I have faith in her that she will do well in school because she has that work ethic I think she got from her mother.

Like most parents in this group, Jessica's mother also has high expectations for her children, as well as a desire to see them become independent. She describes how her family has been able to keep the level of challenge high for their children:

Over the years we've done an enormous amount of traveling, and when we were younger...we did museums...took them to the ballet or to musical things. We started out thinking *we* would educate the kids and if by chance they learned something at school, so much the better.... We've certainly given them a whole lot of additional stimulation and experience in learning, but I could not have done the academic stuff.

Jessica's mother, like many others, is articulate about the purposes behind her parenting decisions. She conveys the need and the ability to expose her children to what she believes are valuable experiences. In turn, Jessica appreciates her mother's motives. In some cases, however, a shared sense of purpose is missing and instead either the child or the parent pushes for his or her own individual goals.

Hank describes his own desires and how they are slightly overshadowed by his parents' expectations of him:

They want me to go to college. They expect it of me....I want to go....I am not sure that I want to go right away though. Maybe take like a semester off or something....I will go to City [the community college]. They have a good architectural program there.

Hank's parents, who were interviewed together, express a strong desire to direct Hank's decisions about his future. They describe their aims and motivation in the following dialogue:

MOTHER: We always tell the kids, they can do anything they want to do. It is up to them how much they want it. And that is very important to let them know.

FATHER: To a kid, that is a meaningless statement. I think that they don't know what it means to be what they want to be....I mean, a sixteen-year-old who is worried about when is the next party, and you say, "You can be anything you want to be."

MOTHER: But we have put the seed in their heads. And they may not know right now what they want to be, but the seed is there...to do whatever they choose to do.

FATHER: I would like to see him get through college. And...we will financially fund that. Whereas, I did not get any financial benefits.

In some instances, the stronger source of adolescent motivation is internal, as Sheila notes when describing how her own expectations surpass those of her parents. She states: "All they ever expect from me is to finish what I start and do the best job that I can....They didn't tell me I *had* to go [to college]....They'd rather I go...but...all my parents really want for me is to be happy...and secure....I think I push myself harder and I expect myself to do better." Whether the motivation and clarity of purpose is shared between parent and child or falls most heavily on one side or the other, these families express a clear sense of direction and what it will take for students to reach their goals.

As these excerpts suggest, families high in both support and challenge express strong beliefs in individuality, in the full development of individual potentialities, and in the right for everyone to achieve happiness. In these families expectations are clearly articulated but are linked to an expressed need for individual freedom; personal fulfillment is joined to a sense of responsibility. There is a sense that love permeates the entire family and that each member is dedicated to the well-being of the others. Yet at the same time, there is also an almost taken-for-granted expectation that each person will be different and will strive to the utmost to do his or her best. It is not easy to keep a system of such complexity going. The families that are able to do it are fortunate in many respects: Parents tend to be more educated and not to have experienced divorce. Yet even these advantages are not enough; these families also seem to have strong convictions about their values and their place in life. They act purposefully and trust their ability to handle the unexpected.

High-Challenge, Low-Support Families

Motivation to succeed occupies a large part of the narrative of both parents and children in this group. The definition of success often goes beyond financial and status achievements to reflect a genuine need to develop any potential to the utmost. Signs of strain include a somewhat excessive competitiveness, even with siblings, and the perception on the students' part that parents are pushing too hard and that their expectations are inordinately high. The situation becomes less than ideal when the family is not communicating and is not mutually involved, so that students find parental expectations arbitrary and external. Hugh describes his family:

> [What kind of things do you do with your family?] Me? I don't do anything with them. Well, maybe. Like if we have to go to a wedding or a funeral, that kind of thing. Or they'll have a party. But nothing social like, you know. I just...don't find a place in the family. I like to be my own person.

His mother speaks of the importance of meaningful work for Hugh when he grows up: "In our family we have a nurse. We have a doctor. We have a lawyer.... I would like Hugh to continue school...[to do] some medical thing.... As long as he does something good, you know I don't mind."

Asked about his parents' expectations of him, another student in this group, Kaz, responds:

> They are very high. They expect straight As....I had straight As last quarter, so now this quarter I don't want to do so well. [Because] they expect it from you. Once you get it once, it's like, get it for the rest of your life, you

know. So I don't want them to expect it. I said, "Wait a minute. I want to enjoy life."

Kaz's father says:

I think he feels the pressure from us. I'm kind of strict...so I tend to push him to study or something. He feels a lot of pressure from us. Now he looks lazy....he tends to be passive, he doesn't want to start new things. That's...what I'm a little worried about.

Another student, Judy, says that the expectation of going to college has been drilled into her since she was two years old, and if she doesn't go to college, her parents "would, like, kill me." Her mother admits ambivalence about her expectations for her daughter's success:

I try to avoid telling her she should do well. I don't think that's helpful. In theory, I feel like if you work hard, however you do is OK. I haven't had to face the situation of a child not doing well. I really don't know how I would react. In theory I'll be accepting, but in reality I'd be really disappointed.

In some families, parents' disappointment at the reality of their child's motivation, academic performance, or future goals may explain in part why their children perceive a lack of support in the home. This disappointment may also be at the root of many parents' desires for their child to do something useful in the future. Adolescents in these families have a solid grasp of what is expected of them, and while they may identify in part with these expectations, they do not appear to embrace them wholeheartedly as their own. And in some cases they reject them.

Low-Challenge, High-Support Families

As with previous groups, parents in these families want their children to do their best, no matter what the outcome. In these families, however, parents seem to emphasize "not wanting to push," and children agree that they are "not being pushed" by parents. Parents yield to their children's interests and often mention their child's interest in social service jobs: teacher, nurse, the helping professions in general. There is much talk about trust and respect in the home, and one gets the impression that family members discuss and share information on a regular basis. Some students in this group complain that parents are too involved in their lives. Trish describes the kind of intense emotional support she gets at home:

> My mom is really protective. She's one of those people, she's constantly worrying about something. She is happy if she has something to worry about.... My mom does everything for me.... She is constantly running around doing things for everybody.... My dad is constantly helping me with school stuff.... but they are not at all those parents who, like, pressure you to do things, and to be the best at things.

And her mother concurs:

> We're not the kind of parents that will give them a reward if they come home with straight As or straight Bs. I just say to them, do the best you can, and if Cs are the best you can do...we won't expect more of you.... and both of us have made it clear to the kids that if they had something that was bothering them there's nothing that they couldn't come and tell us.... It feels good that we've got that kind of relationship.

Steve, a junior in high school, is beginning to think that maybe he should plan to go to college after graduation because "Dad is fascinated with college." He himself is not so sure. He would like to open a restaurant after school, or do "something mechanical," or possibly be an orthodontist. He discusses his plans with his parents occasionally, but he doesn't feel they are pushing him in any particular direction. Steve's mother has this to say about what she expects of her son:

> I just want him to find something that he really likes and do it. He is not going to ever have to worry about money. His father has tons of money

put away [for him.]...millions....I just hope Steve doesn't get dependent on that....I hope he finds something he likes and is good at.

Joanne's mother also wants her daughter to be happy, and when asked about the likelihood of Joanne attending college, replies: "I don't think it's even [a question] in this area. I think kids...most of them, they do go on. I mean, it's just...something they do." This reply is similar to other parents and adolescents in this group, who talk about present and future decisions without much intention or purpose seeming to guide their decisions. Although these families are often warm and close-knit, they tend to lack the boundaries and articulated purposefulness found in families that offer a more challenging environment. The focus of these families is defined in terms of the strength of their internal relationships. Though not perfect, these families seem to offer enviable stability and emotional support, especially in comparison with those low in support.

Low-Challenge, Low-Support Families

This group of families is not well positioned to prepare children for a positive future. Parents are often absent and, even when physically present, seem uninvolved and uncommunicative. Students spend little time with their families. Much more than in the other family types, goals are vague, expectations are phrased in terms of "whatever direction the child takes is all right," and interview questions are often answered with "I don't know."

Typical of students from these families is the interview with Sam, a high school senior who would like to become a lawyer:

[What do you think your mom expects from you?]
  To get good grades.
[What are good grades?]
  As and Bs.
[What else does she expect of you?]
  Responsibility.

[For what?]

Everything.

[What are some big ones?]

Um, keeping the house clean, 'cause I dirty it. Coming home early. Like those are the big ones.

[What about college?]

Yeah, she wants me to go to college.

[Do you talk about the future with her?]

No.

[Why not?]

Because...I don't know. She knows I don't read, I don't, like, get into details. Things like that....She likes [me becoming a lawyer] 'cause it's a good profession....I don't want to be a truck driver or something.

Lisa, a senior, mentions that she expects to finish high school but has no further plans. She never talks with her parents about her future—or about much of anything else. Her mother shares Lisa's hope that she will finish school "so she won't be like me, an ignorant woman." She expects to help with her daughter's education for as long as possible, provided Lisa does not marry, but expresses a sense of helplessness in regard to her daughter's future. She says, "I tell her to finish her studies but if she does not want to, what do you want me to do to her?"

Jarod has more ambitious plans: "I want to be a lot of stuff. When I was younger, like in fifth grade, I wanted to be an astronaut. And then I wanted to be a doctor. Now I want to be a laser technician or a computer scientist." Yet he doesn't talk about these plans with his parents, and his mother, who worries about Jarod's emotional life and low grades, wishes she could help him academically but feels it is his teacher's responsibility.

Another student, Sherry, when asked about her parents' expectations for her, answers: "I don't know....They never talk to me about that." And her mother says: "I don't know....I'd like to see her really rich, because she likes to spend a lot of money....To go into a store and not look at a price tag—just look at a blouse and say, 'That's what I want.' I guess that's what I'd want for her."

Most of the parents in these families have good intentions and try hard, but it is clear from the interviews that many in this group feel somewhat bewildered and defeated. One senses that these parents' expectations are unaffected by realities they see but do not accept. They want the best for their children, sometimes expecting them to be doctors or lawyers even though their children are just scraping by academically. The children of these families seem to face the future alone, although they share their parents' confusion and helplessness.

One also senses that the most detrimental aspect of these families is a lack of spirit, cohesion, and purpose. More interaction between parents and children, more dedication to common goals, might greatly improve the quality of these children's lives and future prospects. Undoubtedly, some of the disadvantages in these families may be the result of a lack of social and material resources. Such disadvantages make it much harder to create a differentiated and integrated family, which in turn seems to impede the children's ability to compete—a vicious cycle. Yet if parents maintain clear values and strong involvement it seems possible to interrupt this cycle, as is demonstrated by the disadvantaged families that appeared in the high-support, high-challenge group.

Parenting and Adolescent Development

Much has been claimed here for the importance of family support and challenge for adolescents—certainly more than can be demonstrated by the empirical findings. Yet these findings, which have correlational rather than causal significance, confirm a great deal of what is known about parenting and child development, and suggesting as well new ways to understand the influence of families on adolescent development. We have seen, for instance, that the most effective families appear to be those that give teenagers the sense that they are loved, together with the sense that much is expected from them. This combination is related to students' self-esteem, as well as to their feeling that their present actions contribute to the future. This combination appears to provide the best setting for teenagers' academic achievement and sense of security. The level of family support that students feel is strongly related to their optimism and sense of well-being at work. The level of challenge they experience in the family is related more to their sense that they are working toward the future and to the amount of time they devote to homework.

These and the other results linking family type to student outcomes were found after controlling for other main variables such as gender, age, race and ethnicity, and parental education. In other words, family dynamic variables can explain adolescent outcomes independent of these structural variables. This suggests that the atmosphere parents create in the family can make a positive difference in their children's adult lives, regardless of what disadvantages the family may suffer. The findings also suggest that it is worthwhile to explore the complexities of family dynamics in greater depth because the way in which children experience interactions at home may have a decisive impact on their future and well-being.

{ 7 }

THE QUALITY OF CLASSROOM EXPERIENCES

David Shernoff, Shaunti Knauth,
and Eleni Makris

HOW DO DIFFERENT types of classroom activities affect the daily experiences of high school students? How do classroom experiences differ by school subject and course placement? This chapter seeks to better understand the nature of learning environments and to identify activities that encourage competency, confidence, and engagement in challenging activities. We believe that instructional activities directly influence students' interest in and engagement with schoolwork and ultimately affect the formation of their future goals. Students' attitudes toward present and future educational opportunities are affected by many aspects of school experiences, including the challenge of school activities, students' perceived abilities to meet them, their desire to participate in them, and the importance they ascribe to them. Classroom activities may vary dramatically in the challenge or enjoyment they provide. Careful study of what happens to students as they move from one activity to another contributes to our understanding of how curricular designs and pedagogical choices enhance or impede opportunities for learning. For example, do students concentrate better when they are listening to the teacher lecture, watching an instructional video, or taking a test? Are individual or group classroom activities perceived as more enjoyable and important to one's future goals? Here we examine how high school students spend their time while at school, especially while in class. We then focus on the extent to which common classroom activities vary in levels of challenge, concentration, enjoyment, importance to future goals, and students' motivation to do the activity. Next, a multidimensional measure of optimal experience, or flow, is used to compare opportunities for optimal learning across school activities. We then examine how students experience school subjects by ability level. Finally, we consider the influence of several individual and background characteristics of students to determine whether the trends we observe are similar for all students.

Where Do Students Spend Their Time in School?

We know that students are in various settings both in and out of classrooms while at school. Exactly how do adolescents spend their time among these settings while at school? Relying on our students' responses to the ESM, we find that a little more than half (55 percent) of their time, or three hours daily, is spent in academic classes, including math, English, history, science, social studies, and foreign languages. Roughly 12 percent of students' time in school is spent in nonacademic classes such as physical education, art, vocational education, and health. A third of students' time at school, approximately two hours per day, is unstructured time spent somewhere on school grounds outside of class—in the lunchroom, gym, halls, student center, library, administrative buildings, or outside the buildings.

The amount of unstructured time students have in American schools is startlingly high, especially in comparison to other countries where time in high schools is not nearly so flexible. In Japanese high schools, for example, students have no study halls or free periods, tend to eat lunch at their desks, and use the library only after class hours. Because Japanese high school students are in a classroom with a teacher every hour of the school day, unstructured time is virtually nonexistent (Rohlen 1983; TIMSS 1996).

Based on previous studies, we suspected that unstructured or unproductive activities will produce few opportunities for optimal experiences or flow. Csikszentmihalyi found that the quality of experience during unstructured time breeds idling, resting, and nonpurposeful activity, which are usually negatively related to flow (1997). In Chapter 5, for example, we saw that productive activities such as classwork, homework, and jobs are the richest source of flow for adolescents, whereas activities such as resting, eating, or watching television rarely produce flow.

Time Spent in Various Classroom Activities

We began our analysis by estimating how students spend their time in their academic and nonacademic classes (see Figure 7.1). Our attempt to categorize activities is admittedly rough, especially since our experiential sample pools data from many different classes and kinds of activities. In addition, teachers often freely mix lecturing, leading discussion, answering questions, and explaining the day's assignments. Nevertheless, we believe these estimates provide a useful reflection of the overall frequency of activities and instructional formats used in classrooms.

According to students' responses to the ESM, the two most frequent activities—taking up almost half of classroom time—are listening to the teacher lecture (23 percent) and doing individual work (23 percent). When combined with doing homework or studying and listening and taking notes, the majority of students' time in class—almost twenty hours per week—is relatively individualized and noninteractive seat work. Students also spend a fair amount of time taking tests or quizzes and watching television or videos. Startlingly small amounts of time are spent in more interactive endeavors. Students reported spending only 5 percent of their time engaged in class discussion and only 3 percent participating in a group project or lab.

144

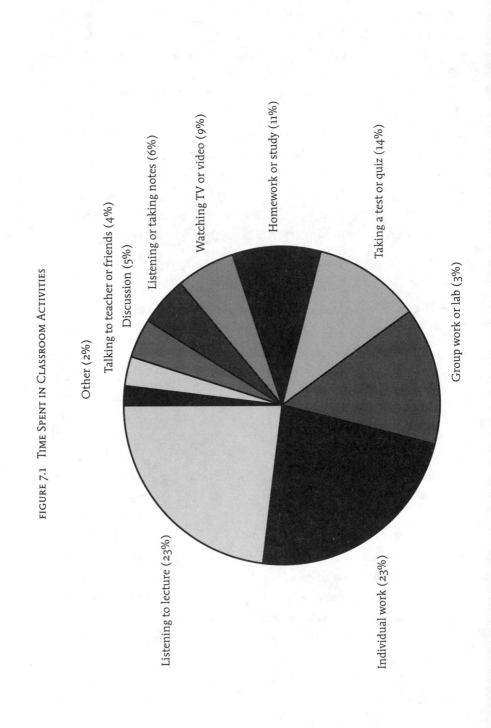

FIGURE 7.1   TIME SPENT IN CLASSROOM ACTIVITIES

Other (2%)

Talking to teacher or friends (4%)
Discussion (5%)

Listening or taking notes (6%)

Watching TV or video (9%)

Homework or study (11%)

Taking a test or quiz (14%)

Group work or lab (3%)

Individual work (23%)

Listening to lecture (23%)

These percentages suggest that students spend about half of their class time (54 percent) on independent work that can be thought of as intellectually challenging: doing individual work, taking a test or quiz, studying or doing homework, or taking notes. Nearly one-third of their time (32 percent), however, is spent sitting and passively attending to information transmitted to the entire class (listening to a lecture, watching television or videos). Students spend minimal amounts of time (8 percent) in activities that could be considered more interactive or engaging, such as participating in a class discussion or a group activity. Relative to the amount of time adolescents spend listening to information designed for the whole class, they spend little time talking individually with the teacher (at most 2 percent).

How Students Experience Different Classroom Activities

We now turn to what students report feeling in various kinds of classroom activities (see Figure 7.2). Not surprisingly, students feel the most challenged when taking tests or quizzes. They are also highly challenged while doing individual and group work. Students feel significantly less challenged while listening to a lecture or watching a television program or video. The same general pattern holds for concentration and importance to future goals. The only difference worth noting is that students did not find listening to a lecture significantly more or less important to their future goals than other activities.

These findings provide two important insights into students' classroom experiences. First, there are substantial differences in the amount of challenge provided by predominant school activities and in the amount of importance students place on them. Second, students' concentration in classroom activities is strongly related to both the level of challenge of the activities and their relevance to future goals.

The trend is almost completely reversed when we compare levels of enjoyment in these same activities. Even though taking tests or quizzes

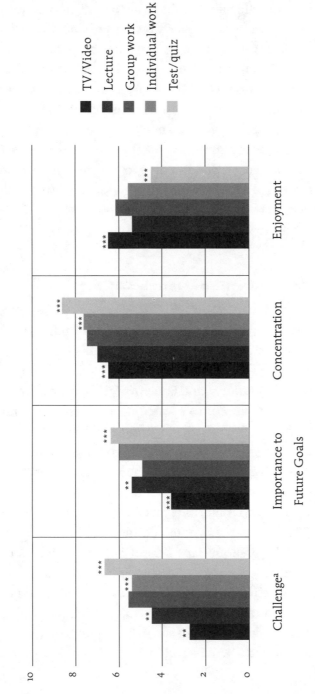

FIGURE 7.2 QUALITY OF EXPERIENCE IN COMMON CLASSROOM ACTIVITIES

*p < .05
**p < .01
***p < .001

(Indictes contrast to the other activities combined.)

[a] An Analysis of Variance comparing mean ESM scores in the five selected classroom activities yielded the following results:

for challenge F = 84.77, p < .001;   for importance to future goals F = 37.37, p < .001;
for concentration F = 36.99, p < .001;   for enjoyment F = 19.73, p < .001

was among the most challenging and important of all classroom activities, it was precisely these activities that students least enjoyed doing. Conversely, students most enjoyed watching television or videos, even though they felt minimally challenged when doing so. Group work, although less challenging and less important to future goals than individual work, was nevertheless reported as more enjoyable, even though these differences were not statistically significant. A similar pattern was found when examining differences in students' wish to do the activity and students' positive affect (the extent to which students feel happy, sociable, proud, and relaxed). One exception was that students reported feeling more positive affect and feeling more in control while engaged in individual work than in other activities. Not surprisingly, they felt themselves to be least in control during lectures, which they did not enjoy or consider important and by which they did not feel challenged.

One of the most disturbing findings concerns the low quality of experience reported while listening to teachers lecture, especially considering that lectures take up nearly one-quarter of all classroom time. Equally troubling in this day of increasing technology use are the significantly low levels of challenge, concentration, and importance associated with watching a video or other audiovisual material, an activity students enjoy. The profile of student responses to taking tests is not surprising. Tests are reputedly the most dreaded and dismal part of a student's existence; students' lack of enjoyment and desire to be doing something else when taking tests confirms this. No other activity, however, quite compares to formal assessments in terms of their perceived importance and the high degree of challenge and concentration they provide. It begins to appear, then, that students find school activities either challenging or enjoyable, but not both.

One activity with positive reports in terms of academic press (i.e., academic challenge, rigor, and relevance) as well as more affective and motivational measures was individual work, a mainstay among classroom activities. Such positive reports may have something to do with the high levels of control that students experience while working by themselves. Although the number of times group work is reported may be too small to obtain a clear reading, group activities also compare favorably with other activities along the affective dimension and occupy an intermediate position with respect to measures of academic pressure.

When Optimal Learning Experiences Occur in Class

Activities that balance a high level of challenge with a high level of skill can lead to the optimal state of engagement called flow. When in flow, students learn to enjoy the challenges that can help them reach their goals. The relation between optimal experiences in school contexts and reported levels of challenge and skill has previously been validated in numerous studies (see Csikszentmihalyi, Rathunde, and Whalen 1993; Moneta and Csikszentmihalyi 1996). Those studies have also found that the balance and intensity of challenges and skills has a positive effect on student concentration. For example, Moneta and Csikszentmihalyi conclude that "if schools are able to provide the student with simultaneously high levels of challenge and skills, then this context is ideal for the optimization of concentration and involvement" (1996, 303).

Under what conditions is flow most frequently experienced in school learning environments? When students are required to do rote learning activities such as copying notes from the blackboard, we expect student engagement to be low, thereby providing few learning experiences. We also expect that presenting students with interesting and challenging problems, such as creating a blueprint or balancing a budget, would be more conducive to learning. When these activities are perceived not merely as busywork but as having purposeful links to future goals, we expect students to be more directly involved and to find flow more often.

Because many of the activities we examined favored either the intellectual or the emotional side of experience, we felt it was important to discover which activities stimulate positive experience in both domains. We created a composite measure of optimal learning experience, or flow, that included measures of challenge and skill as well as concentration and enjoyment. By this measure, tests and quizzes, group work, and individual work all produce above-average levels of flow, whereas listening to lectures and watching television or videos produce little flow. This finding suggests that a diverse array of classroom activities may effectively promote optimal learning. These may include interactions and conversations between students and teachers, as when an English teacher leads a discussion of a short story. Other activities may consist primarily of individual work. These individual and group activities can consist of daily tasks such as solving algebra problems, or ongoing projects such as conducting research and writing a final report. All such activities require students to engage in problem-solving tasks with clear objectives and challenge them to use their abilities to demonstrate their understanding of the subject matter.

By contrast, the more passive activities, in which a general package of information is distributed to all students—through lectures or television programs, for example—present fewer and weaker opportunities for experiencing flow. This finding supports what mindful educators have long observed: Learning is inherently a matter of *doing*. This is not to say that demonstration, observation, and listening do not have their place in the learning process. Rather, it suggests that conventional pedagogy's overemphasis on passive listening to the neglect of opportunities for active engagement may lead to an unproductive investment of time and money in expensive audiovisual equipment and new technologies.

The high levels of optimal experience reported during both individual work and group work deserve special comment. Despite claims by some educators and researchers that group activities are the key to effective education (e.g., Slavin 1983), our data suggest that neither individual nor group work is superior in all instances. Both probably offer their own advantages and potential to stimulate learning. For example, individual work may afford students both control and the opportunity to reorganize and demonstrate what has been learned. Group activities provide students with opportunities to learn from others through language and cooperation. Such opportunities are equally valuable.

What Do Students Think About in Class?

Teachers spend a lot of energy trying to hold their students' attention. Even the most talented students may find themselves daydreaming and have to struggle to keep their minds on class. To be sure, the demands of the classroom compete with social, romantic, or other concerns and interests in the consciousness of the ordinary adolescent. The ESM self-report form asks students what they are thinking when they are signaled. It is thus possible to determine whether students are thinking about academics or something else while in different classroom activities. Nonacademic thoughts, according to students' ESM reporting, include those relating to one's self, friends, romantic interests, eating, going home, or nothing at all. It may come as a surprise to many teachers that students report attending to academics only about half (54 percent) of the time while sitting in a lecture or while watching audiovisuals. Academically related thoughts were experienced much more frequently while in group activities (67 percent of the time) and while doing individual work (63 percent of the time), but these percentages may still be disheartening to most educators. By contrast, students were thinking primarily about academics the vast majority of the time (81 percent) that they were taking tests or quizzes. These results corroborate those based on how students feel while in different class activities. Unstructured activities appear to invite students to daydream, whereas students find greater engagement in individual work and group work, which are usually more structured. One will catch few students daydreaming while taking a test or quiz, which combines high structure with high importance.

Student Experiences in Different School Subjects

We next examine how students experience different school subjects and analyze what activities they participate in during class. Six academic subjects—math, English, science, history, foreign languages, and social studies—and three nonacademic subjects—art, computer science, and vocational education—were selected for comparison.[1]

Although almost every school subject is dominated by listening to lectures and taking notes, there are several notable differences in how time is allocated in various school subjects (see Table 7.1). For example, history classes appear to rely on lectures 33.5 percent of the time, whereas the other academic subjects use lectures 20–28 percent of the time. Science

TABLE 7.1 PERCENTAGE OF TIME FOR COMMON ACTIVITIES IN
SCHOOL SUBJECTS

Lecture
1. Vocational education — 40.0[a]
2. History — 33.5
3. Art — 30.1
4. English — 28.6
5. Math — 27.6
6. Science — 26.9
7. Social science/studies — 21.3
8. Foreign language — 20.0
9. Computer science — 8.0

Group activities
1. Science — 8.6
2. Art — 4.8
3. Foreign language — 3.3
4. Social science/studies — 2.9
5. Math — 2.1
6. English — 2.0
7. Vocational education — 1.6
8. History — 1.3
9. Computer science — 0.0

Individual Work
1. Computer science — 62.5
2. Vocational education — 35.0
3. Art — 30.1
4. Math — 27.6
5. Foreign language — 23.3
6. English — 21.5
7. Science — 18.7
8. Social science/studies — 17.5
9. History — 14.5

Audiovisuals
1. Social science/studies — 17.4
2. History — 15.8
3. Art — 14.4
4. English — 13.8
5. Foreign language — 11.1
6. Science — 8.6
7. Vocational education — 8.3
8. Computer science — 4.1
9. Math — 1.8

Tests/Quizzes
1. Math — 26.3
2. Foreign language — 23.3
3. History — 18.3
4. Social science/studies — 14.6
5. Science — 14.0
6. English — 12.7
7. Computer science — 8.3
8. Vocational education — 5.0
9. Art — 4.8

a The total percentage of time spent on various classroom activities for each school subject does not here total to 100 because not every kind of activity is here reported, but rather four of the most common ones and group activities.

courses, which typically include group labs, use group activities far more frequently (8.6 percent) than do the other academic courses (1–3 percent). Computer science classes are dominated by individual work, with little time allocated to other formats. While in computer science classes, students report engaging in individual work about 62.5 percent of the time, more than twice as much as in other classes. Students also report doing individual work more often in math classes (27.6 percent) than in other academic classes (15–23 percent). Audiovisual aids are used most frequently in social studies (17.4 percent) and history courses (15.8 percent) and very infrequently in math and computer science courses (1.8 percent and 4.1 percent, respectively). Students are tested most frequently in math (26.3 percent) and foreign language courses (23.3 percent) and least frequently in nonacademic courses (5–8 percent).

We next examined how adolescent experiences compare in classes in different subject areas. Students find math courses, which rely heavily on individual work and assessments, to be the most challenging and important to their future goals.[2] At the same time, students report wishing to do math less and enjoying it less than other subjects.[3] They report feeling almost exactly the opposite about art classes. They express the greatest desire to be doing the present activity when they are in art classes,[4] as well as strong feelings of enjoyment and positive affect.[5] Not surprisingly, however, art was found to have the least importance of all subjects to adolescent future goals.[6]

Of all academic and nonacademic subjects, the lowest levels of nearly all affective and motivational measures—challenge, enjoyment, importance—are reported during history class.[7] History classes are more dependent on lectures than other subjects are and rarely employ group activities, but this is probably not the only explanation for the consistently low ratings students report in history class. We suspect that the low ratings also reflect how history classes are presented, structured, and sequenced.

In general, students report more positive affective states in nonacademic classes than in academic ones.[8] Unlike art, however, vocational education and computer science courses are also perceived as important for reaching future goals.[9] The bad news is that these findings are consistent with the stereotypical impression that students on average do not particularly like their academic courses. Students' desire to engage in school activities was significantly lower in academic courses than in nonacademic courses.[10]

Students tended to report higher levels of flow in nonacademic courses such as vocational education, computer science, and art.[11] Among academic classes, the highest levels of flow were reported in math classes, where levels of challenge and concentration were particularly high. Students reported significantly less flow in English, science, and social studies classes, especially when compared with nonacademic classes.[12] Consistent with our previous findings, the lowest levels of flow were reported in history class.[13]

These results suggest that high school students have more positive, engaging experiences while in nonacademic classes than in required academic classes. Although they reported their experiences in academic classes to be more challenging and important, they associated their experiences in nonacademic classes with a greater desire to do activities, as well as higher levels of flow, enjoyment, positive affect, and self-esteem.[14] As was observed with classroom activities, there appears to be a tension between subjects that students find challenging and important and those they enjoy. This pattern suggests that students like nonacademic classes more than academic courses but at the same time do not find them particularly challenging or relevant to their future goals.

Although school subjects obviously differ in many ways other than in the particular activities they most often employ, there seems to be an association between those activities and the reported experiences of students in those subjects. For example, the results suggest that in classrooms flow is strongly related to the amount of time students spend doing individual work. Indeed, the ranking of school subjects by frequency in flow is nearly identical to their ranking according to how frequently students are engaged in individual work.[15] It appears that students experience flow most frequently in those classrooms that challenge them to demonstrate their present skills and future potential.

What Students Say About School Subjects
in Relation to Their Future

We supplemented students' ESM reports by interviewing them directly. Here again, we often observed a tension between what students enjoy in school and what they find important to their future. One student, who aspires to be an architect, responds as follows when asked about her English class:

> It's boring. I like drafting even though the teacher gets on my nerves. I like my drafting and typing class. And plus, I like my [drafting] math class. Math is important in the architectural field.

In keeping with previous findings, here Michelle acknowledges her dislike of traditional academic subjects such as English, her preference for certain nonacademic courses, and the relative importance of math over other subjects. She describes her drafting classes as interesting and absorbing. While engaged in drafting projects, she reports being highly focused on the immediate task, as in the state of flow. She describes herself as feeling immersed, in contrast to the way she experiences school in general. She reports this feeling mostly while in occupationally related school activities:

> I like drafting. I like it because I think that it's interesting. You know it's like once I get into drawing and stuff, I don't think about anything else. It just takes my whole attention, and that's why I like it.

While in these classes, Michelle is aware of her own skills as well as those skills that are needed to complete the assigned drafting projects. In addition to having a clear understanding of her future occupational goal, she also sees the importance and relevance of practical occupational classes, as well as math class, for preparing herself to meet her goals.

Students with clearly defined occupational goals consider occupational problems challenging and essential to preparing for the future. Vocational classes engage them in individual activities that have clearly defined goals and offer immediate feedback. Therefore, if they make a mistake, they can problem solve to find a solution. For example, if Michelle drafted a house and the walls did not make a right angle, she could immediately focus on this problem by redrawing her lines. Such students can track their progress and success in vocational and nonacademic classes, thus reinforcing their feeling that their personal strength lies in occupational rather than traditionally academic school activities.

Another student, Bob, whose career ambition is to become an engineer, also discusses school in terms of his long-term career goals:

> That is my number-one goal: to go to college and get a good job in drafting or engineering. I think the drafting course is the only way I'm going to get out of here [high school] and will help me get a real good job. I like drafting and solving problems.

Bob explains the importance of working together with friends or classmates to solve problems. While in class, he and his friends enjoy the challenge of solving classroom problems by themselves without the teacher's assistance. They enjoy being in control of individual work assignments and finding their own solutions to academic problems. He comments: "I like drafting because I have a few friends in the class. If we are in a group, we brainstorm. I like brainstorming."

Often, Bob and his friends refrain from asking the teacher for assistance, preferring to meet the challenge and solve problems individually or by discussing options among themselves. While in math class, Bob says,

> If we have problems we just ask each other questions…and we just figure out the problems. I like finding solutions to problems. I like using my head to solve problems. I like to think. I like to learn.

Other students particularly enjoy the challenge of academic learning and skill development. They often realize that many professions require a high level of educational attainment, making their academic success critically important to achieving their career goals. When asked about her favorite subject, Maria grudgingly responds:

My English class. I don't like the teacher because she makes us work, but I know that inside I like that class 'cause I know it is going to help me achieve my goals and help me out a lot in the future. She is like the hardest English teacher in the school. She pushes us real hard. She expects too much, but I know I could do it if I just took the time to do the work.

Like other such students, Maria frequently comments on how she almost "loses herself" when engaged in challenging classroom tasks. When the teacher provides her with structured, independent classroom activities, Maria meets the challenge by increasing her skill level, thereby enhancing learning and reinforcing her enjoyment of schooling. Maria also expresses a desire to become an astronaut, but it appears to be more of a distant, secondary goal in relation to the immediate importance of succeeding in high school and college:

The best way to get into the aeronautics field is to take some hard courses that will help you in high school and that way when you get into college, you won't be slowed down by not knowing the stuff. You'll be prepared. That is what school is, a college prep course.

Maria had not missed a single day of school; she had earned a place on the academic honor roll and was already taking several advanced placement courses. Maria has clear occupational goals and believes that success in academics and college is the means to attain her goals.

From observing students' self-reports when they are signaled in class as well as their comments about school in their interviews, it is apparent that challenge and clear relevance to their aspirations are the two fundamental determinants of students' motivation. Independence and opportunities to interact with other students also seem to play an important motivational role. In addition, traditional academic subjects such as math and English, as well as the more occupationally oriented classes, provide some combination of these essential motivators. Students currently appear to find less that motivates them in courses such as history and social studies, subjects that seem resistant to progressing from traditional, lecture-dominated pedagogy to more innovative forms of instruction.

How Classroom Experiences Differ
by Ability Placement

The significance that students attach to particular classroom experiences may be affected by their general enthusiasm for education, their past achievements, and their placement in courses by ability. Course-taking patterns provide an opportunity to learn more about a wide range of student outcomes, including interracial friendships (Hallinan and Williams 1989), self-esteem (Oakes 1985), academic achievement (Gamoran and Mare 1989), educational aspirations (Hotchkiss and Dorsten 1987), and future course taking (Stevenson, Schiller, and Schneider 1994). In a national longitudinal study of eighth graders, Stevenson, Schiller, and Schneider (1994) studied course-taking patterns in math and science and identified three different course sequences for each subject. They concluded that early course-taking patterns in math have a large impact on the courses a student takes throughout his or her high school career. Course-taking patterns in high school also have a strong effect on students' opportunities for postsecondary educational advancement and may prove to be an effective predictor of educational advancement later in life.

Because of the importance of math and science sequencing to educational opportunities and future advancement, three math and science sequences—low, middle, and high—were identified for each grade level.[16] Students reported no statistically significant differences in the levels of challenge, skill, concentration, or enjoyment while in the three math and science sequences. Self-esteem and positive affect, however, were reported to be significantly lower among students in the upper math and science sequences than in the middle and lower sequences. At the same time, the self-esteem and positive affect reported by students in the middle math and science sequence were reported to be significantly higher than that of students in the lowest sequence.[17]

In light of previous research, these results at first appear puzzling and counterintuitive. Indeed, the results regarding self-esteem seem to directly contradict Oakes's (1985) findings that the self-esteem of the students in the lower tracks and sequences suffers the most. We suspect that some students taking upper-level academic classes that are prerequisites for entry into highly selective colleges may feel pressure to do well and, consequently, are more anxious in class than their schoolmates who are in lower sequences. High levels of anxiety may prevent such students from feeling good about themselves in class because they are not sure they are meeting high expectations. In contrast, students who are not in highly competitive, high-stakes classrooms may feel more relaxed regardless of the difficulty level. Therefore, the low self-esteem and affect reported by students in the upper-level math and science sequences may be partially explained by students' attitudes toward schoolwork. Specifically, some students in upper-level sequences may internalize their own expectations regarding school achievement to an extent that diminishes the sense of happiness, pride, or self-worth they would otherwise derive from their achievements.[18]

Individual Differences: Who Experiences Flow in Class

What students experience in school activities may certainly be mediated by their home and community environments. Aspects of family background, such as the educational attainment of one's parents, may affect students' expectations for their own achievements as well as how they view their daily school activities. A student's experiences relating to his or her race may influence that student's view of the fairness or purpose of schooling (Mickelson 1990). Beyond broad demographic and socioeconomic groupings, there are more subtle characteristics that affect learning experiences. Some students, who for whatever reason actively seek out and recognize challenges and are optimistic about the future, may be more likely to pay attention or engage in a discussion, giving them an opportunity to experience flow more frequently than more apathetic or pessimistic students.

What types of students are likely to find their classwork challenging, salient, and enjoyable? Our analysis takes into account gender, race, and the socioeconomic status of the schools. Females, we find, experience much higher levels of flow in school activities than do males (see Figure 7.3). They also experience more enjoyment and higher levels of concen-

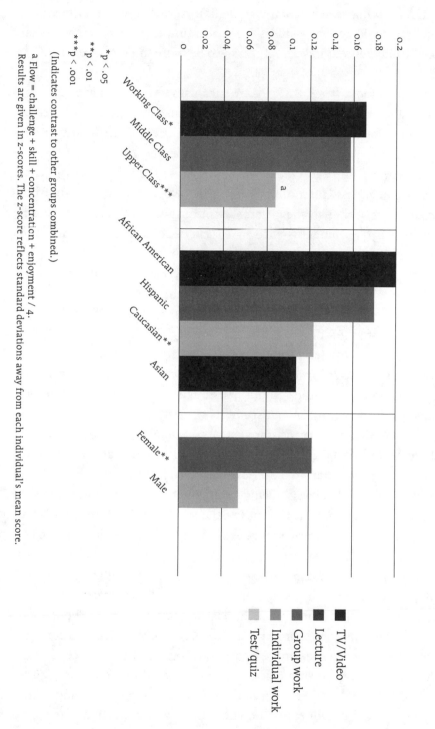

FIGURE 7.3   FLOW IN CLASSROOMS BY STUDENT CHARACTERISTICSa

a Flow = challenge + skill + concentration + enjoyment / 4.
Results are given in z-scores. The z-score reflects standard deviations away from each individual's mean score.

(Indicates contrast to other groups combined.)

*p < .05
**p < .01
***p < .001

tration than males, particularly while doing group work and individual work and while watching videos. They also find classroom activities—especially lectures and individual work—to be more important to their future goals.

With respect to race, African-American students report experiencing significantly more flow than other racial groups. They also report greater levels of enjoyment, motivation, and positive affect. Compared to other racial groups, African-Americans report high levels of enjoyment, particularly while doing individual work. Hispanic students also indicate greater enjoyment and more positive affect while in school than other racial groups, although the difference is not statistically significant. On average, Hispanic students wish to do school activities more often and find them more important.

Caucasian students report significantly lower levels of optimal experiences while at school than do other racial groups, and they experience less enjoyment and positive affect during class activities. They also find school activities less desirable and important to their future goals. Caucasian students find tests and quizzes particularly unenjoyable.

Asian students report the lowest levels of flow during classroom activities as compared to other groups. Although the differences are not all statistically significant, Asian students consistently report lower emotional, affective, and motivational states while in school than all other ethnic groups combined.[19] Asian students report particularly low levels of enjoyment, concentration, and flow while watching television or videos and particularly high levels of enjoyment while doing group work.

As to socioeconomic background, students from the more advantaged communities consistently report lower levels of flow, enjoyment, concentration, sense of importance, and desire to be in school classes than students from less-advantaged communities. One exception was during group activities, for which students from financially advantaged communities report higher scores on such measures. Students from the schools serving less-advantaged communities report more flow in class than students from other communities; they also report enjoying their class more and wishing to do classroom activities more than do other students. The fairly substantial "experience gap" between advantaged students and those with fewer resources is nowhere more apparent than when students are taking tests or quizzes. Like their less-advantaged peers, students from the middle class also report relatively more positive classroom experiences: They tend to feel happy, proud, sociable, and relaxed while in class, particularly as compared to students from the most advantaged communities.

Differences in Student Attitudes and Behavioral Profiles

Subtler student characteristics such as attitudes can also be expected to play a part in how students experience life in classrooms. Numerous individual differences emerge with regard to students' psychological orientations and attitudes. Intrinsically motivated students and those optimistic about the future report higher levels of perceived skill, greater enjoyment and self-esteem, higher concentration, and more positive moods than extrinsically motivated students or those pessimistic about the future. Indeed, analyses show that students of such different psychological profiles tend to rate many of their experiences differently, regardless of whether those experiences occur inside or outside of school. Many of these rather entrenched differences, however, are greatly diminished during group activities as opposed to activities entailing more individual responsibility. Students with a pessimistic orientation regarding the future experience an increased self-perception of skill level during group activities.[20] The very consistent differences reported between optimistic and pessimistic students in terms of self-esteem, affect, enjoyment, concentration, and importance also seem to disappear during group activities.

Consistency of Classroom Experiences Across Subgroups

Differences in individual background characteristics do not affect our central findings regarding the differences in how students experience classroom activities. In fact, differences in background characteristics were relatively small when compared to the differences that were reported *among all subgroups* as students moved from one kind of activity to another. The difference in experience reported while listening to a lecture, doing group work, doing individual work, watching television or a video, or taking a test or quiz was statistically significant across all sociodemographic subgroups and across future orientation and motivation subgroups. In most of these groups, students reported significantly less flow while listening to a lecture or watching audiovisuals and more flow while taking a test or quiz.[21] Regardless of the great diversity of schools that we sampled and of students within them, the activities in which students are asked to participate appear to be the chief determinants of their experience in classrooms.

What Is Missing in Academic Classes?

Schooling, we have found, is primarily a passive and independent activity. Students spend more class time listening to their teacher talk about a subject, taking notes, and doing individual work than doing anything else. There is a great deal of variation with respect to how challenging and important students find common classroom activities. In general, students concentrate harder and appear to learn more during activities that they find both challenging and important.

Unfortunately, some of the most common classroom activities are lacking both in challenge and perceived importance to future goals. Student ESM reports reflect a lack of active engagement in many of these dominant classroom activities. For example, students' concentration drops substantially while listening to a lecture or watching videos. In addition, students clearly indicate that activities like watching television are not relevant to their future goals. Students feel much more challenged when taking a test or quiz. But they do not particularly enjoy such experiences, nor do they feel good while they are involved in them.

Despite the seemingly dull nature of the activities that students are most commonly asked to do, they still feel more challenged in academic classes than in other classes. Even so, they do not appear to find most of their academic classes interesting or enjoyable. Academic classes are positively associated with challenge and importance to future goals, but they do not foster enjoyment, positive affect, or motivation.

The findings concerning the somewhat competing dimensions of intellectual challenge and positive affect raise the question of whether academic classes can be experienced as both demanding and enjoyable. The repetitive, passive, routine nature of activities certainly contributes to the feeling that schooling is something to be endured. Our findings suggest that under certain conditions, some forms of group or individual work can be both challenging and enjoyable. The classroom activities that facilitate flow experiences are those that are well structured, where students are given adequate opportunities to demonstrate their skills and knowledge as autonomous individuals.

Courses that are most conducive to flow experiences tend to be those that emphasize individual work. Individually assigned work may include demanding assignments that require sustained intellectual effort, such as writing a computer program or research paper or creating a piece of art. This work allows a student to set clear goals and to match challenges with skills—conditions that make enjoyable involvement more likely. Group work also appears to have a number of virtues over other instructional formats by involving students and leveling the playing field. By creating common situations for all students, group work minimizes the differences in the ways students experience many other kinds of activities. With the exception of science labs, however, group activities are currently so underutilized that it is difficult to draw more definite conclusions.

The combination of both high challenge and high motivation that is conducive to flow is found most frequently in nonacademic courses such as computer science or vocational and technology classes. In addition, many students find some of the traditional academic classes such as math and English to be challenging, important, and essential to obtaining a level of education necessary for their futures. Regardless of specific classroom activities and school subjects, the experience of flow in schools appears to be closely related to students' perception that schoolwork is important for reaching their goals. Such perceptions vary according to the clarity of students' future goals and their understanding of the training they need to reach those goals. Students who have clear aspirations for the future but are unclear regarding the education and training they need to reach them find occupational activities worthwhile but tend to view academic activities as irrelevant to their goals. Students who have a clearer sense of the education necessary for reaching their goals, and who are confident that they may receive such education, are more likely to find academic activities challenging and rewarding.

Fostering greater engagement in schooling may be achieved not only through structuring activities but also through promoting their connection to students' future goals. This is not to say that all schoolwork should be explicitly linked to future careers, but that the process of developing particular skills and understanding necessary for future success must receive greater emphasis. Currently, school is a place where teenagers typically are assigned tasks rather than being allowed to choose them. Given that schooling is involuntary, a shared sense of purpose between adolescents and adults may be an integral part of fostering engagement in school.

To facilitate flow experiences, schools need to create environments in which students understand both the broader purpose of schooling and the specific purpose of individually assigned tasks. Adults can encourage engagement by becoming involved as mentors and advisers to students as they undertake work that challenges their skills. In school, as in other contexts, adults have the responsibility for assuring that the demands made of adolescents have a clearly defined purpose. In addition to providing support to students, adults also need to give them the freedom to direct their own efforts. With the right sort of commitment from adults, adolescents may become more engaged in school activities.

Part Three

TRANSITIONING FROM HIGH SCHOOL

GUIDING STUDENTS INTO THE FUTURE: THREE SCHOOLS OF THOUGHT

Shaunti Knauth and Eleni Makris

IN EARLIER CHAPTERS we discussed the important role families and communities play in providing students with information about work and postsecondary education opportunities. One of the most important sources of information in high school regarding these issues is the guidance counselor. This chapter examines the role of the guidance counselor. The perception of the high school guidance counselor as a gatekeeper who guides some graduating seniors toward postsecondary education and others toward work (Cicourel and Kitsuse 1963) no longer accords with student aspirations (Schneider, Knauth, and Makris 1995; Rosenbaum, Miller, and Krei 1996). Nearly three-quarters of seniors graduating in 1992 expected to attend a two- or four-year postsecondary school (Green et al. 1995). Although the majority of high school seniors may expect to make this school-to-college transition, high schools vary in the ways they allocate their resources to achieve that aim. How schools allocate resources reflects to some extent the interests of the community as well as the local labor market and opportunities for postsecondary schooling.

Even though all the secondary schools in our sample consider themselves to be comprehensive high schools, in which most students are guided toward some type of postsecondary experience, the schools differ considerably in how they articulate that objective and in the actions they undertake to accomplish it. For example, in one state that has adopted a strong orientation toward work preparation, a high school restructured its academic program to include more courses on career knowledge and specific vocational skills. In another state, a school system restructured its curriculum to encourage all students to attend any one of the many postsecondary schools within the local community. In this chapter we use data from the high school interviews with administrators, teachers, guidance counselors, students, and parents, as well as observations made in the schools, to examine how three different high schools direct their students toward postsecondary education and entry into the labor force.

Opportunity Structures in High Schools: A Function of Resources

School resources are typically thought of in terms of per pupil expenditures or the size of the instructional staff. Equally important, however, are the social resources that schools allocate to their students. Coleman (1988, 1990) referred to these resources as social capital—that is, those intangible relations created by individuals interacting with one another around common positive goals such as increasing the high school graduation rate. The social interactions of school staff, students, and parents serve as a communication channel through which norms, such as the importance of obtaining a college degree, can be strengthened. Strong social ties can also help to discourage actions considered to be inappropriate, such as dropping out of school.

By tracing how a school distributes its resources among its student population, it is possible to determine the relative importance the school places on guiding all or certain students into postsecondary schooling or the labor force. The school may express strong support for having all students attend some type of postsecondary institution. But it may be that only a small proportion of the high school counselor's time is devoted to college counseling, and that most of his or her day is taken up by paperwork or routine course scheduling. The actual time counselors spend with students on specific activities serves as an index of the opportunities those schools give their students to learn about the steps they need to take to move from high school into college or the workplace. What resources a school has to distribute are determined in part by the community in which it is located. Schools are nested within communities that not only determine economic resources through local taxes but also can influence the strength of social resources by providing internships or apprenticeships in local businesses. Thus, if the school steers students to attend four-year colleges after high school graduation, this reflects to some degree the economic and social resources of the community. If there are few jobs for graduating seniors but a wide range of low-cost community colleges, the school may be more inclined to suggest that students attend two-year schools after graduation rather than trying to find full-time, long-term employment.

We have chosen three very different schools—Middle Brook, Del Vista, and Grove—to compare and contrast how school and community resources are allocated to direct students toward different outcomes. The criteria used to select these cases are based on three major characteristics: status of the local economy, school and community demographics, and school orientation toward work and further schooling.

Status of the Local Economy

We suspected that opportunities for adult employment in the local labor market would influence the schools' direction of students toward postsecondary schooling or work. Therefore, the three cases were chosen to represent different labor market conditions. Middle Brook High School is

located in an affluent suburb, surrounded by universities and an un-
changing service economy. Del Vista is located in a coastal city, which
had experienced a dramatic decrease in service and manufacturing jobs
over the previous five years. In contrast, Grove High School is situated in
a sprawling suburb near the city of Feldnor and includes several unincorporated areas that were experiencing a rapidly growing labor market as a
result of the continuing development of family theme parks.

School and Community Demographics

The second consideration was to be able to contrast the allocation of
school resources among schools that serve different student populations.
Geographically, the three school sites are in different regions of the
United States, namely the Northeast, Southwest, and Southeast. Middle
Brook High School is located in a predominantly Caucasian, upper-
middle-class community; Grove's community is predominantly Caucasian and middle class; and Del Vista is situated in a more racially and
ethnically mixed middle-class community. All the schools draw their students from the communities in which they reside, and the racial and ethnic mix of the student populations for each school reflects the
composition of those communities (see Table 8.1).

School Orientation Toward Work
and Further Schooling

The last criterion for selection was based on initial interviews with counselors that suggested distinctive orientations in the allocation of resources to guide students toward future schooling and work. For example,
one of the Middle Brook High School counselors believed that the mission of the school was to teach its students to be "prepared for the world,
not just in math or science" and to be "happy and productive citizens in
the world." The language used to describe the school's mission by the
counselor at Del Vista High School was more specific about the future

and stressed independent decisionmaking. He reported that the school seeks to empower its students by "expanding their horizons" and "having them make up their own decision whether to continue schooling afterward or join the labor force." At Grove High School one of the counselors maintained that the school's role was to prepare its students "to go into the world of work…and have some salable skills."

The attitudes of these counselors are substantiated by the data we obtained one year later from school surveys on the directions that focal

TABLE 8.1   STUDENT AND SCHOOL CHARACTERISTICS BY SITE

Student Characteristics	Middle Brook High School	Del Vista High School	Grove High School
Racial & Ethnic Composition			
African-American	12.0 %	20.6 %	17.0 %
Asian	12.0 %	12.8 %	3.0 %
Caucasian	71.0 %	27.3 %	70.0 %
Hispanic	5.0 %	32.3 %	10.0 %
Other	0.0 %	7.0 %	0.0 %
Parental Education			
Did not complete high school	4.2 %	15.4 %	10.8 %
Completed high school	7.0 %	13.5 %	25.0 %
At least some post–high school education	11.0 %	30.7 %	30.2 %
College degree	20.6 %	19.2 %	19.4 %
Graduate degree	57.2 %	21.2 %	10.4 %

School Characteristics	Middle Brook High School	Del Vista High School	Grove High School
Per Pupil Expenditure (1994–95)	$7,026	$3,299	$3,937
Counselor/Student Ratio			
Total counselors (full-time)	9	7	7
Total students (grades 9–12)	1652	3600	2800
Counselor/student ratio per school	1/184	1/550	1/400

students took after high school graduation (see Table 8.2). Middle Brook High School directs the majority of students into four-year colleges. College attendance is promoted by the counseling center's extensive college preparation programs and literature and the school's per pupil expenditure of more than $7,000 (see Table 8.1). On the other hand, although Grove High School also sends the majority of its graduating seniors on to some type of college, more seniors at Grove (33 percent) enter the workforce directly after graduation than do seniors from the other two schools (see Table 8.2). In contrast, Del Vista High School maximizes its limited resources to send students to college. Del Vista has a highly diverse economic, ethnic, and racial student population, and it is located in a deindustrializing community. With a per pupil expenditure that is $700 less than Grove and almost $4,000 less than Middle Brook, Del Vista sends over 90 percent of its graduating seniors to college. But numbers tell only part of the story. Our case studies discuss how these schools seek to fulfill their mission and how they allocate their resources in guiding students toward postsecondary school or work.

The cases describe the goals of each school's counseling program and explain how these goals relate to the counselors' views of their work, the formal structure of the counseling program (including the activities that the counselors undertake routinely), the ways counselors distribute information formally and informally on postsecondary schooling and

TABLE 8.2   POSTSECONDARY STUDENT OUTCOMES BY SITE

	Middle Brook High School	Del Mar High School	Grove High School
	n = 18	n = 18	n = 18
Attending 4-year college	72 %*a	11 %*	22 %*
Attending community college	6 %**	78 %**	39 %**
Working	17 %	11 %	33 %
Unemployed	6 %	b	6 %

a Percentages may not be equal to 100 due to rounding.

b All of these students did not pursue college and could not work because they did not have a green card. Subsequently, they all returned to their native Mexico, making their employment status unknown.

* p < .001. ** p < .0001 Significance appears among sites by outcomes.

work, and the kinds of encouragement they offer students in relation to those options.

Middle Brook High School: A Tradition of Educating

Middle Brook High School is located in an old, established suburban community of approximately 55,000 people that borders on a large city in the Northeast. Eighty-seven percent of the town's population is Caucasian, 8 percent is Asian, 3 percent is African-American, and 2 percent is "other." It is an affluent community: The official median family income of $61,799 is probably a low estimate, given that the adult population includes 8,000 college students. The level of education among community residents is high: 64 percent are college graduates and 57 percent have doctorates. From 1986 to 1991, the suburb saw an influx of highly educated immigrants, many of whom were employed in white-collar jobs in the neighboring city, which was experiencing moderate growth in its service industry. The majority of elementary and secondary school students attend the local public schools. However, the proportion of students in the community who attend private schools is slightly higher than the national average.

In 1993 Middle Brook High's total student enrollment was near 1,700—about average for a suburban high school (National Center for Education Statistics 1995). Of the students who attended the school, 1,453 lived within the suburb, 149 were bused, and 50 were from out of state or from other countries. Approximately one-fourth of the student population belonged to an ethnic minority. Thirty-three percent of Middle Brook's students spoke a language other than English at home. There were twenty-five different second languages among Middle Brook's population, with Russian the predominant second language. One-fifth of the students participated in English-as-a-Second-Language (ESL) programs.

A Microcosm of the Postsecondary Community

Middle Brook High School lies hidden from a busy street by huge oak trees. The school is accessible by a single winding road, which encircles the four main classroom buildings. Linking these buildings is a large, concrete, multilevel courtyard known as the Quad, which is the central meeting place for the students. One administrator boasts that the founders of Middle Brook School, some two hundred years ago, "designed it to be like the houses of Harvard and Yale." It is not unusual to find students playing guitars or reciting poetry on the Quad. Beyond the Quad are two baseball diamonds and a large playing field, all of which are well maintained.

Students at Middle Brook High School are given considerable academic and personal freedom in school by the staff and faculty. Students often enter classes after they have started, wander around and sit in the halls, hang out in the Quad, or skip class to finish extracurricular projects without anyone questioning them or directing them back to class. Very few personal limitations are imposed by the school administration, and students are allowed to express themselves publicly in many ways, including their clothes and hairstyle. One counselor notes that "rings are also growing in popularity, as are places to pierce them in multiples along the ears, nose, nipple, and anywhere else a hole can be made."

Being allowed to stroll about school unattended and to sit in the Quad during classes foreshadows the freedom college students are given. But with this freedom comes responsibility. If students fail to meet such obligations as doing their schoolwork, they are reminded of the consequences such actions will have on their grades and future. As one counselor states:

> In our school the kids call themselves in [when they are sick]. The parents don't make the judgments about that and then they [the students] have to deal with the consequences. In our school they're expected to be responsible for a lot of things. The expectation goes on the students and we work with them because the parents are still there, the school is still there, so it's a much more of a training during high school for the life skills that you need when you go off to college.

Thus, the school treats its students as college-bound adolescents who are preparing for the autonomy and responsibility of postsecondary schooling. As in college, classroom attendance is not mandatory at Middle Brook, common area passes are not required, and extracurricular involvement is encouraged. As another counselor says:

> We believe in student responsibility for decisions in most or all of the education process. We believe in close relationships between students and teachers and I think we also believe in students not just being prepared for the work but also looking, preparing for social change, or being able to be role models in their own field and in their own lives as they grow.

Interaction between students and teachers is also informal, and students view instructors more as adult friends than as authority figures. Between classes teachers are often in the halls, not patrolling but talking and joking with the students. Students often call teachers by their first names and ask about their families and personal lives. A graduating senior felt that the teachers were largely responsible for the relaxed student-teacher atmosphere and boasts: "Students are eager to talk with their teachers because they have a personal relationship with their teachers. They felt close with their teachers because their teachers care.... And the teachers really get into students' life, ya' know."

The teacher's responsibility not only lies in academic growth but also is extended into the development of the student's personal and social skills. Another graduating senior, who wanted to pursue a career in journalism, was encouraged by her teacher to intern at the local television station. She comments that her teacher helped her by giving her information concerning various aspects of journalism with which she was unfamiliar, and says that she gained confidence through her teacher's encouragement: "She was one of my best teachers. I guess she was the best teacher I've ever had and she thought so positive of me and it made me feel real positive about myself." The teacher in this example was concerned not simply with academics or classroom behavior but also with the well-being and self-esteem of her student. It was this personal contact that was valued by the student. In fact, one primary goal of the school is to encourage close and supportive teacher-student relationships. These relationships are an important and valued social resource of the school, as well as of the parent and student community.

Fulfilling the School's Mission

The formal mission of Middle Brook is to have the students be

> apprenticed to life in its ideal form—life that is devoted to inquiry, guided by reason and compassion, touched by beauty and joy, and informed by justice. We want our graduates to become literate about the full array of human achievement so that they will know and value what it means to do anything well [student handbook].

This formal statement, which emphasizes a humanistic, self-development approach to education, is also articulated by the staff and administrators. One academic guidance counselor comments:

> The mission of our school is to educate students during their adolescence, so that they're prepared for work in all aspects of their lives, that they know about the world, not just thinking about doing well in mathematics but that they're happy and productive citizens in the world and that they care about other people, and not just themselves.

There are numerous ways in which the school fulfills its mission. The school staff helped place one graduating senior as a volunteer in the community's homeless shelter. This is not unusual: The school actively seeks opportunities for the students to work collaboratively with various community groups. The students find these experiences to be personally satisfying. The student who volunteered in the homeless shelter feels that this experience has given him a deep sense of civic responsibility: "I feel my time is well spent. I don't get paid. I do a lot of community service. I don't get paid for that."

This is not an isolated example. The school is committed to providing experiences for the students that increase their exposure to civic participation and responsibility. Each year the school encourages the students, through extracurricular clubs, to select an issue that will be the focus of their activities. For example, in 1993 the school approved a student club that selected gay and lesbian tolerance as their focus. For the entire school year, this club made other students and the community aware of the importance of tolerance toward gays and lesbians by posting flyers, holding open forums for community discussion, and inviting well-known activists to speak at the school. The campaign of tolerance was so well accepted that the community provided financial resources to the club to petition the state to pass anti-discrimination legislation. This example of the school's allowing students to become involved in a controversial issue with real political consequences demonstrates how the school nurtures self-development and leadership by providing a safe forum for its students to learn about societal issues that directly affect their community.

This focus on civic responsibility is complemented by a strong push for academics. By the beginning of their senior year, many graduating seniors have already been accepted into a four-year university and have gained several college credits by taking advanced placement courses. Of the 422 senior graduates from the class of 1993, 89 percent took the Scholastic Aptitude Test (SAT) or American College Testing (ACT) and 31 percent took advanced placement tests. Fourteen were National Merit Scholarship finalists and seventeen were semifinalists.

The Structure of the Counseling Program

The resources allocated for counseling in Middle Brook High School are extensive. Counseling services are available for individuals as well as groups. More than thirty community social service agencies are invited into the school to conduct informational classes about their services. The high school expends enormous resources on its Department of Pupil Support Services, which boasts a staff of thirty-one, including nine guidance counselors, three school psychologists, four social workers, two substance abuse preventionists, three career center advisers, three tutoring center coordinators, three health office nurses, one special educational programs coordinator, and three headmasters. The support staff to student ratio is 1 to 57.

Even though the counseling program allocates tremendous resources to the personal well-being of the students, the underlying efforts are directed at having students further their education. This is not done overtly, and in fact no counselor admitted that the counseling program was directing students toward college. All counselors state that they merely "provided the resources, and the student would have to pursue [them]." As one counselor notes:

> I believe the choices should be the students' and theirs alone and how they arrive there is based on all the adults in their lives and their friends and family.... Hopefully, they will make their own decisions. I will try to present different options, which they can choose from, but I don't think it's our place to discourage or encourage [students] in a certain area or profession.

This philosophy of allowing the students to recognize and pursue their own strengths, while consistent with the school's mission, seems at odds with the sheer number of resources that are directed toward helping students make college choices. The semester course schedule devotes six pages to describing which high school classes meet college entrance requirements. Two full-time career counselors are employed strictly to guide students into the right colleges. The Career Center uses parent volunteers to show students how to access information about colleges on computer and find financial aid information, and the center distributes college handbooks. The center's primary function is to provide students with college information, whereas information on job placement following high school graduation is practically nonexistent.

When visiting the Career Center, we observed students frequently entering and leaving with pamphlets and printouts. There was a sign-up sheet for individual sessions with career counselors. Because this was such a popular service, there was a one-week waiting period for an appointment. The service is advertised by a promotional flyer that is distributed to students at the beginning of each year and posted around the school. A twenty-two-page career and college planning handbook entitled "Choice, Not Chance" is also circulated to all high school students. This handbook breaks down the process of pursuing college admission into sixteen different areas, including criteria for college admissions, college entrance testing dates, schools' competitive reputations, transcript information, financial aid information, ways to pay for college, timetables for decision making, the importance of grades and teacher recommendations, information on interviewing skills, application flowcharts, practice personal statements, alumni connections, and information on twenty-one colleges that encourage visits. Although counselors will not admit that they directly influence their students toward a specific college choice, once a student expresses interest in a particular course of study, the counselors suggest programs and schools that complement his or her interests and personal strengths:

> With the college-bound kids, I try to talk about what schools they would be right in and I'm certainly looking at their past personalities. I try to be realistic with them about what they want to do that will help move them along to whatever goals they're aiming for, or help them set up realistic expectations in order to do what they want to.

Counselors at this school do not hold students' hands through the college application process, but they definitely provide much support and guidance. Each student is called into the counselor's office at least twice a year to discuss college plans. These appointments are made during lunch and before or after school, so that classes are not interrupted.

The counselors maintain constant contact with college recruiters. They keep abreast of the requirements of the local four-year and two-year colleges and devote considerable time to writing letters of recommendation, often working on them at home. One counselor remarks: "That's what I do with all my free time for two months." Significant time is devoted to helping students prepare their personal statements. As one counselor notes: "I would never write their essays for them, [but] sometimes I read them. I make phone calls to colleges on behalf of a student rarely, only in real special needs situations." Frequently, counselors attend conferences conducted by the local colleges. College admission counselors are also invited into the high school twice a year and allowed to conduct interviews with interested students. Students are allowed to spend unlimited time with the college admission counselors and may visit with as many as they like.

Del Vista High School: Everyone Can Succeed

With a population of almost 500,000 (58 percent Caucasian, 14 percent African-American, 24 percent Hispanic, and 4 percent other races), Del Vista is the fifth-largest city in California. As is true for most coastal areas of the state, housing in Del Vista is expensive. The median value of a home is $220,900, making Del Vista the fifth most expensive of the seventy-five largest cities in the United States in 1992. Only 41 percent of the homes are owner-occupied. Rents are also high, at a median monthly rate of $551, the seventh most expensive of the cities. Despite the high cost of housing, Del Vista, as well as the rest of the state, is experiencing rapid deindustrialization. The downsizing of the defense industry has led to a statewide loss of jobs and has severely affected Del Vista's local market.

The Del Vista Unified School District has a total enrollment of 75,464 students and consists of fifty-seven elementary schools, fifteen middle schools, and seven high schools. In the school district overall, the percentage of Hispanic students has been rising and the percentage of Caucasian students has been falling. The percentage of Caucasian students in the school district decreased by almost 50 percent from 1984 to 1992, from 40.1 percent to 24.2 percent. The students at Del Vista come from two different communities. The inner-city students, who make up the majority, are bused in daily from throughout the city. The rest live in the middle-class neighborhood surrounding the school. The total student population of Del Vista High School is about 3,600. By the school's estimate, between one-half and three-quarters live in single-parent homes. A third of the students speak English as a second language, and 30 percent take part in the school's ESL programs.

Because Del Vista's students have very different levels of family resources, the school is forced to address two prominent societal issues, diversity and limited socioeconomic resources, which place a great demand on the school for special educational services. Additionally, because Del Vista is near the Mexican border, many of the students are new immigrants. Del Vista uses many of its resources to provide these students with ESL services and special counselors to offer support and help them gain access to special services provided by the community. Thus, the diversity of the student body is acknowledged by the administration as a special need, and substantial resources are allocated to assist students to succeed in school.

The school itself, built in the mid–1950s, is a combination of one- and two-story buildings positioned around two quads. Typical of many California high schools, the main quad contains the almost obligatory oak tree surrounded by benches and lawn. There are also several tennis courts and a baseball diamond on the school grounds.

The Counseling Philosophy: Great Expectations with a Dose of Reality

A phrase often repeated among the staff at Del Vista High School is, "Every student succeeds." Success is most often described in terms of academics. The mission statement of the school reads: "The Mission of Del Vista High School is to provide all students with an exciting, energetic learning environment that encourages academic excellence and the development of personal qualities and skills necessary for success in life." In addition to helping students attend college, the counseling staff describe themselves as the go-between for students, parents, teachers, and administrators, acting to ensure the students' future success, whether it be "just graduating from high school, getting a job, going to junior college, going to a university, [or] ... achieving success in their personality development and social relationships." One of the counselors describes his rewards from counseling as "helping someone get a scholarship, or getting into a better school than they may have set their sights on."

Students at Del Vista are not separated into the college bound and non–college bound. Rather, most students are encouraged to go to college, even though many of them do not fit the typical profile of the college-bound student. The counselors report that the parents and the students share their views on directing the children to college. Describing the expectations of parents, one counselor says:

> [N]o matter what their culture or socioeconomic status is, all parents— there are probably exceptions, but I'd say the majority of parents—want something a step above where they are in life. If they didn't make it through high school, they want the kids at least to get a high school diploma, if they graduated from high school they want their kids to go the next step, which is junior college at least.

The same counselor points out that most of the students hold similar expectations: "[They say] 'Of course I'm going to graduate,' and then they say, 'Of course I'm going to a four-year college.' I think they want the most they can get—even if it's in small increments."

The counselors at Del Vista High School talk of students' need to interact with counselors about college:

> A good third of the students are probably the first in their family to go to college. And consequently, they have no one in their families to ask what college is like. These students really need learning centers or to work with college counselors.

In contrast to their constant emphasis on reaching for academic success, the counselors also describe their role as providing students with a dose of reality. As one puts it:

> If you know all the student's test scores and the student is getting Ds and barely scraping by and they want to be a doctor, you have to, you can subtly try to lead them into maybe thinking about becoming a radiation technician or a licensed vocational nurse or maybe something you think they really could be successful at.

The counselors repeatedly expressed their concerns about dispelling unrealistic expectations and providing correct information on career preparation.

Support, Accommodation, and the Usual Caseload

How, and how much, do counselors actually enact their philosophy of academic success for all, and how is their philosophy influenced by the mission of the school? There are only seven counselors in the school, giving each counselor a caseload of 550 students. Each counselor is assigned an entire entering class, which he or she must follow from their matriculation in ninth grade to their graduation. The school believes that having one counselor who will monitor and follow a student's progress throughout a four-year period will give the student a sense of consistency and will help to establish an interpersonal relationship with an adult outside the family. Counselors comment that keeping the same students has real advantages, particularly for writing college recommendation letters, because they "really know the students." Despite the large caseload, the counselors maintain that they do know and in fact do see every student at least twice a year.

Del Vista High School has several stated goals for their counseling program: career planning, college planning, and personal development. In addition to assigning classes, the counselors also take responsibility for meeting those goals. For example, to fulfill the goal of college planning, one counselor establishes and maintains contact with college and university admissions officers to monitor scholarship opportunities and college testing. For career planning, another counselor contacts local businesses to create employment opportunities for students who want to find jobs after graduating from high school. In regard to personal development, the counselors provide support and suggestions to students in their interactions with their parents. Interestingly, several counselors express concern about parents who apply too much pressure on their children to achieve good grades and to enroll in the best colleges. The counselors believe that half their time is spent helping parents form realistic expectations for their children and teaching them parenting skills.

A key feature of Del Vista's counseling program is its intervention activities with students at risk. Del Vista sees the need to reach out to such students and has created programs to keep them from dropping out. In the ninth grade the counselors examine the grade transcripts of every student to determine who is low on course credits. The counselors believe that by catching such students before the tenth grade and showing them how they can make up the missing credits, students may stay in school longer and eventually graduate. Despite these assiduous efforts, the dropout rate for the school is a high 25 percent. To bring its dropouts back to school, Del Vista also offers a range of second chances. The counselors maintain that at least half the students who drop out are back in school within a year. Most of these students return to the night school program provided by and housed in Del Vista High School. In the early 1990s the size of the night school graduating class was about 500, in contrast to the regular day school graduating class of about 750. Graduates from the night program receive a high school diploma and have a graduation ceremony complete with robes and tassels.

The majority of Del Vista's graduates go on to community college (see Table 8.2). One reason the junior college system is so popular is that the local community college has used its financial resources to provide what the high school counselors refer to as a "signing bonus." Any student with a 3.5 grade point average (on a 4-point scale) who attends Del Vista City Community College automatically receives a small cash award. This incentive allows many students to enroll who otherwise could not afford to attend college. Although the community college calls the signing bonus a scholarship, it is really a one-time offer that is not based on academic performance or merit. It is not based on the assumption that the student who receives the bonus will stay in college or will continue his or her studies after the first semester. Its purpose is to entice students to enroll and thus increase the community colleges' enrollment.

The community colleges also attract students by offering many courses and programs that easily fit into their schedules. Students who receive bad grades or do not like the community college's requirements can simply transfer to another of the many two-year colleges in the area, an option that the junior college system in California offers its students. As one counselor explains:

What I've heard from my students is that they all go to Del Vista City College and if they're not successful, they'll drop. They may be on probation for a year and if they don't make it they'll drop that school and go on to the next junior college and try again, and on to another as long as their parents support them.

It may be that the provision of second chances at Del Vista High School reflects the second-chance philosophy of the community college system.

College Counseling: Emphasis and Information

The high school counselors spend much of their time ensuring that students graduate from Del Vista High School and are able to begin college. To increase the likelihood of students attending college, counselors try to involve parents in the application process. For example, the counselors hold a college information night for eleventh graders and their parents. Also, many counselors belong to state and national college admissions associations, attend their conventions, and network with college admissions counselors to learn what qualities they are looking for in entering students.

The counselors see themselves as playing an integral role in the application process. They write letters of recommendation, a task described as "extremely time-consuming." These are not form letters. As one counselor notes, he tries to show in each letter that the student did something unique at the school that demonstrates the student's maturity and particular strengths. The counselors also give special instructions to students on how to write the college essay. More important, they feel compelled to appeal cases when students do not get into the college of their choice. According to the counselors, such appeals are rarely successful in the California state system of colleges and universities. But, as one counselor observes, "for those few that you really are willing to fight for, I think it's worth it."

Special attempts are made to reach the school's minority populations. A Hispanic college representative is in the school every Friday. Additionally, the California state college system has a representative at the school three days a week to talk to groups of students, and a junior college counselor comes to speak with students once a week. Out-of-state schools have a minor presence in the high school. The Ivy League schools and most competitive colleges do not come to the school, although the school does advertise when college representatives are in the Los Angeles area.

Counseling Toward Work

Del Vista offers several options for students who choose to work during high school, including the Regional Opportunity Program and the Job Training Partnership Act Program. For minority students whose families qualify as low income, the school has combined its community resources to develop a job training partnership program that offers credit for work and attempts to link work experience to school through a weekly morning review class. The school also has partnership programs with local businesses, such as Southern California Edison, in which students earn credit by working for companies in the afternoon after attending their morning classes. In addition, certain classes allow students to leave the school for two hours a day to go to a site where they study such fields as landscaping, banking, or finance.

Del Vista High School deliberately decided not to have one major vocational center or program but rather to rely on community resources and have business personnel work onsite with the students. On Saturdays, for example, students can attend a class on banking that is taught at the school, and in the second semester students actually work in a bank. From the perspective of one counselor, some of these programs do nothing more than keep the students on the attendance rolls. Another finds advantages, saying:

> for students that may be thinking of something other than academic college, such as technical college or trade school, this gives them a chance to do the job training. And if they're not going on to school at all after high school it's perfect for those students to try a job now and see if they like it.

In general, the counselors view the work programs as successful because they meet the needs of certain students. The banking program, for example, almost always results in employment at a bank for students who enter the labor force directly after after high school graduation. However, counselors express concern about the work programs because so many of the students who use that option are already credit deficient, and to graduate they have to make up those credits. Taking two hours a day off to go to work cuts into the time available for taking classes.

Although there are clear graduation requirements, and the process of meeting the requirements is highly institutionalized, at Del Vista transitions from high school to work are not handled in any systematic way. According to counselors, a potential employer will occasionally call the high school to ask about a student's attendance record but not about grades. Unlike colleges, employers rarely ask for letters of recommendation and are not concerned about the students' academic performance. Counselors talk about wanting information from employers, saying that it would be useful if employers would contact the school and discuss what they are looking for in their employees. Employers do call the school about available job openings. The school places the job descriptions on a bulletin board, but students must contact potential employers themselves. No classes are offered related to the job hunting process; there are no practice interviews or sessions on preparing resumes.

Grove High School: School As a Road to Work

Grove High School is near the city of Feldnor, located in a southeastern state. Feldnor, a medium-sized city, has expanded rapidly around several large family theme parks whose tourism fuels the local economy. Many of the tourism-related jobs do not require advanced education, allowing fairly easy access to the labor force. Throughout the 1980s, an average of 1,721 people per month moved into the surrounding county. The city itself grew by just under 30 percent between 1982 and 1991. Within the county, the greatest increase in population has been in the unincorporated areas. The majority of Feldnor's population, 78.6 percent, is Caucasian, 12.4 percent is African-American, and 9 percent is Hispanic. The median family income for 1992 was $38,900, which is $900 above the national average.

The Feldnor area is experiencing two significant trends: an expanding population and a restructuring of its labor market around a service economy. Feldnor's schools have been forced to deal with the impact of these changes.

The Community and the School

Low and sprawling, Grove High School includes a huge parking lot and a large single-level main building decorated in primary colors. Built in the 1960s, the main building is made up of three wheel-shaped wings that meet at the media center. Open-style classrooms spiral out around the center of each wing. A two-story addition behind the main building houses the ninth-grade class, and a new ninth-grade center was under construction nearby.

Feldnor's student population increased by 35 percent from 1982 to 1991, and the impact on Grove was visible in the rows of one-room "temporary" classrooms behind the main school building. The temporary classroom area, which resembled a mobile-home park set on a sandy lot, was called the Outback by students and school personnel. Small spray-painted kangaroo silhouettes ran across many of the outside walls of the temporary classrooms, painted by students as part of the administration's effort to build a feeling of school. Teachers and administrators, however, complained about the isolation of these classrooms, and the teachers working in that area carried walkie-talkies to compensate for the lack of phone and intercom lines.

The makeup of the student body, shown in Table 8.1, is similar to that of the surrounding community. Although the majority of Grove's students are Caucasian, school personnel often mention the impact of what they see as increasing cultural diversity among students, which is usually viewed as a source of difficulties for the school. As one counselor puts it:

> Our area is just changing so drastically. There's a little community, a little school, and then all of a sudden it's three thousand and you've got all

these diverse populations of people. There's cultures all mixed together, and no one knows what to do with anybody and no one understands, you know.

She describes a variety of cultural clashes, not only between students of different ethnicities but also between the rural population and the "newcomers" to Feldnor:

The...we call them the rednecks, the McCoys, have trouble understanding the Puerto Ricans who are coming down from up north and New York. And then you've got the black kids, and you've got the preppie white kids, and it's a *real* difficult mix.

Although the tensions between groups are described as a problem at Grove, there have been no programmatic attempts by the school to build accord among groups. Addressing the needs of particular groups also does not seem to be a priority for school personnel, in comparison with Del Vista, where the perspectives and circumstances of lower socioeconomic Hispanic students are explicitly addressed.

The School Philosophy: Many Paths, One Destination

The school's educational philosophy is often described as "being based on individual needs." Teachers and administrators frequently use this phrase when discussing Grove's curricular opportunities, saying that a wide range of options in coursework is necessary to respond to the wide variety of student interests. An examination of Grove's curriculum, however, suggests that although the school does offer a multiplicity of course options, a common goal for the majority of students is preparation for work.

Grove's orientation toward academics and vocations is embodied in its curriculum guide, a primary source of information for students. The school's philosophy of offering choice in coursework is visible in the guide. Under "Language Arts," for example, there are forty-two courses available, with titles that include English IV, Word Processing, and four levels of Newspaper. The range of courses is not unexpected in a comprehensive high school, as the well-known analogy of the "shopping mall high school" makes clear (Powell, Farrar, and Cohen 1985).

At Grove, however, preparation for an occupation is offered as a unifying framework for the myriad of options. The bulk of the curriculum guide is devoted to explaining tech-prep, a curriculum that integrates vocational and academic classes. The aim of tech-prep is to prepare students to enter the labor force or continue their vocational training and academic coursework in two-year community college programs. In Grove's guidebook, twenty-two pages detail twenty different tech-prep options, such as agricultural mechanics, drafting technology, and clerk typist. For each option the sequence of courses needed from ninth through twelfth grade is laid out. By contrast, a brief description of honors courses takes up one page.

This schoolwide orientation, which emphasizes further schooling for a minority of students and preparation for work for the majority, can be seen not only in how Grove structures curriculum opportunities but also in how the school allows students to spend their school days. Students in the upper grades can take part in a dual enrollment program in which they split their class time between attending classes at Grove and working at a nearby vocational training center. Provisions are also made to allow for students' participation in the labor force while still in high school. One year an extra class period called "zero period," which began at 6:15 A.M., was added to the school's daily schedule so that students could attend a full day of classes before leaving for a full-time afternoon job. Grove's allocation of staff time also reflects the school's focus on preparing students for work. The school staff includes a full-time tech-prep coordinator, who is responsible for helping teachers and administrators implement the program. There is no comparable position for the school's program of honors courses.

Counseling Philosophy and Tasks:
Many Individuals, Much Paperwork

When asked to articulate their philosophy, Grove's counselors reiterate the school's focus on individual needs. "I think that individual counseling [is] for our department probably a top priority," says one Grove counselor; most of the counselors agreed with this assessment. The counselors note that their attitude toward student needs and their correct role in the school is to provide emotional counseling and support for students. The focus on individual contact with students rests on the beliefs that helping students work through personal difficulties is a primary goal of counseling and that students have very distinct needs and so should be dealt with individually. Teenagers' needs for developmental support, counselors often note, are strengthened by the difficult circumstances of teenagers' lives today, which include family breakdown, the constant portrayal of violence and sexuality in the media, and violence in some parts of the local community.

Grove's guidance counselors express frustration, however, that other tasks actually limit their opportunity to offer individual emotional and developmental counseling. Barriers are created, the counselors say, primarily by the amount of time spent completing paperwork, particularly logging students' courses and grades and drawing up students' class schedules twice a year. The paperwork required of Grove's counselors may well be greater than that at our other sites. In fact, in response to complaints from schools that their counselors had too much paperwork, a state law was passed that limited the percentage of time that counselors could be asked to spend on record keeping. But the comments made by Grove's counselors suggest that they view academic coursework as an unimportant part of students' personal development. This perspective no doubt contributes to their frustration with assigned tasks. The low regard that the counselors have for student scheduling is evident in the following remarks by one of the counselors:

> For instance, right now we're dealing with scheduling, with making sure that we have all the student schedules for next year in the computer.

Unfortunately, you know, they could hire a secretary, not demeaning a secretary, but they could hire a secretary or somebody, a high school graduate, to come in here and do the scheduling.

The lack of training needed for scheduling, the counselor goes on to explain, is due to the stationary nature of student placement, "because basically all you see is if Johnny Jones is in regular English as a junior, Johnny Jones is in regular English as a senior. I mean, you basically don't have to have a master's degree to figure that out."

Academic coursework, in the view of this counselor, is a static pattern through which students must pass, and his dealings with it are an impediment to his desired work of alleviating students' immediate emotional distress. This is in contrast to the counselors at Middle Brook and Del Vista, who consider tracking and guiding students' curricula to be an integral part of their work.

A lack of focus on academics is also apparent when counselors talk about the efforts they make to have contact with students outside counseling activities. One counselor, for example, serves as the coach for the girls' basketball team. The counselors feel that it is very important for students to see that school personnel are interested in the student "as a person." They contrast this with seeing only "a student, someone sitting in the fifth row of a classroom." The counselors seem to consider time spent in class as negating individuality rather than adding to teenagers' self-development.

Ironically, an uncertified adviser carries the most responsibility for emotional counseling. The Student Assistance Team Coordinator is the person to whom students turn for help with serious emotional issues. He began his career at Grove as an art teacher and became known for relating well to the students, a personality characteristic that is similar to that of his predecessor, who originated the position. The coordinator is well-known throughout the school and is mentioned by teachers, administrators, and students as being extremely effective in dealing with students' emotional difficulties. Students are sent to him or seek him out on their own. He also makes classroom presentations on drug prevention. The large demand for his services confirms the guidance counselors' views that students need assistance with emotional issues and increases the guidance counselors' frustration that their time for such developmental work is restricted by other demands on their time.

Counseling for the Future

Given the counselors' focus on teenagers' current emotional well-being, what guidance do they give in planning for the future? Describing students' educational goals, several counselors, as well as administrators, emphasize the need for students to be "realistic" as early as possible in their high school years. As an assistant principal describes it, almost every ninth grader expects to attend college. Knowing that a smaller proportion will actually go, counselors should help students to reach realistic expectations for further work and schooling as soon as possible, rather than having to adjust through experiences of disappointment. The view of coursework as a static pattern appears to carry over to the development of intellect and competence, which is seen as determined before high school and unaffected by the high school experience.

College, however, is seen as the obvious option for a specific group of students at Grove. Teachers, administrators, and counselors often use words such as "talented" or "elite" when talking about the students they expect to attend college. The school's honor program has been "strengthened" along with tech-prep. One counselor describes the principal's goal in fortifying the honors program: "She's really pushing the honors program and trying to meet the needs of the advanced students as well as the students who I think could be potential dropouts."

At Grove 22 percent of the students go on to attend four-year colleges or universities (see Table 8.2). Yet the counselors do not seem to consider college counseling to be one of their central tasks. Some responsibilities for college guidance have actually been transferred to parent volunteers. One counselor describes the arrangement in positive terms:

> We have a great principal who is extremely supportive of guidance. She does all…she can do to try to alleviate a lot of the burden from us. We used to

[have] kids coming in here for college applications, things like that, and she gave us a classroom, and parent volunteers man it now. If a kid comes and says I need an application, or I need a college catalogue or I need this, that, those people over there every day, they can give 'em all the information.

The counselors' role in the college application process begins only when students have a clear sense not only that they want to attend college but of where they want to go: "Then if they have information about the school in particular, then they can come see us."

The Question of Academics

Grove's counselors state clearly that the interactions they prefer to have with students do not pertain to students' current schooling. What value, then, do counselors assign to schooling—that is, the daily classroom experiences and its outcomes? For one counselor, the outcomes of academic coursework have little value when students enter the world of work: "If you don't go to college and you haven't taken any vocational courses, you don't have a whole lot of job training. The fact that you got an A in World History, that means diddly squat when you go to get a job."

The counselors tend to view schooling as a means to an end—employment—but do not emphasize time in school as of value in itself. One possible result of this view is reflected in the experience of a student who dropped out of Grove in his junior year:

> When I first started high school I had a lot of problems. When I was in the eleventh grade most of them went away and I was ready to go to school then, you know, I was ready to be taught. Well, I went to my guidance counselor and asked him what I had to do to graduate. Well, he looked up my records and he told me "Well, unless you're going to be here until you're 21 there's nothing you can do to graduate."

Unwilling to accept the counselor's view, the student suggested possible plans for his high school completion:

I was like, "Not even if I take night classes, not even if I take all seven classes?" No. I said, "All eight because now they have a zero period—and summer classes?" And he said, "Even if you do all that that's what I was saying, you'll still be here until you're 21 to graduate." And I was like, "What should I do?"

The counselor's response was to encourage the student to leave high school: "And he said, 'If I was you I'd get my GED and learn some trade.'"

The counselor's assessment of the student's time frame for high school completion may be entirely accurate. Yet his advice illustrates a lack of belief in the value of completing a full curriculum or remaining in a high school setting. This is in sharp contrast to Del Vista, which employs a range of means, including an on-site night school, to keep students connected to high school. The socialization value of completing high school as opposed to obtaining a Graduate Equivalency Degree (GED) has been suggested by a recent study of adolescents who received an equivalency certificate. The study found that the completion rates of postsecondary schooling and training programs are far lower for those awarded a GED than for regular high school graduates (Cameron and Heckman 1993).

Against the counselor's advice, the student reentered the Grove High School program. His reentry was difficult, given his heavy course schedule and what he describes as an unsupportive atmosphere. The student thought back on the advice of his counselor:

I just went back to school and I was doing my work and then I thought, "I wake up this early in the morning and I go to school and I do my work and I act all nice all during the day and I don't worry about people aggravating me or teacher belittling me or all that stuff and I do my work because I want to become something" and, you know, it finally got to me that I'll be there till I graduate, and I'm like 21, and no college is going to accept me or anything. So I went and talked to people and they said you can get your GED and go to a community college. So I quit and went to a vocational center to get my GED.

The counselor's advice in this instance appears to have dampened the student's motivation. The student seems to have assimilated his counselor's views of schooling, condensing his academic coursework and focusing on entry into the workforce.

Grove's allocation of its resources between school and work differs from Middle Brook's and Del Vista's. Only a small group of students is funneled into an honors program, and counselors spend much of their time assisting these students with college recommendations. The majority of resources, however, are allocated to directing students into the labor force. The place of school and schooling in this process is a confused one.

Three High Schools—Three Schools of Thought

Middle Brook, Del Vista, and Grove high schools impart distinctly different messages about the relationship between school and students' future plans. Using data gathered through the Experience Sampling Method (ESM),[1] we can examine how students themselves perceive this relationship. On each ESM report students were asked "How important was [what you were doing] in relation to your future goals?" Students' responses were significantly different at the three schools.[2] School is considered most relevant to future goals by Del Vista's students (6.23 on a 9-point scale) and least relevant by Grove's students (5.37). The views of Grove's students are not surprising, given the emphasis the school places on work rather than on postsecondary schooling and the lack of value assigned to the high school experience in general. That Del Vista's students perceive a higher level of importance than Middle Brook's students (5.45) is more surprising. One might expect the strongest correlation to be seen at Middle Brook, because of its setting in an academic community and its focus on sending students to competitive four-year universities. Our results, however, suggest that the "total citizen" ethos of Middle Brook and the assistance given to students in finding internship and volunteer activities allows adolescents to see activities other than schooling as important to future goals. For students at Del Vista, academic success is emphasized as the central, if not the only, avenue to future success, and its students reflect that message in their views of their daily school experiences.

Our case study analysis also suggests that the three schools have distinct attitudes about the role school personnel should play in guiding students toward future options. Middle Brook emphasizes creating close relationships between students and school personnel, relationships that focus not only on academic achievement but also on civic and creative development. The relatively low ratio of students to school personnel allows Middle Brook the resources to build such relationships. Del Vista also emphasizes adult-student contact, but with the different aim of informing students about their academic progress and directing them toward finishing high school. The limited personnel resources of Del Vista suggest less individual contact between students and adults in the school than might be possible at Middle Brook. Grove places value on relationships between school personnel and students, as illustrated by the example of directing students toward parent volunteers for initial college guidance, so that counselors can devote more time to emotional counseling.

Our sociometric survey of the relationships in students' lives allows us to examine variation in the extent to which students report advisory relationships with adults in their school.[3] When asked whether they went to school personnel for advice, Middle Brook's students were more likely to say that they went to two or more adults in their school, whereas Del Vista and Grove students were more likely to report going to only one or no adults within their school for advice.[4] Middle Brook's orientation and rich personnel resources appear to have created a strong network of adult support for its students.

This evidence shows that the availability of resources and the unique manner in which those resources are allocated by individual high schools greatly influence each school's mission, which in turn influences the postsecondary experiences of its students. One way in which the school's mission and ethos is translated to students is through the high school guidance counselor. Counselors are not gatekeepers who sort and restrict student access to postsecondary experiences. Rather, they transcend their own philosophy and incorporate the school's mission by directing students either into college or directly into the labor market according to school resources and community expectations.

At Middle Brook High School, located in an affluent community, the school's staff expects that the overwhelming majority of the student body will matriculate at four-year colleges. In fact, 72 percent of the graduating seniors did enroll in four-year postsecondary schools. At Del Vista High School, located in a deindustrialized, racially and socioeconomically mixed community, the school relies heavily on the resources of the community and the uncomplicated enrollment process of the local community colleges to help the seniors continue on to postsecondary studies. Seventy-eight percent of graduating seniors enrolled in a local two-year college. At Grove High School, located in a community with an expanding service economy, the school's staff expects graduates to be prepared for the world of work. This school accomplishes that goal by developing a strong tech-prep curriculum and creating school-to-work opportunities. A third of Grove's graduating seniors directly enter the work force, thus sustaining the community's labor demands by providing a new group of prepared workers.

{ 9 }

PATHS AFTER HIGH SCHOOL

James Roney and Rustin Wolfe

WHAT BECAME of the 219 seniors from the first year of the study after they graduated from high school? What choices did they make? Did they continue their education or did they enter the workforce? What factors influenced these choices? To answer these questions, we interviewed these students nearly a year after graduation, in the spring of the second year of the study. One year is not a long time, of course, so it is difficult to know how definitive the steps that young adults have taken during that time will be. Nevertheless, the transition out of high school is crucial. Not long ago, it was in the late teenage years that people commonly married and embarked on a lifelong career (Schneider and Stevenson 1999). Today, however, such lasting commitments rarely take place immediately after high school graduation. Instead, we find that more than three-quarters of the high school graduates in our sample continued their education in some form, although most also worked part-time.

These figures may not surprise us, but it is worthwhile to stop a moment to consider the implications of such trends. If one is interested in knowledge or committed to a career that requires further study, then the college years are essential for career development. Without further schooling, life chances are going to be severely constricted. For those whose future careers do not require college, the college years will be just an extension of the adolescent moratorium that already takes up such a large part of young people's lives. Most college students seem to find a way to compromise: While they are in school, they begin to work part-time, thereby starting to assume adult responsibilities while deciding which career is most suitable to their interests and abilities.

So it is vital to determine what paths our students took in the years after high school graduation. Our telephone interviews showed that a year after high school graduation 79 percent of the seniors were enrolled in some institution of higher learning. That figure is high: In another national longitudinal study, the postsecondary attendance rate in the fall after high school graduation was 62 percent (NELS:1988-94). A little more than half (55 percent) of the seniors in our sample matriculated to four-year colleges. Nearly one in four attended a community college; slightly more than one in five did not attend any postsecondary institution. (See Figure 9.1.)[1]

We were also interested in how many college students were employed during at least some part of the year after high school graduation. A total of 70 percent of all respondents at two- and four-year colleges reported being employed during some part of the school year. Most young people, even those enrolled in college, work in some capacity after high school. Among those high school graduates who did not attend postsecondary school, only seven were not working. They were looking for jobs, had joined the military, or were traveling abroad.

This threefold division—no college, two-year college, and four-year college—encompasses a broad range of different paths that young people can take after high school graduation. The types of jobs available to a young adult will vary greatly, however, depending on whether he or she obtains an associate degree from a two-year institution or a bachelor's degree from a four-year college. Moreover, among four-year colleges,

FIGURE 9.1 SENIOR SAMPLE ONE YEAR AFTER HIGH SCHOOL GRADUATION

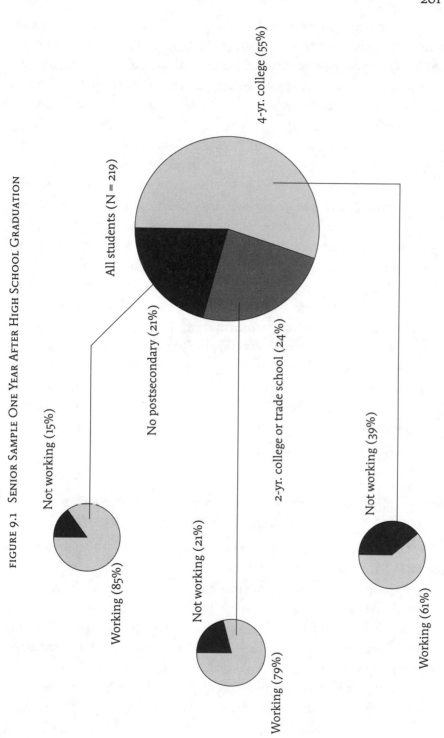

there are distinctions that can limit or enhance adult work opportunities. College and university degrees are valued differently depending on the prestige of the school that issued them. In this respect, U.S. institutions of higher education are also stratified. We therefore decided to examine which characteristics of students predicted their enrollment in more or less prestigious institutions.

To obtain a finer distinction among the colleges and universities attended by the graduates in our study, four-year schools were divided into two categories: "very selective" and "less selective." These categories were drawn from *Barron's Profile of American Colleges* (1994), which distinguishes the selectivity of colleges on the basis of students' SAT and ACT scores, the high school grade point average (GPA) and class rank of incoming freshmen, and the percentage of applicants accepted. The "very selective" group included institutions such as Harvard (where four of the seniors in our study were admitted), the University of Illinois at Urbana-Champaign (five), and Cornell University (three). The "less selective" group, according to *Barron's* ratings, included such schools as Eastern Illinois University (three), Kansas State University (four), and the University of Massachusetts at Boston (three). Seventy-nine of the graduates in the sample attended "less selective" colleges, and forty-one attended "very selective" schools.[2]

Background Characteristics and Paths
After High School

The first question we asked with respect to the paths taken by students was: What is the relationship between a young person's identity and background and the path he or she has taken one year after leaving high school? Data from the interviews are revealing (see Table 9.1).

Gender, we discovered, makes little difference, with the exception that women are slightly over-represented in very selective four-year institutions. A student's race or ethnicity does make a difference, but perhaps not as much as might be expected. A disproportionately large number of young African-Americans were not enrolled in any type of postsecondary

TABLE 9.1   Postsecondary College Attended by Student Background and Characteristics

	Not in College	2-Year College	4-Year Colleges	
			Less Selective	More Selective
N = 219				
Gender[a]				
Male	20 (21%)	26 (27%)	35 (36%)	15 (16%)
Female	26 (21%)	27 (22%)	44 (36%)	26 (21%)
Social class of community[b]				
Lower	14 (26%)	15 (28%)	24 (45%)	0
Middle	26 (31%)	34 (40%)	24 (28%)	1 (1%)
Upper	6 (7%)	4 (5%)	31 (38%)	40 (49%)
Race[c]				
Asian	0	4 (19%)	8 (38%)	9 (43%)
Hispanic	7 (30%)	8 (35%)	7 (30%)	1 (4%)
Black	17 (33%)	11 (22%)	19 (37%)	4 (8%)
White	20 (17%)	29 (24%)	45 (37%)	27 (22%)
Father's education[d]				
No college	15 (32%)	14 (30%)	16 (34%)	2 (4%)
Some college	1 (4%)	8 (30%)	13 (48%)	5 (19%)
B.A. or higher	3 (5%)	9 (15%)	22 (37%)	25 (42%)
86 missing subjects				
Mother's education[e]				
No college	16 (29%)	13 (23%)	21 (37%)	6 (11%)
Some college	4 (11%)	10 (28%)	17 (47%)	5 (14 %)
B.A. or higher	3 (6%)	9 (17%)	19 (36%)	22 (41%)

[a] Row percentages are presented within cells.

[b] Chi-Square = 1.00.5, 6 df, p < .00001

[c] Chi-Square = 25.17, 9 df, p < .01

[d] 86 missing subjects
Chi-Square = 35.94, 6 df, p < .00001

[e] 74 missing subjects
Chi-Square = 24.66, 6 df, p < .001

institution (33 percent). Of the 45 percent who enrolled in four-year colleges, fewer than one in four attended very selective schools. Caucasians,
who made up 57 percent of the respondents, make up more than 60 percent of the students enrolled in very selective schools, and very few chose
not to attend any postsecondary school. All the Asian-American students in the sample went on to some type of higher education, and 43
percent attended very selective colleges and universities, a much higher
representation than other groups achieved. More Hispanic students
attended two-year colleges than any other category of postsecondary
institution.

The two indicators of an individual's social class—parental education
and social class of the community of the high school attended—showed
strong differences in terms of postsecondary education, but again the
findings are not as straightforward as one might have expected. Young
adults whose parents went to college but did not complete a degree program are poised to surpass the educational attainment of their parents.
The majority of these students were enrolled in four-year institutions.
Turning to our measure of community social class, postsecondary attendance patterns for adolescents in middle-class neighborhoods are less
promising. A substantial proportion of students from these communities
are attending community colleges.

The Impact of School Experiences

The knowledge that young people acquire throughout the teenage years is
obviously related to their later options for higher education. We next investigated how certain high school experiences are related to college enrollments. Table 9.2 depicts results from logistic regression models
constructed to predict the influence of academic and background variables on year 2 outcomes. The results differ slightly depending on the type
of outcome considered.

None of the background variables exerted a significant influence on
the odds of attending some form of college versus none at all. Since
nearly three-quarters of the students from poorer communities nonethe-

less attended college, social class was clearly not an insurmountable obstacle to postsecondary education.

Academic performance, as measured by the students' courses and grades, is an important predictor of college enrollment. We categorized mathematics and science courses according to their level of difficulty, with the highest level mathematics sequence starting with pre-calculus (see Chapter 7). Students who reported taking average level mathematics classes were over five times more likely to attend college than those who took remedial math classes. Likewise, those students at the bottom end of the grade point distribution were less likely to attend college. Students who reported GPAs above about 2.5 and who had taken average mathematics classes were very likely to attend some form of college the year after graduation. Taking remedial mathematics courses was associated with a greater likelihood of two-year as opposed to four-year college attendance. The social class of a student's community was a very strong predictor of

TABLE 9.2   LOGISTIC REGRESSION MODELS TO PREDICT COLLEGE OUTCOMES WITH ACADEMIC VARIABLES

	Model 1 N = 140 No College vs. Any College[a]	Model 2 N = 115 2 Yr. vs. 4 Yr. College	Model 3 N = 86 Very vs. Less Selective 4 Yr.	Model 4 N = 140 4 Yr. College vs. All Others
Background variables				
SCC		+	+	+
Pared				
Gender				
Race		(Asian) -		
Academic variables				
Math sequence	+	+		+
Science sequence		+	+	+
Grades	+			
% correct[b]	88	88	81	86

[a] All independent variables are entered simultaneously into each of the respective models. Only significant predictors are noted within cells of the table. Positive signs indicate that a higher value for the independent variable is associated with greater odds of attending the more competitive college category.

[b] Percentages of subjects correctly classified.

the type of school attended among those who went on to college. This influence is clearly visible from the percentages depicted in Table 9.1.

But with regard to science courses, enrollment in the highest science course sequences predicted attendance at more selective schools. Students enrolled in advanced science courses in high school—that is, who took at a minimum advanced chemistry or physics— were 4.5 times more likely than those who took the average science sequences to attend four-year as opposed to two-year colleges. Among those students at four-year schools in year 2, the influence of science courses was even more dramatic: Those enrolled in an advanced science sequence in high school were 17 times more likely to attend a very selective college than were those students who took the average science sequence.

Similar logistic regression models were constructed to examine the effects of more experiential variables when identity and background characteristics were held constant. These models are depicted in Table 9.3. The "openness to experience" variable predicted attendance at some type of postsecondary institution versus none at all. Students who spent more time performing paid work as high school seniors were more likely to attend two-year rather than four-year colleges. Finally, students who reported spending more time socializing with friends and peers were less likely to attend very selective as opposed to less selective four-year colleges and universities.

Predicting college attendance is complicated by the fact that a large number of relevant variables interact in complex ways to influence this outcome. These interactions cause variables that are significant in one predictive model to drop out as important influences when examined with new combinations of independent variables. Consequently, only those statistical models that deal with these interactions between variables are likely to have any chance of presenting a meaningful picture of the determinants of postsecondary outcomes.

We therefore constructed a path model to account for some of the ways the independent variables in Tables 9.2 and 9.3 interact to influence college enrollment. This model is presented in Figure 9.2. To capture the different types of postsecondary outcomes within one model, we looked at year 2 status as an interval scale variable (see Figure 9.2 for the coding

of this variable). It is questionable whether type of postsecondary outcome is truly an interval variable, and the path model should be looked at
as an approximation of what would likely be found using multiple models
with distinct dependent variables, as in Tables 9.2 and 9.3.

The path model was constructed using three levels of independent
variables, with each level conceptually prior to the subsequent level. The
variables on the far left side of Figure 9.2 represent characteristics largely
beyond the control of individual students and causally prior to subsequent
variables. The amount of time students spend on homework, for instance,
cannot influence their parents' education. The next layer of variables—

TABLE 9.3   LOGISTIC REGRESSION MODELS TO PREDICT COLLEGE OUTCOMES
            WITH EXPERIENTIAL VARIABLES

	Model 1	Model 2	Model 3	Model 4
	N = 118	N = 88	N = 66	N = 101
	No College vs. Any College[a]	2-Yr. vs. 4-Yr. College	Very vs. Less Selective 4-Yr.	4-Yr. College vs. All Others
Background variables				
SCC		+		+
Pared	+		+	
Gender				
Race				(black) +
Social, family, and psychological variables				
% in play				
% in socializing with peers			−	
% in paid work		−		−
Family challenge				
Family support				
Openness to experience	+			
TV time				
% correct[b]	92	80	82	77

[a] All independent variables are entered simultaneously into each of the respective
models. Only significant predictors are noted within cells of the table. Positive
signs indicate that a higher value for the independent variable is associated with
greater odds of attending the more competitive college category.

[b] Percentages of subjects correctly classified.

amount of time spent on homework and percentage of ESM responses coded "more like play"—represent student outcomes that mediate the academic performance variables that more directly affect the odds of college attendance. These performance variables appear in the next layer: grade point average, science course sequence, and math course sequence. These academic performance variables were entered into an ordinary least squares (OLS) regression model along with all of the other variables in Figure 9.2 to predict college attendance outcome. This is the final, direct model. In the previous layers, OLS models include as independent variables all variables in prior layers; for example, all of the variables to the left of "SCISEQ" (science sequence) are entered simultaneously to predict science sequence. Arrows are drawn from only those variables that exert statistically significant influences within the respective models.

The path model indicates that science and mathematics course sequences are significant predictors of college enrollment. The amount of time a student spends with his or her peers negatively affects college enrollment. Homework operates in the opposite direction. The more time spent on homework, the more likely a student is to attend college. Social class of the community, as seen in our other models, has a direct influence on college enrollment. What is important to learn from Figure 9.2 is that taking advanced science and mathematics courses is influenced by family support and challenge, parent education, and time spent in perceived play activities. (See Chapter 4 for definitions of play and work.) Even controlling for background variables such as social class and parents' education, the amount of perceived family challenge has a direct positive effect on science sequence, which in turn directly affects college enrollment. Family support, however, actually has a negative influence on the likelihood of taking advanced science courses.

What Determines the Paths
Taken After High School

The results indicate that the best predictor of whether a senior will go on to college or will try to find a full-time job is high school GPA. The best

FIGURE 9.2   A PATH MODEL FOR PREDICTING COLLEGE ENROLLMENT

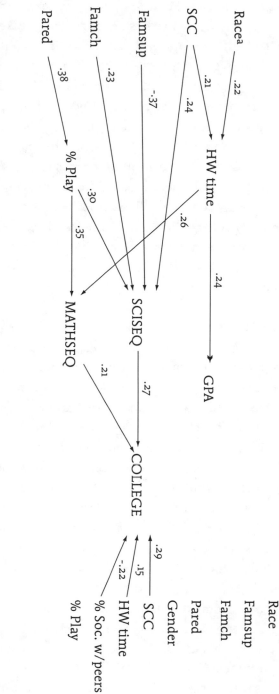

a The final model for direct effects on college status (represented by all arrows pointing directly to "COLLEGE" with arrows drawn only for significant predictors) has n = 99 (out of 140 students in the sample with ESM data) and explains 64 % of the variance. "COLLEGE" is a continuous variable with 1 = no college, 2 = 2-yr. college, 3 = less selective 4-yr., 4 = very selective 4-yr.

predictor of whether a senior will go on to a four-year college (as opposed to a community college) is the math/science sequence taken in high school. To predict whether a senior will matriculate in a highly selective college rather than a less selective one is rather complicated. Chances of getting into the top colleges are significantly higher for students who come from affluent schools, whose parents are well educated, who have maintained good grades, and who have a playful attitude toward life.

In some respects, these results are encouraging. They suggest that the direct contribution of social class to a young person's future is limited to entrance to the most selective schools. A child from an uneducated family or from a poor high school can still realistically look forward to attending a community college or to one of the less selective four-year schools. A student's background, however, also has indirect effects. Each of these disadvantages makes it less likely that he or she will get into the best postsecondary educational environment.

The results, however, also point to strategies that may help adolescents overcome the obstacles of an impoverished environment. The most obvious way out is by doing well academically. Good grades are almost a sure key to college acceptance, and usually the better the grades, the better the college. Of course, to say that a student should get better grades is a truism without much force behind it because poor grades are related in a vicious circle to a poor environment. Nevertheless, there is an opportunity to break out of this circle for those who have enough ability and motivation.

Taking high-level math and science courses will also facilitate a student's chances of getting into a four-year college. Of all the factors we measured, this one was second only to the wealth of the community in which the high school was located in influencing educational paths. Clearly, if the high school does not offer calculus or advanced science courses, this option is not open to students. All too often, however, the courses are offered but students fail to take them.

Another way to overcome the disadvantages of one's background is through higher expectations. As shown in our model, higher family challenge increases the likelihood of taking the high course sequences that lead to college enrollment. Upward social mobility, especially through academic means, is usually the result of high norms and expectations in the family. Openness to experience and a playful attitude toward life are more subtle personal orientations that provide an added advantage for getting into more competitive colleges.

What do these complex patterns finally add up to? Interpreting evidence is always difficult in the social sciences. From one perspective, it is encouraging to know that entrenched "ascriptive" characteristics, such as a student's ethnic origin, gender, and class position, are not as great an obstacle to college attendance as one might have feared, except at the most prestigious schools. A young person still has the opportunity to attend a more competitive college providing that he or she performs well in high-level courses. From a more pessimistic viewpoint, one might get discouraged at the cumulative handicap of a disadvantaged background that deprives young people of access to the kind of information that would facilitate their continued education. Perhaps the most useful way of interpreting these data is to acknowledge that the playing field is far from level, while taking into account the ways in which inequities of access to higher education can be overcome. Such a realistic attitude is the first step toward a more equitable distribution of resources.

Essentially, this initial phase of our study has confirmed that, for most young Americans, the transition to productive occupations has been postponed many years beyond high school graduation. Apparently, the main decision of the last few years of high school is not which career to pursue but which college to attend. The main task of high school is not to prepare students for jobs but to prepare them for further education. What young people need most to take advantage of the opportunities at this stage is good grades in advanced science and math courses, broad knowledge of the world of work, and high ambitions. It also helps to face the future with curiosity and enthusiasm and to have parents who are challenging.

These are some of the essential tools for negotiating successfully the delayed transition to a productive adulthood. Whereas in the past most jobs required more brawn than brains, the reverse is now true. Perhaps for the first time in human history, this is a generation that will make its living from the manipulation of abstract symbols rather than material energy. And this reversal inevitably implies that higher education will play a larger role in preparing young people for the labor market.

We have discussed the paths students take exclusively in terms of what types of schools, if any, they enter after graduating from high school. This focus on higher education is justified because colleges now prepare the majority of young people for entry into the labor force. At the same time, it should be recognized that no matter how important, the choice of a college is only one aspect of this transition. First of all, paths taken one year after high school are by no means final. Some students will leave college before graduating, and others who are now working will decide to earn postsecondary degrees. In this respect, the flexibility of the American system of higher education is ideally suited to provide second chances and a diversity of options.

Second, higher education is not the only asset that a young person needs to lead a happy and productive life. Many careers do not require postsecondary education. Achieving a fulfilling and stable relationship with a spouse or partner and making a commitment to family and community are equally or more important in the long run. Skills and abilities that help a young person to advance academically may not always be the same as those needed for personal fulfillment. During follow-up phone interviews, former high school seniors were asked, "Overall, how satisfied are you with your life?"—a question that has been widely used as one of the measures of the overall quality of a person's life (Myers 1992; Diener in press). Educational expectations and GPA—which are positively related to enrollment in more selective colleges—show a significant *negative* relation to overall life satisfaction. It is possible that ambition and academic success set expectations too high, leading to dissatisfaction. While family support and a sense of optimism about the future during high school do not help young people get into more selective colleges, they are positively related to life satisfaction after high school graduation.

Once the transition to a full-time occupation is completed, an entirely different set of skills and abilities may become essential for success. In these later stages, elements of character and personality that are not salient for the transition to college may become important. To what extent this is true, however, cannot be ascertained one year after leaving high school; it is a question that can only be answered over the course of a career.

MAKING THE TRANSITION
TO ADULTHOOD

T HE TRANSITION FROM youth to productive adult careers is shaped
by two quite distinct causal factors. The first consists of the social
forces that provide opportunities and put limits on what a person can do.
Parents pass on to their children not only their genes but also their social
and cultural capital. Families, schools, and communities offer varying
levels of support that can influence teenagers' futures. Given the same
amount of personal effort, a young person born to wealthy, educated parents will have more financial and social resources to expend on obtaining
an advanced degree than the child of a single mother living in an economically depressed urban area.

Personal effort is the other variable that influences the outcome of
adult careers. For whatever reason—genetic, environmental, or sheer
luck—some young people develop higher ambitions, more enthusiasm
and optimism, and better habits for using mental energy. A teenager
who has acquired such personal characteristics will have a better chance
to attain a position of responsibility and power in the adult world. Conversely, a youth who lacks such traits might never realize the promise

that an advantaged social position might have afforded. Social mobility is in large part due to differences in the focus and energy that each individual brings to his or her preparation for the future.

Schools are the main arenas in which children prepare themselves to take on the responsibilities of the adult world. Teenagers acquire much of the knowledge, attitudes, values, and habits that will help them become productive adults in classrooms. Of course many other influences also shape what kind of adults they will become: what happens or fails to happen in the home, what they see on television, what they hear from peers at the mall. But in terms of the hours spent and the resources that are invested, from the time children are five years old until they are eighteen the school is the main institution outside the family where anticipatory socialization for adulthood takes place.

Previous approaches to studying young people's school-to-work transitions were based on two fundamental assumptions that once seemed sound but now are questionable: first, that clearly structured and differentiated adult careers exist that correspond to particular traits, or skills, of young people and, second, that young people are generally motivated and prepared to pursue adult careers. Given these premises, schools were expected to channel young people into careers corresponding to their interests and abilities. High schools provided career counselors whose primary responsibility was to match students according to their traits with the jobs best suited for them. Students were given a battery of tests and inventories that mapped their occupational skills and preferences and then were steered toward existing jobs and careers with appropriate profiles.

In the past few decades, however, the assumptions on which school-to-job policies were based appear to have changed drastically. Adult careers have become less stable and less clearly delineated. Even some of today's most prevalent high-tech jobs, like computer programming, are in danger of becoming much more scarce as program-writing software renders lower-level computer-related jobs obsolete. It is increasingly more difficult to count on careers that will make stable, predictable demands on workers, and as a result it has become harder to make meaningful matches between traits of persons and occupations.

Moreover, the sense of urgency that once prompted young people to begin productive careers soon after high school graduation seems definitely less acute now than it had been in previous generations. Instead of clear occupational goals, most adolescents plan to pursue higher education in the hope that their vocational goals will become clearer along the way. Continuing in college even without any sense of vocation is especially true of youth from affluent families. Inflated expectations regarding careers and their financial rewards, as well as a lack of familiarity with career options and their requirements, are another aspect of the increasing disjunction between youth and the realities of the workplace (Schneider and Stevenson 1999).

Given these changes, we decided to focus on issues that have been infrequently investigated in the past. In looking at the social context, we did not limit ourselves to examining the effects of the usual structural variables: parental education, occupation, and family composition. Instead we focused on less tangible but perhaps equally important factors, such as the peer network, opportunities to learn and practice job-relevant behavior, and the amount of support and challenge the family provides. In terms of personal characteristics, instead of considering school achievement and job expectations as major factors, we looked at less easily measured traits such as optimism, self-esteem, and the tendency to find pleasure in challenging activities. We surmised that these social supports and personal traits best prepare young people to find a productive place in a rapidly changing, insecure adult work environment.

Personal Strengths for a Productive Adulthood

It is useful to begin by considering the complex nature of personal traits that facilitate future productive involvement in the world of work. In one sense, personal traits can be seen as *dependent variables* caused by enabling social conditions. For example, a child who is assiduous in his or her studies might be so because of an academically demanding family environment. In another sense, traits can be seen as *independent variables* that predict later success. In this case, the child's perseverance, whatever its origin, is indicative of future involvement in productive adult work. Finally, a trait can be seen as being a desirable *outcome* regardless of its effectiveness in reaching a later goal. From this perspective, persevering in schoolwork is valued on its own merits whether or not it leads to desired consequences. In what follows we assume that the traits discussed are valuable in and of themselves and that they are also useful as means for achieving adult career goals. Whether this last assumption is accurate, however, cannot be determined on the basis of the first year of our study. Such conclusions will have to wait for analyses of longitudinal data collected when young people in the study are farther into adulthood.

Accurate Information Leading to Realistic Expectations

Perhaps the most basic personal prerequisite for a successful transition to productive adulthood is knowledge of career options. This is not as simple as it seems. As we mentioned before, the types of jobs available and the kinds of preparation required for them have become highly volatile. Even medicine, one of the oldest and most traditionally structured professions, is undergoing upheavals as specialties come into and fall out of favor and as the profession as a whole strives to redefine its identity in the context of a changing health care system.

Knowing what various careers entail is made even more difficult by the images created by the mass media. Teenagers grow up watching on-screen lawyers spending most of their time arguing cases in court, doctors saving lives under dramatic circumstances, athletes being venerated, and entertainers being fawned over. Accountants and insurance salespeople are rarely shown in heroic roles; rather, they are usually portrayed as fumbling drudges. The vast majority of the jobs in the labor market—those held by electricians, construction workers, service employees, clerical workers—are shown with few redeeming features, as way stations from which to escape to more glamorous occupations.

One important finding of this study is that by the sixth grade teenagers have developed stable and consistent images of what is work and what is play. The term "work" is generally used to identify activities that are obligatory and unpleasant but important for the future. Activities that adolescents call "play" are voluntary and pleasant but relatively unimportant. As adolescents grow older, they label more of what they do as being like work, and they increasingly dislike those things. It appears that today's children learn from the culture around them that work might be necessary but is not something one would wish to do for its own sake. Only money and glamour make work palatable.

Not surprisingly, the teenagers in our study seem rather confused about what to expect from their future jobs. Many teens, even by the end of high school, hold strangely incongruous ideas of what they might do when they grow up: "Well, I think I will be a psychiatrist. Or perhaps a model—unless I become a stewardess—I like to travel a lot" is representative of how many adolescents think about their future prospects. Expectations are severely upward biased. If the actual division of labor conformed to students' expectations, there would be at least ten professionals for every blue-collar worker. An inordinate number expect to become professional athletes, singers, actors, and entertainers, although the frequency with which these "expressive" careers are mentioned declines with age. Adolescents' ideas of what different jobs entail and of how to enter various careers were vague. Students in general seem to have unrealistic career expectations and to underestimate the educational requirements for those careers (Schneider and Stevenson 1999). Many say that they expect to become lawyers or doctors without expecting to go beyond four years of college. Finally, income estimates were wildly inflated—about the only realistic figures were those of students who planned to become teachers and who ranked themselves at the bottom of the expected pay scale.

Clearly this disjunction between knowledge and reality is disturbing. Sooner or later one might expect disillusionment to set in when the bubble of inflated expectations bursts. How can young people be prepared to look at their future careers more realistically? This question is not as easy to answer as it seems. If being "realistic" means accepting the status quo and resigning oneself to one's family's position in the social hierarchy, then we would not want children to be realistic in that sense. Individuals who succeed against odds are by definition unrealistic, and without them the world would be a much poorer place.

Perhaps the best solution is to separate the issue of career knowledge into two components, one cognitive, the other motivational. At the cognitive level, which includes knowledge about jobs as well as the skills and preparation required for them, it pays to be well informed and realistic. At the motivational level, each child should be encouraged to reach as high as possible, but with full knowledge of the demands and opportunities involved. The combinations to be avoided are resigned realism or uninformed enthusiasm. But if a child can obtain a reasonably clear picture of what the world of work is like, even as it shifts and changes, and at the same time he or she can hold on to a personal dream, no matter how ambitious, then that child is well positioned to enter the transition to adulthood.

Relevant Work Experience

Children in our society differ a great deal in terms of their exposure to work-relevant activities. Some grow up surrounded by unemployed adults, with few role models and no access to apprenticeship in mainstream jobs. Others are surrounded by successful professionals, are exposed to a variety of occupations, and have a chance to help in a relative's store, plant, or office. Our learn-do measures have shown that adolescents have very few opportunities to gain experiences that might translate into future careers. By the end of high school most teenagers have done some paid work as babysitters, lifeguards, or fast-food servers, even though these jobs are not usually the kind around which vocations are built. Actual work experience related to a future career is extremely rare. What compensates for lack of direct experience is the opportunity to learn something relevant to a vocation. A middle-schooler who begins to read biology and chemistry can feel that she is on course for becoming a scientist even if she has never set foot in a laboratory.

But direct experience is still desirable. Children typically begin to form vocational images through play. Many of these—the typical childhood notions of becoming a cowboy, nurse, astronaut, or firefighter—are developmentally predictable and are soon forgotten. But some of them survive longer: A large number of the would-be architects in our study (3 percent of all adolescents) were attracted to that profession because after building model airplanes they went on to help build bookshelves, garages, and home extensions—and they enjoyed those activities.

In addition to play, early family experiences can serve as starting points to vocational identities. Teenagers who want to be physicians often have physicians for parents or have spent time caring for an ill sibling. They might have worked part-time in a doctor's office or volunteered in a local hospital. Teenagers who plan careers in engineering typically have helped parents or relatives assemble machinery such as a car engine, television set, or lathe.

Only a few adolescents discover an activity that they can be fully involved in while still in school and that can also lead to an adult career. For example, a boy in our study was listless and bored until age fifteen, when he discovered a fascination for koi ponds. He began designing rocky pools for Japanese carp, learned to build them, became an expert on various pumps and types of fish, and in a few years had a bustling business installing koi ponds in neighborhood backyards. A girl in the study decided to become a "Celtic scholar" after a visit to Ireland and volunteered her time in museums sorting artifacts as she continued to learn more about her vocation. But by and large such opportunities are rather rare and open to few.

In principle there is no reason why young people should not have the chance to learn directly, hands-on, what it means to be a nuclear engineer, oceanographer, plumber, or physician. But in practice adolescents have become extremely sheltered from adult work. In the nineteenth century children needed to be protected by child labor laws against exploitation by owners of mines, factories, and sweatshops, but it seems that now we have gone too far in separating children from work. We mainly train them to be consumers—of abstract information, entertainment, and mostly useless products—with too little regard for concrete, active engagement with the environment. What is needed is an opportunity for youth to experience the joys and responsibilities of making things happen, without being prematurely drawn into monotonous work.

Involvement in Academic and Extracurricular Activities

For students who have a genuine interest in and motivation for careers in which abstract knowledge is a prerequisite, high schools can be a place to learn relevant career information. But unfortunately, even the most committed young scholars and scientists have trouble with the structure of the educational establishment. In a study of one hundred creative individuals in the arts and the sciences, these eminent men and women had few good words for the secondary schools they attended (Csikszentmihalyi 1996). They remembered few stimulating and caring teachers, and the standardized, mass-produced instruction itself seems to have left few memorable traces. Even Nobel Prize-winning physicists and chemists had hardly a good word to say about their schooling.

Of course, there are many reasons to study and do well in school besides obtaining the information one needs for a career. School can foster habits of industriousness, discipline, and order. It is probably for those reasons that children from disadvantaged backgrounds, whose home lives and communities are unsafe and unpredictable, are happier in school than are their more affluent peers (Schmidt 1998). Above all else, schools provide the certification that degrees confer and that opens up the doors of further training and desirable careers. Therefore there is no question that doing well academically is essential for a successful transition to the world of work, however flawed secondary schools might be.

But in addition to the academic curriculum, schools also provide the opportunity to engage in activities that are halfway between the spontaneous play of childhood and the serious work of adulthood. In many ways, extracurricular activities compensate for the lack of work experience that is so endemic in American society. Working on the school newspaper, building sets and rehearsing for the school play, competing on a varsity team or taking care of athletic equipment, and playing in the school orchestra require almost adultlike skills and responsibilities, and they take place in a voluntary, usually enjoyable setting. Several studies have shown that participation in such activities improves a student's grade point average and other measures of academic success in adolescence (Eccles and Barber in press; Marsh 1992; Schmidt 1998; Schneider, Swanson, and Riegle-Crumb 1998). Other positive effects on the development of youth have been found as a result of participation in civic and service activities (Youniss and Yates 1997).

In the study of creative persons, several Nobel laureates mentioned that their vocational interest started when a teacher asked them to set up a lab after school hours or offered to publish a story of theirs in an intramural literary magazine. It is often these incidental episodes of real-life involvement that constitute the most formative influence of schools. Not surprisingly, extracurricular activities are the ones that students perceive as being simultaneously like work and like play, and the ones they see as both important to the future and enjoyable in the present. Unfortunately, the opportunities for this sort of engagement are the first to disappear from schools when budgets are cut.

Optimism and Self-Esteem

Having clear vocational goals, work experience, and accurate information are not enough to guarantee a smooth transition into productive adulthood. A child must also develop positive personal traits and attitudes, including an optimistic disposition, an internal locus of control, and self-esteem. Optimism—or the tendency to view the future as conforming to one's desire—has long been thought necessary to avoid failure and to confront obstacles effectively; it has been shown to buffer depression, illness, and academic failure (Scheier and Carver 1992; Seligman 1991). Self-esteem has recently been considered so important educationally that the California legislature has *mandated* that its schools raise students' levels of self-esteem.

Vital as such traits are, they are by no means unproblematic. An optimistic disposition, when out of touch with reality, can prevent a person from taking the best course of action. At the extreme, the personality variable dubbed John Henryism, after the mythical railroad worker who thought he could outdo a steam hammer, describes people who think they can control all events in their lives through hard work and determination. Those who score high on the John Henryism scale but are low in socioeconomic status are apt to develop high blood pressure (James et al. 1987). In our study, minority youth from disadvantaged backgrounds scored higher on optimism than their more affluent peers. It is probable that for them to succeed, they have to inflate their expectations more than the wealthy do. But one has to wonder what happens if and when their hopes are dashed.

Self-esteem has lately been seen as a panacea for everything that is going wrong with young people. The popular wisdom is that if we could just raise students' self-esteem, they would turn into brilliant scholars and successful professionals. Few stop to think, as William James did more than a hundred years ago, that self-esteem depends on two things: what one has actually accomplished and what one expects to accomplish (James 1890). A person might have high self-esteem for one of two reasons: either because he or she has accomplished much or because he or she has expected little of himself or herself. All too often, high self-esteem reflects the complacent attitude of a person with low ambitions. It is difficult to argue, however, that young people should not be optimistic and should not hold themselves in high esteem, even though the best students, and those who enjoy the best social circumstances, tend to be lower on both traits. Perhaps being jaded about the future and about oneself is a luxury that students with social and economic advantages can afford to have. Students with limited resources would be truly disadvantaged if they were less than enthusiastic.

In our study these traits—optimism and self-esteem—were generally related to other measures of well-being. Optimistic students and those with high self-esteem were happier, more sociable, and more involved. Yet these positive characteristics did not seem to have much bearing on longer-term effects such as academic performance or career knowledge. While these characteristics seem to improve the quality of life in the present, the jury is still out as to their contribution to career development.

Curiosity and Interest

Although one-time measures of general dispositions such as optimism may be difficult to interpret, the results of repeated measures of daily experience provided by the ESM give a clearer idea of the personal traits that contribute to a successful transition from school to productive adulthood. For instance, when a teenager repeatedly feels that what he does is play, he signals an open, experimental attitude toward life; when another feels that her activities are more like work, she reveals a responsible, persevering attitude. Both of these have distinct advantages. Work orientation seems to be optimal, at least in the short run; the students who have it are involved in their studies and report a higher quality of experience overall. Play orientation, more typical of boys and those in economically advantaged families, might bring better results later, as students move on to college and career.

The most problematic condition occurs when teenagers say that what they do is neither like work nor like play. In a typical week more than one-third of students' lives is made up of such moments, and nearly 20 percent of the sample report "neither" as the prevalent condition. Disengaged students experience the worst of all possible worlds. They don't enjoy what they do in the present, and they do not think that what they do will be helpful in the future. Their achievement in school is low, and their participation in outside activities is minimal. Here we begin to see the personal price that children in the lower socioeconomic strata have to pay: more of them end up in this disengaged condition.

Why is it that some young people feel that what they do is neither enjoyable nor useful? Certainly objective conditions in the environment are part of the explanation. Without opportunities for interesting engagement, without stimulation, it is easy to fall into an apathetic condition in which what one does has no meaning either in the present or in the future. On the other hand, the environment is not absolutely deterministic. Every person has the opportunity to bring different personal meanings to daily experiences. To see the universe in a grain of sand might be difficult, but it is not impossible. Even under the most constraining conditions, some teenagers develop enough interest in and curiosity about the world around them to create chances for playfulness or productive engagement.

The opposite state of being disengaged is when students say that what they are doing is both like work and like play. At those times they feel happy and energized, and they also feel that what they are doing is important. One goal of education should be to increase the occurrence of such conditions because they provide the best balance of learning and enjoyment. Currently less than 10 percent of the average teenager's life includes such moments. They tend to occur most often during involvement in hobbies, sports, and extracurricular activities.

The most prevalent trait of creative individuals (Csikszentmihalyi 1996) still lively into the ninth and tenth decades of life is the intense curiosity and interest in everything that is happening around them. Many such persons were born into poor and disadvantaged families. How such engagement can be started and maintained throughout life is one of the most important questions for the social sciences to answer.

Learning to Like Challenges

One way to increase engagement is by encouraging young people to take part in activities that challenge their abilities and give them opportunities to increase their skills. Csikszentmihalyi refers to such balance as being in a flow state, when an adolescent is so absorbed in an activity that he or she loses track of time and feels at one with the activity. Spending time in flow promotes learning and the acquisition of skills. Persons who seek out challenges that are equal to their expanding abilities are more likely to develop a positive view of their lives (Adlai-Gail 1994; Csikszentmihlayi, Rathunde, and Whalen 1993; Hektner 1996). Such self-directed persons strive to achieve goals that are intrinsically motivating. Having such goals means that the activity itself brings enjoyment and satisfaction.

When adolescents are in flow, they report feeling greater levels of concentration, enjoyment, happiness, strength, motivation, and self-esteem. Flow offers highly positive experiences and seems to have long-term consequences for young people's lives. Adolescents who are in flow are most likely to feel that what they are doing is important to their future goals. Such experiences may be developmentally beneficial because they provide the rare combination of enjoyment of the task at hand and perceived relevance to the future.

Given the beneficial effects of flow, it is important to understand the contexts in which flow is most likely to occur. Contrary to conventional understandings about school, we find that young people are most likely to experience flow in their classes and when they are doing homework. Teenagers also experience flow when they are working at their jobs and participating in sports and hobbies. Less structured activities like watching television and listening to the radio, although still enjoyable, are less likely to produce flow. Although flow is more common in school than in other contexts, the overall frequency with which it happens is much less than we would hope, given its beneficial effects.

Our schools and the activities in classrooms are not necessarily organized to produce opportunities that would allow students to be in a flow-like state. It seems to us that the challenge for educators is to consider how we can organize learning opportunities in high school classrooms that will provide more chances for students to experience flow. Our results with respect to flow and other personal characteristics suggest that certain contexts of adolescents' lives can be restructured to provide a more optimistic sense of the future, enhance their self-esteem, and challenge them to increase their skills.

Social Supports for a Productive Adulthood

Personal traits are not only acquired genetically but are also shaped by social supports in families, peer groups, communities, and schools. All these contexts work together and severally to influence adolescent career development. Even teenagers who are optimistic, have high self-esteem, and consistently engage in activities that promote flow can find themselves in colleges that do not meet their expectations because they lacked support and direction from their family or their high schools. A talented teenager with supportive parents may not be admitted to the college of his or her choice because the high school did not offer rigorous courses required by selective colleges or failed to provide accurate and timely information about college entrance exams.

Gender, Class, and Ethnicity

Being born a boy or a girl, belonging to a racial or ethnic minority, or having wealthy or poor parents all influence how young people form views about their future and the social and economic resources they have to make their dreams reality. Only a few decades ago, most females expected to graduate from high school, get married, and raise a family, but not have a career (Coontz 1992). Today, the expectations of adolescent females are dramatically different (Schneider and Stevenson 1999). Young women are not considering the dilemma of whether to work or to have a family. Both girls and boys expect that their spouse or partner will work and will share childcare responsibilities. Teenagers, regardless of gender, race or ethnicity, or social class, expect to work, marry, have children, and retire at age sixty-five (unpublished tabulations, first-year data set).

Girls, who typically receive better grades in school than boys do, appear to be capitalizing on their academic efforts. Whether one is a boy or a girl matters little with respect to college attendance. In fact, we find that girls are more likely to attend highly selective colleges than boys are. Females are also more likely than boys to aspire to professional jobs. If the occupational dreams of our teenagers come to pass, future astronauts, heads of major corporations, and presidents of the United States are as likely to be females as males.

Race and ethnicity also appear to have little systematic impact on educational and career plans. Most teenagers, regardless of their family background, expect to obtain at minimum a bachelor's degree and have high-power jobs in medicine, law, or business. The educational dreams of many minorities are not just dreams: African-Americans are more likely than Caucasians with similar grades and family resources to attend four-year schools.

Although the future dreams of our teenagers do not vary by gender, race, and ethnicity, what happens to them after high school graduation appears very much to be influenced by family and community social class characteristics. Even though we find that students in families with limited resources are more likely to work hard in school and expect to attend college and receive a degree, these qualities are not enough to gain them entrance to competitive colleges. Students whose families have limited social and economic resources more often attend two-year institutions, where the likelihood of obtaining a bachelor's degree is significantly reduced (Adelman 1994; Schneider and Stevenson 1999). On the other hand, students in more advantaged families with high levels of education are more likely to be admitted to the most selective four-year postsecondary institutions in the country.

Although "good" students in financially advantaged households are more likely to attend selective colleges, their attitudes toward their high school academic courses were not positive. When in high school, these students perceived their academic classes as boring, and they were less optimistic about their futures. Feeling unengaged in school, these students tended to place more importance on the outcome of the instructional task than on the challenge of the activity itself. Such students were more likely to worry about their performance in their academic classes and believe that those courses were directly relevant to their futures.

Academic classes are boring for nearly all teenagers, but getting good grades matters more for students whose families are highly educated and have considerable financial resources than it does for other students. If one's parents have the economic resources and are willing to spend them, receiving good grades—especially taking advanced-level courses where an A counts more than in a regular class—increases the odds of getting into a highly competitive college. Thus, in spite of their personal feelings toward school or specific classes, students in families with economic resources direct their energies toward acceptance by a selective college, and they are more willing to suffer through anxiety, boredom, and lack of control to get good grades to reach that aim.

Although we can do little to change a parent's job or give direct subsidies to the home in the form of financial aid, we should not consider the effects of social class as unalterable. While the general trend for students from disadvantaged families and communities is not to attend elite colleges, we find that there are some teenagers who succeed despite being in severely disadvantaged communities. What seems to mediate the consequences of social class are interactions in the family and actions taken by the school that not only offer support but also provide direct advice on how best to maximize one's talents for future career success.

The Family Environment

Recently, considerable attention has been devoted to the lack of importance of the family in the development of youth into adulthood (Harris 1998). Our findings challenge this claim and provide concrete evidence that families matter in an adolescent's career development. Despite the popularized notion that young people feel alienated from their families, we find that most young people love their parents and count on them for support and encouragement when making choices about the future.

Nearly all the students in our study see their parents as loving and supportive. Yet merely giving adolescents love and support without providing opportunities to be responsible for their behaviors, encouraging them to do their best, and recognizing accomplishments can be problematic for many students. Students whose families have high expectations, who are treated in an adult manner and treat other members of the family similarly, are more likely to attend competitive colleges.

Traditional sociological models (Blau and Duncan 1967; Sewell and Hauser 1975) placed considerable importance on parents' educational expectations for their child when predicting adult economic and social success. We find that most of the parents in our study expect their children to attend college regardless of their economic resources. Not unlike their adolescent children, the parents in this study see college as the minimum level of education they hope their child will achieve. These findings are consistent with those of larger national longitudinal studies such as NELS:1988–94 (Green et al. 1995). Are there other actions, then, that parents can take that may influence students' future plans?

Contrary to some school reform efforts, which suggest that parents of schoolchildren should become more involved with their children's education by participating in school programs (U.S. Department of Education 1994), we find that it is what parents do and what they communicate to their teenage children at home that appears to be more beneficial to their educational and career plans. Parent discussion with adolescents about courses, plans, and colleges is important for all teenagers. Parents who frequently communicate with their teenagers about school experiences and high school plans are not only providing information but also indicating that they are interested and involved in the adolescents' lives.

Parenting does not end when a teenager gets a driver's license. Our work demonstrates the continued role of families in the formation of young peoples' career plans. Parents of adolescents need to be more, not less, involved in their children's lives, frequently communicating with them about the world of adult work. Parenting responsibilities include learning about adolescents' talents and interests. These interests need to be channeled into real-life experiences. The role of parents in the lives of adolescents is one of finding opportunities to help children learn about work and educational opportunities. One way they can do this is by looking locally within their community for places that would be willing to take an intern or provide paid employment in an area of interest to the adolescent. If a young person enjoys photography, it is not enough to visit a photography exhibit; the parents should encourage the child to pursue his or her passion, perhaps by finding an internship with a neighborhood photographer or arranging for the child to take pictures for a local newspaper.

The Local Community

The local community can be a tremendous resource for helping young people learn more about adult work. Teenagers growing up in affluent communities find many opportunities for productive paid employment. Schools working with local communities make arrangements for internships in hospitals, data processing firms, and town government. Sometimes those jobs that involve high levels of responsibility and interaction with adults result in paid employment. A high school senior in a wealthy suburb showed exceptional talent in filmmaking at the local high school. The school arranged with the village to have the student videotape all government board meetings for the public access television station.

But for young adults growing up in economically disadvantaged communities the situation is very different. It is difficult for the high school to find work opportunities for teenagers because there are few local businesses. Examples of jobs available in these communities included domestic help for hotels, clerical work in a mortuary, and working at a fast-food restaurant. In communities where few people are working, information about employment opportunities is severely limited. Lack of information regarding where to apply for a job, how to apply for a job, and how to conduct oneself in an interview places a student at a real disadvantage. Students in these types of neighborhoods would probably be better served working outside their communities, where they can expand their knowledge of adult work opportunities, interact with other adults working full-time, and develop habits that are consistent with a productive work ethic.

Community resources also influence college choices. In the wealthy communities, students are much more likely to attend four-year than two-year postsecondary institutions. One factor that appears to encourage attendance at two-year institutions is the local availability of such colleges. We find, for example, that wherever there are extensive community college opportunities, special efforts are made by the high school to encourage high school graduates to attend two-year schools. From the students' grades, attitude, course selection, and parent education, we would expect that if they lived in a wealthier environment they would probably attend four-year colleges. Furthermore, if the parents had obtained a college degree, the students would be more likely to attend a highly selective rather than a less selective college.

Programs designed to improve the standard of living need to recognize that community resources not only provide direct income benefits to the parents but also have implications for the children. Our findings clearly show the relationship between local resources and teenage work opportunities. Moreover, they demonstrate how communities can have a direct influence on college choice. This is important because the road to a college degree beginning in a two-year college can be arduous and may not necessarily result in a bachelor's degree (Schneider and Stevenson 1999).

The Peer Network

Not surprisingly, young people enjoy being in each other's company. The importance of being with many friends is even greater for younger teenagers in comparison to older ones, who enjoy spending time with one close friend. Although young people feel happiest and most engaged in the company of their friends, these friendships do not appear to be connected to future goals. Typical social situations, such as hanging out at the mall or going over to someone's house to listen to music and eat pizza, are times when young people talk about each other but do not necessarily formulate ideas about their future.

Time spent in unstructured activities with friends, although enjoyable, does not appear to give young people strong social support to overcome personal or school adversities (Schmidt 1998). On the other hand, time spent in school or outside of school in more structured types of activities appears to have more positive effects on students' career goals. Students who participate in extracurricular activities and take leadership roles appear to have a clearer understanding of what they would like to do with their lives after high school. Extracurricular activities in school may provide opportunities to help students think about their futures.

The School Curriculum

Perhaps one of our most disturbing findings concerns how high schoolers experience their academic classes. The relatively unengaged time that teenagers spend listening to their teachers lecture is particularly troublesome, given that such experiences are so unenjoyable and boring. For a society that will increasingly rely on the ingenuity and creativity of young workers, it appears that we are socializing teenagers in ways that are inconsistent with future needs. Whereas students find teachers' lectures boring, they find group work engaging and challenging, and group work is what employers want workers to be able to do (SCANS 1992). Yet this is exactly the type of activity lacking in the high school curriculum.

The courses a student takes in high school seem to be directly related to the type of college he or she attends. Taking advanced-level math and science courses increases the odds that a student will attend a more selective college. Students who take more math and science courses at advanced and honors levels are more likely to attend competitive universities, whereas students who take a minimum number of these courses are rarely admitted to them. Given that a college degree is the goal of the majority of secondary school students, how little time they actually spend in subjects that prepare them for higher education is disturbing. In a typical week a student spends only three hours a day in math, English, science, and history classes combined.

Vocational Counseling

The counseling that young people are receiving in high school is nearly entirely directed at college preparation. Today's high schools are focused on college entrance even in poor urban communities where the performance of the students is below grade level. Vocational programs are nearly nonexistent, and the students taking more applied courses such as mechanical drawing, electronics, or applied health have their sights on going to college. The notion that high schools need to be developing tighter links with the workplace makes sense only in the context that the general purpose is to expose students to work-related possibilities after college rather than job placement after high school.

It has been argued that vocational programs are what keep many teenagers in school (Arum 1998). Yet very few students are actually enrolled in such programs. For example, in a high school with a total enrollment of 3,500, only 124 students were in the vocational program—this in a school that sends the majority of its graduates to community colleges and technical vocational schools. Students find vocational classes more enjoyable than academic subjects, but they do not find them intellectually challenging. To compound the problem of low enrollments and lack of intellectual rigor, many of the teachers of these courses encourage their students to attend community college, where it is assumed they can get the type of training they need for the jobs they desire. The relationship between high school and community college for students in vocational programs needs further study. Do students who are taking vocational classes and are being encouraged to attend community college have the preparation to succeed in two-year colleges?

What do these data from the first year of our study suggest about the future? First, young people who have positive, flexible views about their futures are building personal strengths that should help to make them resilient as they move through college and eventually face an uncertain and volatile labor market (Bills 1995). The job market for these young adults will be one in which credentials and training for jobs are likely to require more and more education. Job security is unlikely to be assured even in the professions. Under such conditions, young adults who remain optimistic and seek challenges will find it easier to cope with an unstable working world.

Second, although social supports matter, they are not necessarily constraining and can be altered to capitalize on individual interests and skills. Families continue to influence adolescents' life plans, and we expect this influence to continue into adult life. Students are best prepared in high school when they take rigorous courses, participate in extracurricular activities, and have meaningful part-time jobs. All these experiences develop knowledge and skills that will help them in whatever careers they pursue. The technological demands of the twenty-first century will require that young adults have greater intellectual capacity than in the past. We must not downplay the importance of technology and mental acuity for all persons choosing professional as well as nonprofessional careers.

Implications for Educational Policy

What do these results mean for educational policies? Career counseling, it seems, can no longer be limited to matching traits with slots but should help youth to develop flexible attitudes, creative problem-solving techniques, and fundamental habits that will allow them to prosper during changing times. These goals cannot be achieved by counselors alone but need to involve the entire educational institution as well as families and communities. The role of counselors might become that of providing information to principals, teachers, parents, and curriculum developers about the needs and realities of the workplace and about strategies for best preparing teenagers to meet future opportunities.

   Our findings lead us to make the following recommendations:

1. *Develop high school curricula in academic subjects that stress creativity, flexibility, and emotional intelligence.* In the future it will be essential to establish more links between disciplines, to see commonalities among different subjects, and to master synthetic as well as analytic approaches to learning. Only then will young adults be able to move effortlessly from one job to another as market conditions change. At the same time, abstract academic learning should be presented in a context of personal and social responsibility.

2. *Encourage high schools to provide more instructional time in academic subjects and to use that time in ways that are intellectually engaging for the students.* Compared to other societies, ours spends much less time exposing students to academic subjects. And when students do take courses in such subjects, they are often inattentive and bored. Schools should place less reliance on passive instructional formats such as lectures and audiovisual presentations. Group projects should be utilized more widely, taking advantage of teenagers' natural inclination to work together with peers. Other instructional formats that engage students' attention are individual work and testing.

3. *Restructure school-to-work programs in high schools so that students come to realize that productive employment in the future will require continual training and learning.* Postsecondary education is becoming a lifelong activity. This applies to all forms of adult work, in

both industry and the professions. Change rather than stability will characterize the workplace. We need to develop in young people a passion for lifelong learning. We need to communicate that education and work are useful, challenging, and enjoyable—more so than entertainment and consumption.

4. *Encourage intrinsic motivation and teach children to enjoy what they do for its own sake, not just for the sake of getting good grades.* Children who enjoy overcoming challenges will seek out challenging situations in their adult lives. They will be more likely to seize new opportunities, to seek new ways of doing things, to work on tasks that have unclear solutions, and to inspire others to work on difficult problems. These are the characteristics that the workforce of the future will most urgently need.

5. *Clarify the links between time use and future job options.* Currently much of teenagers' time is wasted in activities that fail to provide either immediate or delayed gratification. Children who develop habits of discipline for their psychic energy are well positioned to take on whatever opportunities arise and to make new ones when there are none. Teachers, parents, and counselors should spend more time advising young people about the links between time use (such as television watching and socializing) and future job options. It is particularly important to make sure that children do not fall into the habit of feeling that what they do is meaningless— neither like work nor like play. In this respect, parental example and other adult role models are enormously important.

6. *Find situations that are more play-like for disadvantaged youth.* Students who perceived their life in more play-like terms were more likely to matriculate in selective postsecondary schools. The importance of play in the lives of young people as well adults is well established, and it will become ever more important in the rapidly changing labor market of the future. The spontaneity and creativity associated with play is something we should support for all children, especially as this quality builds self-confidence and

educational attainment. Yet it would appear that we are not able to provide enough opportunities for being playful to young adults of limited financial means.

7. *Encourage parents to become more actively involved in their teenage children's lives.* Parents should understand that the time young people spend outside of high school provides many opportunities for the acquisition of knowledge and skills. To benefit from these, parents must learn more about their children's interests and find opportunities to communicate high expectations as well as unstinting support. This kind of parental involvement requires time and attention, but without it teenagers will have a difficult time realizing their potential.

An essential goal in the transition from school to a productive adult life is to develop curiosity and interest not only in learning but in life as a whole. This is no mean task, since currently schools often do the opposite: dampen curiosity and lead students in the direction of cynicism and disinterest. The condition to be avoided at all costs is the one in which teenagers feel that what they do is just a waste of time. Attractive goals to strive for, and the skills to reach them, are the tools young people need most.

The best antidote against disengaged boredom is a combination of hard work and playfulness. To the extent that teenagers can develop intrinsic motivation—through self-directed exploration of knowledge, through extracurricular activities—they will learn to enjoy what they do for its own sake. Young people who learn to work hard and play hard are likely to go on learning. They will enjoy overcoming challenges and prosper even under adverse conditions, instead of swelling the ranks of the disillusioned and the unemployed. The best insurance for the future is preparing generations of skillful, enthusiastic, and purposeful young men and women.

SITE DESCRIPTIONS

Bayside is a neighborhood located in a major midwestern city in the midst of a dense and diverse population. Bayside High School has a student population of nearly 1,200, the majority of whom are of Hispanic origin, and reflects many of the characteristics typical of inner-city schools, including a high dropout rate and a low daily attendance rate. Whereas the high school draws students from all over the city, the two Bayside elementary schools we studied serve only students from the district. Both elementary schools contain sixth-, seventh-, and eighth-grade classes and primarily serve Hispanic students.

The city of **Betton** has long been one of the major manufacturing centers of the Midwest. Our research was conducted in an elementary school, a junior high school, and a high school in the Northern Hills school district. Two-thirds of the students in the district are African-American, and the three schools we studied were all located within a mile of one another. Northern Hills High School is home to 1,700 students, the majority of whom would be considered middle class.

Curie Science School is a magnet mathematics and science school located in the Northeast in one of the largest cities in the United States. The neighborhood surrounding the school is in poor economic condition, but the school itself is largely isolated from its surrounding community, drawing its students from a wide variety of neighborhoods around the city. Whereas the neighborhood surrounding Curie is largely African-American and Hispanic, Curie's students are primarily Asian and Caucasian. Although it is a public school, students must pass an entrance exam to attend. Curie is recognized as one of the top high schools in the country.

The **Cedar** school district serves a small midwestern city and its surrounding residential areas. The district is largely blue-collar, although it has recently been experiencing a severe decline in the manufacturing sector. Cedar High School, with an enrollment of 1,400 students, is one of the more racially and ethnically diverse schools in the city, which is overwhelmingly Caucasian. We also studied an elementary school in the district and a junior high school that feeds into Cedar High School.

Central City is a large midwestern city that has experienced a slight economic decline over the last decade. Central City School District was formed as a result of a desegregation policy dating from the mid-1970s. Audubon Academy, formerly a predominantly African-American school, is now a college preparatory school whose student population must conform to the integration decision. Students are admitted to Audubon based on grades, test scores, and teacher recommendations. We also studied three public schools in Central City: Roosevelt High School and two of its feeder middle schools. The student population of Roosevelt High School is nearly 50 percent African-American and is predominantly middle class.

The East Coast city of **Crystal Port** is among the twenty largest cities in the United States, with one of the largest African-American populations. The Crystal Port economy is largely service related, and the population of the city has declined steadily since the 1980s. Marshall High School and its feeder middle school are located in the inner city. The student populations of both these schools are predominantly African-American. At the time of its inception Marshall High School was a premiere school for African-Americans, but urban decay and other problems have plagued its inner-city neighborhood, and we were told by many that Marshall is now "the worst school in Crystal City." Both the high school and the middle school experience serious problems with student attendance and safety.

The West Coast city of **Del Vista**, with a population of almost half a million, has experienced rapid growth in the past twenty years, particularly among South Asian and Pacific island populations. The city has long had a highly specialized industrial economy, but drastic cutbacks in government contracts have caused economic decline in this area. Del Vista remains, however, the fifth most expensive of the seventy-five largest cities in the United States. Del Vista High School has approximately 3,600 students, more than half of whom are bused in from inner-city neighborhoods. In both the high school and its two feeder middle schools, a significant portion of students have limited English skills.

Grove High School and its feeder middle school are near the city of **Feldnor**, located in a southeastern state. Feldnor, a medium-sized city, has expanded around several large family theme parks whose tourism fuels the local economy, and the area has grown rapidly since the 1980s. The population of Feldnor is about 83 percent Caucasian. The student populations of both Grove High School and its feeder middle school have increased since the 1980s, and their student body is largely reflective of the city as a whole.

Forest Bluff is a growing, suburban, white-collar community. An overwhelming majority of its residents are Caucasian, and the median family income is more than double the national average. The high school is the only public high school for the area, and in appearance and resources it is similar to many small colleges. Its only two feeder schools are modern, clean, and attractive, and its students have above-average achievement scores.

Maple Wood is an upper-middle-class suburb located on the outskirts of a midwestern city. As one of the city's older and more proximal suburbs, Maple Wood has a distinct urban flair uncharacteristic of most suburban communities. Maple Wood's proximity to the city's business district has made the community an attractive living choice for many white-collar workers. The village of Maple Wood is recognized as one of the few areas in or around the city that has been successfully integrated economically, racially, and ethnically. The Maple Wood School District is considered among the best in the United States. We studied Maple Wood High School, with an enrollment of 3,000 students, one of its feeder junior high schools, and two elementary schools in the district.

Metawa is a rural midwestern town that has had a fairly stable economy since the 1980s. Adults in the community hold a wide variety of occupations, including white-collar professional jobs and craft/operative jobs. Metawa High School serves 1,300 students from a 225-square-mile area. We also studied the town's only public junior high school and one of Metawa's six elementary schools.

Middle Brook is a relatively affluent suburb of a northeastern city. Since the late 1980s, the suburb has seen an influx of highly educated immigrants, many of whom are employed in white-collar jobs in the neighboring city, which has been experiencing moderate growth in its service industry. Although the student population at Middle Brook High School and the feeder middle school we studied is predominantly Caucasian, approximately one-third of the students speak a language other than English at home.

INSTRUMENTS

Date _____ Time you were beeped _____ am/pm Time you answered _____ am/pm

As you were beeped . . .

Where were you? _____

What was on your mind? _____

What was the main thing you were doing? _____

What else were you doing? _____

Was the main thing you were doing . . .

More like work ( )   More like play ( )   Both ( )   Neither ( )

	not at all								very much	
How well were you concentrating?	0	1	2	3	4	5	6	7	8	9
Were you living up to expectations of others?	0	1	2	3	4	5	6	7	8	9
Was it hard to concentrate?	0	1	2	3	4	5	6	7	8	9
Did you feel self-conscious or embarrassed?	0	1	2	3	4	5	6	7	8	9
Did you feel good about yourself?	0	1	2	3	4	5	6	7	8	9
Did you enjoy what you were doing?	0	1	2	3	4	5	6	7	8	9
Were you living up to your expectations?	0	1	2	3	4	5	6	7	8	9
Did you feel in control of the situation?	0	1	2	3	4	5	6	7	8	9

Were you doing the main activity because . . .

You wanted to ( )   You had to ( )   You had nothing else to do ( )

Describe your mood as you were beeped:

	Very	quite	some	neither	some	quite	very	
Happy	o	o	o	o	o	o	o	Sad
Weak	o	o	o	o	o	o	o	Strong
Passive	o	o	o	o	o	o	o	Active
Lonely	o	o	o	o	o	o	o	Sociable
Ashamed	o	o	o	o	o	o	o	Proud
Involved	o	o	o	o	o	o	o	Detached
Excited	o	o	o	o	o	o	o	Bored
Clear	o	o	o	o	o	o	o	Confused
Worried	o	o	o	o	o	o	o	Relaxed
Competitive	o	o	o	o	o	o	o	Cooperative

Who were you with?

( ) alone   ( ) teachers   () If you were with friends,
( ) mother   ( ) classmates, peers   what were their names?
( ) father   ( ) strangers   _____
( ) sister(s) or brother(s) ( ) friend(s) How many?____ _____
( ) other relatives   female () male ()   _____
( ) others _____   _____

Indicate how you felt about the main activity:

	low							high	
Challenges of the activity	1	2	3	4	5	6	7	8	9
Your skills in the activity	1	2	3	4	5	6	7	8	9

	not at all					very much			
Was this activity important to you?	1	2	3	4	5	6	7	8	9
How difficult did you find this activity?	1	2	3	4	5	6	7	8	9
Were you succeeding at what you were doing?	1	2	3	4	5	6	7	8	9
Did you wish you had been doing something else?	1	2	3	4	5	6	7	8	9
Was this activity interesting?	1	2	3	4	5	6	7	8	9
How important was it in relation to your future goals?	1	2	3	4	5	6	7	8	9

If you had a choice . . .

Who would you be with? _____

What would you be doing? _____

_____

Since you were last beeped, did you do any: (estimate to nearest quarter/hour)
(Please circle o if you haven't done the activity.)

TV watching	o	1/4	1/2	3/4	1	1 1/4	1 1/2	1 3/4	2 hours
Chores, errands	o	1/4	1/2	3/4	1	1 1/4	1 1/2	1 3/4	2 hours
Paid work	o	1/4	1/2	3/4	1	1 1/4	1 1/2	1 3/4	2 hours
Hanging out with friends	o	1/4	1/2	3/4	1	1 1/4	1 1/2	1 3/4	2 hours
Homework	o	1/4	1/2	3/4	1	1 1/4	1 1/2	1 3/4	2 hours

. . . has anything happened, or have you done anything which could have affected how
   you feel?

Any comments? _____

VARIABLE LIST

Descriptions of Variables

I. Dependent Variables

Non-Sport Extracurricular   Ranges from 0 to 9, based on participation in each of nine categories of school-based, nonathletic activities.

School Trouble   Ranges from 0 to 24, based on degree of trouble experienced in each of six categories of school-related disciplinary problems.

Job Knowledge Score   Rasch score constructed from twelve true-false items about a wide range of jobs and work-related terms. The range of items includes topics especially relevant to blue-collar and craft jobs (e.g., "an apprentice is a new worker who is assigned to learn a trade from a more skillful worker"), as well as topics relevant to expert professions (e.g., "most lawyers spend their working days in courtrooms"). The informal economy is not represented in the scale.

Educational Expectations   From question—"As things stand now, how far in school do you think you will get?"—response categories are: 1 = less than high school graduation; 2 = high school graduation only; 3 = less than two years of vocational, trade, or business school; 4 = two years or more of vocational, trade, or business school; 5 = less than two years of college; 6 = two or more years of college; 7 = B.A.; 8 = M.A. or equivalent; 9 = Ph.D., M.D., or equivalent.

Occupational Expectations Duncan Socioeconomic Index Score of the first occupation the respondent expects to have. From question—"What do you think you will do [after you finish school]?"—responses were coded into U.S. Census Detailed Occupation Categories. Duncan Socioeconomic Index Scores were merged into the census occupations. In some analyses the job categories themselves were used.

ESM Variables Measuring Quality of Experience In addition to the raw scores, person-level z-scores were computed for all quality of experience variables. Computed as such, an individual's weekly mean on a given item is 0, and scores above or below 0 indicate one's deviation in score from one's own personal mean.

Concentration Response on a ten-point scale to: "How well were you concentrating?"

Living up to Others' Expectations Response on a ten-point scale to: "Were you living up to others expectations?"

Ease of Concentration Response on a ten-point scale to: "Was it hard to concentrate?" Reverse coded.

Feeling Good about Self Response on a ten-point scale to: "Did you feel good about yourself?"

Enjoyment Response on a ten-point scale to: "Did you enjoy what you were doing?"

Living up to Own Expectations Response on a ten-point scale to: "Were you living up to your expectations?"

In Control   Response on a ten-point scale to: "Did you feel in control of the situation?"

Happy   Response on a seven-point scale rating happiness.

Strong   Response on a seven-point scale rating strength.

Active   Response on a seven-point scale rating how active respondent feels.

Sociable   Response on a seven-point scale rating how sociable respondent feels.

Proud   Response on a seven-point scale rating how proud respondent feels.

Involved   Response on a seven-point scale rating how involved respondent feels.

Excited   Response on a seven-point scale rating excitement.

Clear   Response on a seven-point scale rating how clear respondent feels.

Relaxed   Response on a seven-point scale rating relaxation.

Cooperative   Response on a seven-point scale rating how cooperative respondent feels.

Challenge   Response on a nine-point scale rating the challenge of the activity.

Skill   Response on a nine-point scale rating the respondent's skills in the activity.

Important to You   Response on a nine-point scale to the question: "Was this activity important to you?"

Easy   Response on a nine-point scale to: "How difficult did you find this activity?" Reverse coded.

Succeed   Response on a nine-point scale to: "Were you succeeding at what you were doing?"

Wish   Response on a nine-point scale to: "Do you wish you were doing something else?" Reverse coded.

Interest   Response on a nine-point scale to: "Was this activity interesting?"

Future Importance   Response on a nine-point scale to: "How important was [the activity] in relation to your future goals?"

Why Doing Activity   Response to: "Why are you doing [main activity]?"

> 1 = Wanted to
>
> 2 = Had to
>
> 3 = Nothing else to do
>
> 4 = Had to and wanted to
>
> 5 = Wanted to and nothing else
>
> 6 = Had to and nothing else
>
> 7 = All

Alone   Dummy variable indicating that student was alone.

Composite Variables from ESM Each of the following variables was constructed as a result of factor analysis, and they are consistent with factors named and used previously in other ESM studies by Csikszentmihalyi and others.

Mood A signal-level measure calculated as the arithmetic mean of the scores on the scales for "happy," "strong," "active," "sociable," and "proud." Computed for both raw scores and z-scores.

Salience A signal-level measure calculated as the arithmetic mean of the scores on the scales for "challenge," "future importance," and "importance to self." Computed for both raw scores and z-scores.

Self-Esteem A signal-level measure constructed as the arithmetic mean of the scores on the scales for "living up to the expectations of others," "living up to your own expectations," "feeling good about self," "succeeding at present activity," and "feeling in control." Computed for both raw scores and z-scores.

Potency A signal-level measure constructed as the arithmetic mean of the scores on the scales for "strong," "active." and "excited." Computed for both raw scores and z-scores.

Affect A signal-level measure constructed as the arithmetic mean of the scores on the scales for "sociable," "proud," "happy," and "relaxed." Computed for both raw scores and z-scores.

Motivation A signal-level measure constructed as the arithmetic mean of the scores on the scales for "enjoyment," "interest in present activity," and "wish to be doing present activity." Computed for both raw scores and z-scores.

The State of Flow, Anxiety, Relaxation, or Apathy These are dummy variables calculated at the signal level that are constructed using z-score measures of challenge and skill. For each of the variables, a value of 1 indicates that a person is in that particular state when the signal went off, and a value of 0 indicates that a person was not in that state. The percentage of time spent in any of these states can be calculated by aggregating the data to the person level.

Flow = 1   when z-scores for challenge and skills are both above 0.

Anxiety = 1   when z-score for challenge is above 0 and z-score for skill is at or below 0.

Relaxation = 1   when z-score for challenge is at or below 0 and z-score for skill is above 0.

Apathy = 1   when z-scores for challenge and skills are both at or below 0.

Intensity of Flow   A continuous signal-level measure constructed as the geometric mean of challenge and skill (raw scores). The intensity of flow score is computed by taking the square root of the product of the challenge and skill scores for a given signal.

Intrinsic Task Motivation   From factor analysis of five measures, each on a five-point scale. Students were asked, "When working on a difficult task such as homework, how important is _____?" The intrinsic factor comprises "enjoying what I'm doing," "being interested," "being challenged," "being good at it," and "learning something new."

Extrinsic Task Motivation   Calculated as Intrinsic Motivation above. Comprises "preparing for secure job," "getting information for making money later," "not falling behind," "learning something to use later," and "living up to parents' expectations."

Social Task Motivation   Calculated as Intrinsic Motivation above. Comprises "impressing friends," "doing better than others," and "getting respect from others."

Optimism   Arithmetic mean of how powerful and confident one feels when thinking about the future (five-point scale).

Openness to Experience Arithmetic mean of how curious and enthusiastic one feels when thinking about the future (five-point scale).

Pessimism Arithmetic mean of how empty, angry, and doubtful one feels when thinking about the future (five-point scale).

II. Independent Variables

Female Dummy variable with male as the excluded reference category.

Parent's Education Education level of more highly educated parent (or the one present, if only one is present). Response categories are 1 = did not finish high school; 2 = high school graduation or GED; 3 = vocational school, junior college, or other two-year school; 4 = some college; 5 = B.A.; 6 = M.A., or equivalent; 7 = Ph.D., M.D., or equivalent.

Parent's Occupational Status Duncan Socioeconomic Index Score (see Nakao and Treas, 1994) for the higher status employed parent or guardian, if both parents are present. If only one parent or guardian is present, the SEI score for that parent or guardian.

Parent Occupation This series of six dummy variables is based on a collapsing of the sixteen categories for parents' occupation on the NELS questionnaire. The dummy variables represent the occupation of the family's principal earner (father, if present and employed; otherwise mother).

Professional I

Professional II

Manager

Laborer

Blue Collar

Lower White Collar

Number of Siblings   Number of siblings the respondent reports living with him or her.

Intact Family   Dummy variable coded 1 if respondent lives with both "Mother" and "Father." The reference category is all other living arrangements (e.g., with stepfather and mother, with adult male guardian, etc.).

Family Support   Composite variable computed by summing affirmative answers to the following items from the Teenage Life Questionnaire.

Positive support items:

1.   Others notice when I'm feeling down, even if I don't say anything.

2.   I feel appreciated for who I am.

3.   If I have a problem, I get special attention and help.

4.   I do things I like to do without feeling embarrassed.

5.   I am made to feel special on birthdays and holidays.

6.   No matter what happens, I know I'll be loved and accepted.

7.   We enjoy having dinner together and talking.

8.   We compromise when our schedules conflict.

9.   We are willing to help each other out when something needs to be done.

10. We try not to hurt each other's feelings.

11. Our home is full of things that hold special memories.

Negative support items:

12. It is difficult to relax and be myself.

13. The only time I'm noticed is when there is a problem.

14. Day-to-day life is disorganized and unpredictable.

15. There are many fights and arguments.

16. Others can't be counted on.

Total support = (sum of items 1 to 11) – (sum of items 12 to 16)

In Chapter 11 a Rasch measure of family support was computed using only the positive support items.

Family Challenge Composite variable computed by summing affirmative answers to the following items from the Tecnage Life Questionnaire.

Positive challenge items:

1. We enjoy playing competitive games.

2. We express our opinions about current events, even when they differ.

3. We ask each other's ideas before making important decisions.

4. It's important to be self-confident and independent to earn respect.

5. Others expect to be good at what they do.

6. Individual accomplishments are noticed.

7. I'm given responsibility for making important decisions affecting my life.

8. I'm expected to do my best.

9. I try to make other family members proud.

10. I'm encouraged to get involved in extracurricular activities.

11. I'm respected for being a hard worker.

12. I'm expected to use my time wisely.

Negative challenge items:

13. We have few interests and hobbies outside of the home.

14. Others lack ambition and self-discipline.

15. It's hard to find privacy when I need to concentrate and finish some work.

16. I don't care if others think I'm "soft" or lazy.

Total challenge = (sum of items 1 to 12) – (sum of items 13 to 16)

In Chapter 11 a Rasch measure was computed using only the positive challenge items.

GPA Ranges from 0.5 to 4.0, with 0.5 representing grades "mostly below D" and 4.0 representing "mostly As."

College Prep Track Voc/Tech Track Pair of dummy variables with general track as the excluded reference category.

School Adviser The number of school adults (e.g., teachers, counselors) the respondent reports going to for advice.

SCC—Social Class of the Community Based on census information. Each site has been rated for SES on a scale of 1 to 5, with 1 being Poor and 5 being Upper Class. Here are the values for each school:

SCC

Value	Schools
1	Bayside, Crystal Port
2	Metawa, Cedar
3	Feldnor, Del Vista, Central City, Betton
4	Maple, Middle Brook, Bridgeway
5	Forest Bluff

Main Activity Primary activity when signaled. By aggregating the signal-level file, the percentage of time spent in various activities can be calculated. Activity categories include maintenance (e.g., grooming, eating), work, school, etc.

Like Work or Play Is the main activity more like work, play, both, or neither?

Expectations about Future Life A series of six questions asking what the chances are that respondents will graduate from high school, go to college, have a job that pays well, have an enjoyable job, own a home, and have a better life than their parents. Responses were on a five-point scale from "very low" to "very high."

Expected Job Response to: "List five jobs you expect to have."

Wished-For Job Response to: "List five jobs you would like to have."

Learn Score   Level of knowledge acquired while doing activity related to expected or wished-for job.

Do Score   Level of skills used while doing activity related to expected or wished-for job.

"Learn-Do" Score   "Learn" score + "Do" score.

Relevant Activity with Family   Indicates that what respondent is learning or doing is done with family members.

Relevant Activity with Friends   Indicates that what respondent is learning or doing is done with friends.

Relevant Activity at School   Indicates that what respondent is learning or doing is done at school.

Relevant Activity in the Community   Indicates that what respondent is learning or doing is done in the community.

Occupational Values   Responses to: "For the job you expect to have in the future, how important are the following to you?"

> Helping people
>
> Working to improve society
>
> Having lots of free time
>
> Working closely with other people
>
> Building or creating things
>
> Having lots of money
>
> Working with your hands

Being famous

Teaching others

Having few responsibilities

Working outdoors

Learning new things

Expressing yourself

Maintaining high ethical and moral standards

Working with animals

Not having to sit at a desk all day

Original responses to these items were on a five-point scale (not at all important to very important). Responses were standardized relative to individual and group responses.

Fitscore   Job knowledge scale based on patterns of responses to questions of the following form: "Pick the 2 jobs that go together the best, and cross out the one that belongs the least: economist, bank teller, sales clerk."

Time Spent on Homework   Sum of time spent on homework, in school and out of school. Each ranges from 1 (none) to 8 (over fifteen hours).

Race   Response to: "Which best describes you?"

1.   Asian, Pacific Islander

2.   Hispanic, regardless of race

3.   Black, not of Hispanic Origin

4.   White, not of Hispanic Origin

5.   American Indian or Alaskan Native

Advanced Course Taking A measure of a student's curricular placement relative to the schoolwide curricular structure, based on advanced courses taken in English, math, and science.

Mathematics and Science Course Sequence Three-level measures of course-taking patterns in high school. For both math and science, Sequence A is definitely college preparatory, Sequence B is probably college preparatory but would not be acceptable by the most prestigious universities, and Sequence C is not college preparatory.

NOTES

CHAPTER TWO · THE DESIGN OF THE STUDY: SAMPLE AND PROCEDURES

1   In the base-year study, students were signaled on a weekly schedule. To accommodate all the schools, the signaling schedule for the schools occurred from October through December.

2   The ESM form used by Csikszentmihalyi, Rathunde, and Whalen (1993) in other adolescent studies was modified slightly for this study to learn how sample members felt about different forms of work—school work, chores, paid work—and future goals. The items eliciting affective and cognitive states use Likert-type response scales. Coding of ESM data was done by trained coders using a detailed coding scheme. (An example of the ESM form is in Appendix B. The coded categories for all measures are found in the variable list in Appendix C.)

3   Because the ESM relies on self-reports, it is open to distortions produced by social desirability or denial. We took pains to assure our respondents that their individual ESM data would never be accessible to persons other than the project staff and that the anonymity of the ESM data, like that of all the data that we collect, would be preserved. A high proportion of our respondents cooperated in the ESM procedure and gave veridical responses.

4   For each site, the team captain prepared a case report containing the following information: (1) a general description of the schools and community, a count of the sampled focal and cohort students, racial and ethnic percentages for the samples, school, and community, as well as observer impressions; (2) a detailed accounting of any variations in procedures or changes in methodology that occurred at the site; and (3) recommendations on methodology, instruments, site management, researcher-school relations, and areas for future study for the next wave of data collection.

5   Within the focal sample, the interviews had a response rate of 95 percent, although the response rate among the focal students for the ESM was only 71 percent. With respect to the other instruments, the focal students tended to have slightly lower

response rates than the cohort sample. The lowest response rate among the focal students was 77 percent for the Friends Form. The overall response rate for both samples for the three instruments—COS, the Teenage Life Questionnaire, and the Friends Form—was 87 percent.

6   School grade level serves as a measure of students' age. Students' gender, race and ethnicity, and grade in school were identified when selecting students for the study. For the purposes of this analysis, coding of students' race or ethnicity is based on responses to the following question in the Teenage Life Questionnaire: Which best describes you? (1) Asian or Pacific Islander; (2) Hispanic, regardless of race; (3) Black, not of Hispanic origin; (4) White, not of Hispanic origin; (5) American Indian or Alaskan Native. Coding of parents' level of education was based on responses to the following question in the Teenage Life Questionnaire: How far in school did your parents go? (1) Did not finish high school; (2) Graduated from high school, but did not go any further; (3) Graduated from college; (4) Master's degree or equivalent; (5) Ph.D., M.D., or other equivalent professional degree. Students were asked to indicate separately the highest level of education completed by each parent (mother and father). For purposes of this analysis, responses for mother and father were combined, and coding reflects the highest level of education obtained by a student's father or mother.

7   To assess educational expectations, students were asked "As things stand now, how far in school do you think you will get?" (Teenage Life Questionnaire). Response options for tenth and twelfth graders included: less than high school graduation, high school graduation, some college (including two-year colleges and trade or vocational programs), college graduation (from a four- or five-year program), master's degree or equivalent, and Ph.D., M.D., or other advanced or professional degree. The response options for sixth and eighth graders were simplified to make it easier for younger students to respond to this question. The response options for these students were: less than high school graduation, high school graduation, college graduation, and advanced degree (law school, medical school, etc.). To compare responses to this question across students from different grades, response options were collapsed into the following categories: less than four years of college, four-year college degree, advanced degree (master's, professional degree, or Ph.D.). These categories are presented in Table 2.2.

CHAPTER THREE · ENVISIONING THE FUTURE

1   ANOVAS were run comparing educational expectations by race and ethnicity ($F = 8.44$, $p < .001$).

2 A Chi-Square analysis of occupational aspirations by gender was highly significant: χ^2 (15, 3883) = 607.5, p < .001.

3 This statistical transformation was devised by Rustin Wolfe. It normalizes the distribution of each value's importance within and across subjects, allowing the distribution to more closely resemble the ipsative measures commonly found in values instruments. The assumption is that the importance of a value is more meaningful in relation to other values and in relation to other subjects than in the abstract. Through two sets of z-scores, raw scores for each item become relative to a subject's scores on other items, and, in turn, relative to other subjects' scores on that particular item. To compute these scores, for each subject the mean of all sixteen value scores is subtracted from the scores of each particular value; the sum is then divided by the standard deviation of all sixteen value scores. Next, for each value, the mean of all subjects' scores is subtracted from each particular subject's score, and the sum is divided by the standard deviation of all subjects' scores. In effect, the final value score represents how important a subject found a particular value in relation to how important he or she found the other values and represents this value in relation to other subjects' relative values.

4 An analysis of variance comparing mean openness-to-experience scores by grade in school yielded the following results: F = 11.02, p < .001. An ANOVA of mean pessimism scores by grade in school was also highly significant: F = 7.12, p < .001.

5 ANOVAs were run comparing mean optimism scores by race/ethnicity (F = 9.01, p < .001) and social class of community (F = 7.19, p < .001). Post hoc tests were then conducted comparing the optimism scores of students from different racial/ethnic groups (Caucasian, Asian, African-American, Hispanic) and those from communities with different socioeconomic profiles. Compared to students from other groups, African-American students and lower SCC students had the highest optimism scores.

6 ANOVAs were also run comparing mean openness-to-experience scores by race/ethnicity (F = 4.14, p < .01) and by parent education (F = 4.38, p < .01).

CHAPTER FOUR · IMAGES OF WORK AND PLAY

1 An analysis of variance comparing mean percent of time spent in "play-like" activities by gender yielded the following results: F = 5.5, p < .05.

2 An ANOVA comparing mean percent of time spent in "neither work-like nor play-like" activities by gender produced similar results: F = 4.6, p < .05.

3 An ANOVA comparing mean percent of time spent in "play-like" activities by students' race/ethnicity was statistically significant: F = 13.01, p < .001.

4   An ANOVA comparing mean percent of time spent in "neither work-like nor play-like" activities by students' race/ethnicity was also significant: $F = 9.81$, $p < .001$.

5   Comparisons of percentage of time spent in "play-like" activities by parents' level of education was significant: ANOVA, $F = 9.05$, $p < .001$.

6   There are no large differences by age, gender, ethnic background, or socioeconomic status with respect to the types of activities perceived as like both work and play. This leveling suggests that the image of what is meant by work and play is well established by the sixth grade and is broadly shared throughout the population.

7   For both self-esteem and salience, composite measures were calculated as averages of students' responses on a ten-point scale.

8   Positive affect was calculated as the average of each of these items on a seven-point scale.

9   This item was measured on a ten-point scale.

10 A comparison of mean self-esteem standardized scores by type of activity (i.e., activities seen as being "more like work," "more like play," "like both work and play," or "like neither work nor play") was highly significant: ANOVA, $F = 78.27$, $p < .001$.

11 An analysis of mean enjoyment standardized scores in "work-like" activities by grade was statistically significant: ANOVA, $F = 3.65$, $p < .05$.

12 ANOVAs were run comparing the quality of experience by gender in play-like activities. For these activities females had lower mean standardized scores for each of the following measures: concentration ($F = 5.91$, $p < .05$), competitiveness ($F = 11.73$, $p < .001$), and challenge ($F = 9.39$, $p < .01$).

13 ANOVAs were run comparing mean quality of experience by gender in activities perceived as being like neither work nor play. In these activities, the mean standardized scores for females were lower than those of males for happiness ($F = 4.40$, $p < .05$) and cooperation ($F = 11.9$, $p < .001$) and were higher than males for concentration ($F = 8.25$, $p < .01$) and challenge ($F = 9.21$, $p < .01$).

14 Mean standardized scores for "wish to be doing" an activity were lower for females than for males for activities that were perceived as being like both work and play (ANOVA, $F = 3.90$, $p < .05$).

15 A comparison of mean self-esteem standardized scores in work-like activities by race/ethnicity was statistically significant: ANOVA, $F = 11.09$, $p < .001$.

16 An ANOVA comparing mean self-esteem standardized scores in work-like activities by parent education was also statistically significant: $F = 5.74$, $p < .001$.

17 While the work and play analyses adjust for individual differences in scale use, our data suggest that adolescents from less-privileged communities generally report higher levels of happiness. Teens from poor and lower-middle-class communities reported average happiness scores of 5.4, while teens from higher classes reported happiness scores around 4.9 (ANOVA, $F = 13.1$, $p < .001$).

18 Caucasians perceive work-and-play activities as more challenging than Hispanics do. A comparison of mean challenge standardized scores in "work-like and play-like

activities" by race/ethnicity was statistically significant: ANOVA, F = 3.89, p < .01. Not surprisingly, there is a progressive increase in the level of challenge from sixth through twelfth grade. An ANOVA comparing mean challenge standardized scores in "work-like and play-like activities" by grade level was statistically significant: F = 3.73, p < .01. This increase in the challenging quality of activities often seen as both work and play confirms the impression that these are opportunities for teenagers to master higher levels of ability.

19   Although these differences were small, they were statistically significant. See note 2.

20   An ANOVA comparing mean time spent in "neither work-like nor play-like" activities by race/ethnicity was statistically significant. See note 4.

21   A comparison of mean "negative affect" standardized scores in "neither work-like nor play-like activities" by gender was statistically significant, with females reporting greater negative affect in these activities: ANOVA, F = 6.61, p < .01.

22   We calculated z-scores for the percentage of time spent by each person in work-like and play-like activities.
      Workers are those whose z-score for work was greater than or equal to 1.
      Players were those whose z-score for play was greater than or equal to 1.

23   A Chi-Square analysis of hours worked by grade was statistically significant: χ^2 = 48.2 p < .001.

24   A Chi-Square analysis of hours worked by race/ethnicity was statistically significant: ^{2} = 24.4, p < .05.

25   A Chi-Square analysis of hours worked by SCC was statistically significant: χ^2 = 59.1, p < .001.

26   An ANOVA comparing mean "ability to concentrate" standardized scores by gender in activities coded as paid work was statistically significant: F = 4.19, p < .05.

27   A comparison of mean enjoyment standardized scores by grade for activities coded as paid work was also statistically significant: ANOVA, F = 5.43, p < .05.

CHAPTER FIVE · LEARNING TO LIKE CHALLENGES

1   Several modifications of this measure have been used; see, for example, the recent methodological summary by Moneta and Csikszentmihalyi (1996).

2   Another way to measure sources of flow in daily activities is by assigning a flow value to each individual response. First, a continuous measure of flow is created by taking the geometric mean (the square root of the product) of the ESM challenge and skill scores for each response. This measure of flow increases as challenge and skill increase, and it decreases as challenge and skill become more discrepant. Thus, the geometric mean provides a measure that captures both the theoretically proposed and the empirically validated aspects of the relationship between challenges

and skills. This measure of flow at the response level can then be averaged for each person to produce an individual-level flow measure that is sensitive to both the amount and the intensity of flow experienced. In the analyses focused on the flow experience, this measure is used directly and ranges in value from 1 to 9. In analyses focused on the autotelic personality, individuals are ranked according to their average level of flow, and then bottom and top quartiles are compared in terms of activities and quality of experience.

3   With the exception of the "Other" category, all other comparisons were significantly different at p < .01.

4   It is also noteworthy, although irrelevant to the present argument, that both groups describe a generally more positive experience in leisure than in productive activities: They enjoy leisure more, they feel happier, stronger, more motivated. However, levels of concentration and perceived importance to the future are higher in productive activities, although levels of self-esteem remain the same.

5   See Chapter 4 for a more detailed discussion of the specific items that are included within each of these factors.

6   A more detailed discussion of sources of motivation—intrinsic, extrinsic, and social—is presented in Chapter 4.

7   See Appendix C for a description of these variables. See Chapter 3 for a detailed discussion of learn-do scores.

CHAPTER SIX · FAMILIES AND THE FORMING OF CHILDREN'S OCCUPATIONAL FUTURE

1   Other studies examining these issues in more diverse populations support this conclusion. For instance, the work of Baumrind (1987, 1989), and the work of those who have extended her widely recognized ideas about authoritative parenting (see Lamborn et al. 1991; Steinberg et al. 1992), show that parents who are both responsive and demanding facilitate adolescent development, including school achievement.

2   Sixteen of the questionnaire items were used to create one index of perceived familial support ($\bar{x}$ = 5.2, sd = 3.8), and the other sixteen items were used to create one measure of challenge ($\bar{x}$ = 5.9, sd = 3.4). The indices were summed, resulting in factor reliabilities for support and challenge of alpha .81 and .74, respectively. The correlation between the support and challenge indices was equal to .65. This relatively high correlation might suggest that only one dimension of families was being measured. Additional information, however, suggested that this was not so. For instance, middle school students perceived more family support (t = 4.92, p < .001), but not more challenge (t = .90, ns), than high school students. This suggests that

as adolescents get older, they perceive their parents as providing less emotional support, while expectations for challenge remain constant. It would seem that the indices of support and challenge capture different aspects of the family system.

Preliminary factor analyses, using tetrachoric correlations because of the dichotomous coding, supported our decisions regarding the items used as measures of support and challenge. However, these factor analyses originally indicated three rather than two clear and distinct factors. In addition to the positive support and challenge items, all the negatively worded items grouped on one factor, regardless of item content. This result was deemed an artifact of the either-or questionnaire format (i.e., it was apparently harder for the adolescents to "totally" agree with a negative statement about their family, as opposed to the less threatening but unavailable option of "partly" agreeing with it). Thus, the negatively worded items were sorted back onto either the support or challenge factor, based on item content and a priori theoretical expectations.

3 Based upon the number of hours sampled by the ESM, each percentage point in the following analyses can be interpreted as equivalent to one hour per week. The family groups spent the following amounts of time with family members during the week of experience sampling:

HS/HC: $\bar{x}$ = 25.9 percent
HS/LC: $\bar{x}$ = 29.0 percent
LS/HC: $\bar{x}$ = 25.1 percent
LS/LC: $\bar{x}$ = 24.8 percent

Contrasts between the various family groups, adjusting for adolescent grade and gender, revealed the following significant differences (one-tailed tests):

HS/LC v. HS/HC: t = -1.51, p < .10
HS/LC v. LS/HC: t = -1.67, p < .05
HS/LC v. LS/LC: t = -1.92, p < .05

Thus, adolescents from supportive but nonchallenging families spent about three to four hours more time with family members than adolescents from the other groups.

4 The following percentages reflect time the adolescents spent alone:

HS/HC: M = 22.2 percent
HS/LC: M = 21.2 percent
LS/HC: M = 24.7 percent
LS/LC: M = 22.3 percent

Contrasts between the groups, adjusting for grade and gender, revealed the following differences (one-tailed tests):

LS/HC v. HS/HC: t = -1.84, p < .05
LS/HC v. HS/LC: t = -1.69, p < .05
LS/HC v. LS/LC: t = -1.57, p < .06

Thus, adolescents from challenging but nonsupportive families spent two to three hours more per week in solitary activities than adolescents from the other groups.

Overall, adolescents from the HS/LC families spent the most time with family members, and those from the LS/HC group spent the most time alone.

5 All the results summarized in the table and subsequent analyses were conducted while holding constant the individual characteristics of the respondent and the respondent's family that correlate with the support or challenge scores. These characteristics include age, gender, racial and ethnic background, school grades, and parental education. Controlling on these factors ensures that the attitudinal results primarily reflect the inner dynamics of the family rather than other factors.

6 Alpha values for these factors were: (1) positive attitude toward teachers (alpha = .82), (2) positive attitude toward students (alpha = .58), (3) feelings of security (alpha =.57), and (4) school cohesiveness (alpha = .46). Alpha values for the latter three factors were somewhat low, but this is due to the small number of items on the factor. The average corrected item-scale correlations for items on the three scales is approximately r = .35.

7 Although only a small amount of variance in the attitudinal measures was accounted for by family support and challenge, Eta statistics showed that in general, support accounted for approximately three to four times the amount of variance accounted for by challenge.

8 Most of the control variables were significantly related to the attitude measures. Higher student grades were positively related to feelings of security (p < .01), but negatively related to perceptions of school cohesiveness (p < .001); higher parental education was related to positive attitudes about teachers (p < .001), and other students (p < .01) but negatively related to school cohesiveness (p < .001). Finally, with Caucasian adolescents as the comparison group, there was a complex mix of ethnic background effects: Asian-American students reported more positive attitudes toward teachers (p < .001), other students (p < .01), and feelings of security (p < .05); African-American students reported less positive attitudes toward teachers (p < .01), while Hispanic students reported more positive attitudes toward them (p < .05).

9 For homework in school, only ethnic background produced a significant effect as a co-variate: Caucasian adolescents spent more time doing homework in school than African-American adolescents (p < .05). For homework outside of school, most of the co-variates were significant: Older adolescents did more homework (p < .001); females did more homework (p < .05). In comparison to Caucasian students, Asian-American students did more homework (p < .001), and African-American students did less (p < .01). Higher parental education was associated with more time doing homework (p < .001).

10 It is interesting to note, however, the difference between the ESM estimates and the questionnaire time estimates in terms of the total amount of time all adolescents spent doing homework: The ESM estimates suggest about twelve hours, and the questionnaire estimates about six to nine hours. This difference is likely due to error

variance in either the questionnaire or the ESM estimates.

11   For recent grades, older students reported lower grades (p < .001); girls reported higher grades than boys (p < .001); higher parental education was associated with higher recent grades (p < .001); and in comparison to Caucasian students, Asian-American students reported higher recent grades (p < .001), and Hispanic and African-American students reported lower recent grades (p < .001). For cumulative grades, girls reported higher grades (p < .05); more parental education was associated with higher grades (p < .001); and in comparison to Caucasian adolescents, Asian-American students reported higher cumulative grades (p < .001), and Hispanic and African-American students reported lower cumulative grades (p < .001).

12   Chronbach's alpha for these items is α .90.

13   The correlation for these items ("importance to self" and "importance to future") is r = .69.

14   A 2 x 2 MANCOVA (high/low support by high/low challenge) examining the relationship between family type by students' mood while doing schoolwork yielded the following results when these co-variates were adjusted for: Family support was significantly related to students' moods in schoolwork (F (1,599) = 6.51, p < .02), but family challenge was not (F (1,599) = 1.76, ns); there was no interaction between support and challenge and students' moods in schoolwork (F (1,599) = 0.0, ns). Students in higher grades reported lower moods (p < .001), as did students whose parents had achieved higher levels of education (p < .001). African-American students reported higher moods than did Caucasian students (p < .05).

15   A 2 x 2 MANCOVA (high/low support by high/low challenge) examining the relationship between family type by students' feelings of salience yielded the following results when these co-variates were adjusted for: Feelings of salience were significantly related to family challenge (F (1,599) = 9.01, p < .01), but not with family support (F (1,599) = 1.76, ns); there was no interaction between support and challenge (F (1,599) = 1.25, ns). Female students reported that productive activities were more salient (p < .01), and Hispanic and African-American students reported higher salience than did Caucasian students (p < .01).

16   Post hoc contrasts for mood, adjusting jointly for the co-variates, showed that the HS/HC group differed from the LS/HC (p < .05) and the LS/LC groups (p < .001); for salience, the HS/HC group differed from the LS/LC group (p < .001).

CHAPTER SEVEN · THE QUALITY OF CLASSROOM EXPERIENCES

1   The following combinations of class types were made to derive the classifications of

school subjects: English combines English, English composition, literature, and reading; science combines general science, biology, chemistry, physics, and earth science; social science/studies combines political science, civics, geography, world culture, psychology, social studies, sociology, anthropology, and ethnic/multicultural studies; computer science combines computer science and programming; art combines music, fine art, photography, drafting, graphics, applied art, and drama; and vocational education combines agriculture, shop, vo-tech, domestic arts, home economics, business skills, and career exploration/counseling.

2   An ANOVA comparing mean scores while in the selected school subjects produced the following results: for challenge: $F = 13.14$, $p < .001$; for importance to future goals: $F = 13.80$, $p < .001$. Students reported the highest levels of challenge and importance in math, which significantly contrasted with the other subjects combined on both variables, at $p < .001$.

3   An ANOVA comparing mean scores in the selected school subjects produced the following results: for wish: $F = 10.82$, $p < .001$; for enjoyment: $F = 18.41$, $p < .001$. Math significantly contrasts with the other subjects combined, at $p < .001$ for enjoyment and $p < .05$ for wish.

4   The F-value for this ANOVA comparing mean scores for the variable wish is reported in note 3. The highest mean score on this variable was reported in art classes, which significantly contrasts with the other subjects combined on this variable, at $p < .001$.

5   The F-value for the ANOVA comparing mean scores for the variable enjoyment is reported in note 3. A similar ANOVA for the variable affect yielded the following result: $F = 6.93$, $p < .001$. Art significantly contrasts with the other subjects combined, at $p < .001$ for enjoyment and $p < .01$ for affect.

6   The F-value for the ANOVA comparing mean scores for the variable importance to future goals is reported in note 2. The lowest mean score on this variable was reported in art classes, which significantly contrasts with the other subjects combined on this variable, at $p < .001$.

7   The F-values for these ANOVAs are reported above. The lowest mean score for the variables enjoyment, importance to future goals, and challenge was reported in history class. These means significantly contrast with the other subjects combined, at $p < .001$ for enjoyment and $p.< .01$ for challenge.

8   The mean score for the variables wish and enjoyment in vocational education and computer science courses were ranked second and third only behind art courses, compared to all of the selected subjects. The mean scores during vocational education classes significantly contrast with the other subjects combined, at $p < .001$ for the variable enjoyment and $p < .01$ for the variable wish. During computer science classes, the contrast is significant, at $p < .01$ for enjoyment and $p < .05$ for wish.

9   While mean scores for the variable importance to future goals was the lowest of all subjects in art classes and significantly lower than other subjects combined, at $p <$

.001, the mean scores on this variable in computer science and vocational education classes were not significantly lower than the other courses combined. In fact, they were higher than those reported in foreign language and history classes.

10   The mean score for the variable wish was higher in art, vocational education, and computer science courses than for all of the academic subjects. The contrast is significant for art, at $p < .001$, vocational education, at $p < .01$, and computer science, at $p < .05$.

11   An ANOVA comparing mean scores in the selected school subjects on the variable flow produced the following results: $F = 7.66$, $p < .001$. The highest mean scores on this variable were reported, in descending order, in vocational education, computer science, and art classes. The mean scores reported in all of the academic subjects were lower. The reported flow was significantly higher than the other subjects combined, at $p < .001$ in vocational education classes, $p < .05$ in computer science classes, and $p < .001$ in art courses.

12   Reported levels of flow were significantly lower than for the other subjects combined, at $p < .01$ in social studies/science classes, $p < .01$ in science classes, and $p < .05$ in English classes.

13   The lowest mean score on the variable flow was reported in history class, which significantly contrasts with the other subjects combined, at $p < .001$.

14   A t-test comparing mean scores in academic classes versus nonacademic classes yielded the following results. Students reported higher challenge in academic courses: $t = 2.43$, $p < .05$. Students reported more importance to future goals in academic classes: $t = 5.05$, $p < .001$. Mean scores were higher in nonacademic classes for the following variables: flow, $t = -3.66$, $p < .001$; enjoyment, $t = -9.91$, $p < .001$; affect, $t = -6.73$, $p < .001$; and self-esteem, $t = -3.93$, $p < .001$.

15   A ranking of subjects by their mean scores on the variable flow is as follows: (1) vocational education, (2) computer science, (3) art, (4) math, (5) foreign language, (6) English, (7) science, (8) social science/studies, (9) history. The ranking of subjects by frequency of employing individual work, given in Table 7.1, is the same, with the sole exception that computer science is first and vocational education is second.

16   Using the methodology of Stevenson, Schiller, and Schneider (1994), individual course-taking patterns were categorized into one of three course sequences. Course patterns were examined separately for tenth and twelfth graders, and separate math sequence groupings were developed for each grade. The upper-level sequence refers to course-taking patterns that are preparatory for highly competitive colleges. The middle-level sequence refers to course taking that may be accepted by colleges, but probably not the most competitive ones. The lower-level sequence is not college preparatory. Using mathematics as an example, three sequences were defined for tenth graders as follows: The upper sequence included all students who have studied at least one higher level mathematics course, such as trigonometry, pre-calculus, or calculus; the middle sequence included all students who have studied algebra

and geometry but not higher math courses; and the lower sequence included all students who have taken algebra or geometry (but not both), and have not taken higher level classes. The lower sequence also included students who have taken math courses other than algebra, geometry, trigonometry, or calculus (e.g., general math, pre-algebra, and business/consumer math). The twelfth-grade mathematics sequences were defined as follows: The upper sequence included all students who have studied calculus; the middle sequence included all students who have taken all or some combination of algebra, geometry, and trigonometry; and the lower sequence included all students who have not taken algebra, geometry, trigonometry, calculus, or pre-calculus.

17 An ANOVA comparing mean scores while in upper, middle, and lower math and science sequences yielded the following results: for affect, $F = 6.37$, $p < .01$; for self-esteem, $F = 7.29$, $p < .001$. For both variables, the mean score in upper level sequences is significantly lower than in the lower and middle sequences combined, $p < .01$. For both variables, mean scores in the middle sequences is significantly higher than in the other sequences combined, $p < .05$ for affect and $p < .01$ for self-esteem.

18 To test this hypothesis, we used our earlier classification from Chapter 5 that distinguishes students who see what they do as more like work from those who see their activities as more like play. In addition, some students disproportionately reported that more of their experiences were like both work and play. We refer to these students as "balanced." Others were in the high extremes in terms of reporting that their experiences felt neither like work nor like play; we call these students "disengaged." In an ANOVA, we compared the quality of experience among workers, players, balanced, and disengaged students while in class. Consistent with our previous findings, results showed that workers report significantly higher levels of flow ($F = 15.84$, $p < .001$), self-esteem ($F = 4.18$, $p < .01$), and importance to future goals ($F = 25.59$, $p < .001$) than do other students. Reporting more negatively are the players, and the most negative reports come from the disengaged group, whose responses are significantly lower than are other students' on these measures. To test the hypothesis that student affect and self-esteem in the high math and science sequences is related to students' attitudes towards work, we re-examined these measures while looking specifically at any differences reported by workers, players, balanced, and disengaged students while in different math and science sequences. Results indicate that both players and balanced students taking the high sequence report more positive affect than their counterparts taking the lower sequence. The opposite is true for workers. Workers in the high sequence report significantly lower affect than workers taking the lower sequence. In addition, they report lower affect than do the other students in the upper sequences. Both differences are significant,

at p < .001. The same pattern can also be observed while examining students' report-ed self-esteem, even though workers report higher self-esteem than other students do in most situations. We conclude that not all students report lower levels of affect and self-esteem in the upper math and science sequences. Rather, these reports are particularly low among students who are highly focused on work and do not per-ceive activities as spontaneous and play-like.

19 Previously, Asakawa and Csikszentmihalyi (1998) found that Asian-Americans from the sixth, eighth, tenth, and twelfth grades reported relatively more positive experi-ences than Caucasian Americans while studying. When studying, Asian-American adolescents enjoyed what they were doing significantly more in addition to perceiv-ing the importance of what they were doing to attain their future goals. We do not believe the results reported here are inconsistent with these previous findings. Rather, they are the product of comparing Asian-American adolescents to other ethnic and minority groups combined (not only to Caucasians) during all class-room hours (not only during individual study).

20 In a series of t-tests, we compared perceived skill and self-esteem of students with optimistic future orientations to those with pessimistic future orientations in each of our selected classroom activities. In every activity except for group work, opti-mistic students report a higher mean score than those of pessimistic students. This difference is significant, at p < .001, while listening to a lecture and doing individu-al work. The self-esteem of optimistic students is also higher than pessimistic stu-dents while taking a test or a quiz, at p < .01. Because such comparisons were not nearly as pronounced when comparing z-scores, which are relative to each student's mean score, we can deduce that optimistic students most likely report much higher skill level and self-esteem in many activities, not only those in classrooms. However, there is no significant difference in the reported skill level and self-esteem while in group activities. In fact, the mean skill and self-esteem reported by pessimistic stu-dents is slightly higher than those reported by optimistic students. We believe that group activities may reduce perceived differences in skill level associated with indi-vidualized activities, which in turn reduces differences in how students feel about themselves.

21 A series of ANOVAS comparing the level of flow reported in our selected classroom activities separately for each subgroup yielded the following results: males, F = 8.50, p < .00; females, F = 12.19, p < .001; Asians, F = 3.45, p < .01; Hispanics, F = 2.44, p < .01; African-Americans, F = 6.09, p < .001; Caucasians, F = 12.37, p < .001; working class, F = 6.18, p < .001; middle class, F = 6.78, p < .001; upper class, F = 11.14, p < .001; mostly As for reported grades, F = 7.00, p < .001; As and Bs, F = 7.57, p < .001; Cs and lower, F = 4.12, p < .01; optimistic future orientation: F = 12.31, p < .001; pessimistic future orientation, F = 7.12, p < .001; intrinsically motivated, F = 8.21, p < .001; extrinsically motivated, F = 11.46, p < .001.

CHAPTER EIGHT · GUIDING STUDENTS INTO THE FUTURE: THREE SCHOOLS OF THOUGHT

1 The Experience Sampling Method is discussed in Chapter 2.

2 An ANOVA comparing average future importance by site was significant: $F = 6.2$, $p < .01$.

3 The sociometric Friends Form is described more fully in Chapter 3.

4 An ANOVA comparing the average number of advisory relationships with adults in school by site was significant: $F = 3.4$, $p < .05$.

CHAPTER NINE · PATHS AFTER HIGH SCHOOL

1 We included the two students who attended proprietary schools in the two-year college category.

2 *Barron's* classifies colleges and universities on the basis of a six-tier competitiveness scale from most competitive to noncompetitive. We distinguished the top four competitive categories as very selective and the bottom two as less selective.

REFERENCES

Adelman, C. 1994. *Lessons of a Generation: Education and Work in the Lives of the High School Class of 1972.* San Francisco: Jossey-Bass.

Adlai-Gail, W. S. 1994. Exploring the Autotelic Personality. Ph.D. diss., University of Chicago.

Amabile, T. M. 1983. *The Social Psychology of Creativity.* New York: Springer-Verlag.

Arum, R. 1998. Invested Dollars or Diverted Dreams: The Effect of Resources on Vocational Students' Educational Outcomes. *Sociology of Education* 71 (2): 130–51.

Asakawa, K., and M. Csikszentmihalyi. 1998. The Quality of Experience of Asian American Adolescents in Academic Activities: An Exploration of Educational Achievement. *Journal of Research on Adolescence* 8 (2): 241–62.

Astin, A. 1997. *The American Freshman: Thirty Year Trends, 1966–1996.* Los Angeles: Higher Education Research Institute, University of California Los Angeles.

Bachman, J., and J. Schulenberg. 1992. *Part-time Work by High School Seniors: Sorting Out Correlates and Possible Consequences.* Monitoring the Future Occasional Paper 32. Ann Arbor: Institute for Social Research, The University of Michigan.

Barron's Profiles of American Colleges. 1994. New York: Barron's Educational Services.

Baumrind, D. 1987. A Developmental Perspective on Adolescent Risk Taking Behavior in Contemporary America. In *Adolescent Social Behavior and Health*, edited by C. E. Irwin. San Francisco: Jossey-Bass.

Baumrind, D. 1989. Rearing Competent Children. In *Child Development Today and Tomorrow*, edited by W. Damon. San Francisco: Jossey-Bass.

Bills, D. 1995. *The New Modern Times Factors: Reshaping the World of Work.* New York: State University of New York Press.

Blau, P., and O. Duncan. 1967. *The American Occupational Structure.* New York: Wiley.

Bordin, E. S. 1943. A Theory of Interests as Dynamic Phenomena. *Educational and Psychological Measurement* 3:49–66.

Bordin, E. S. 1990. Psychodynamic Model of Career Choice and Satisfaction. In *Career Choice and Development*, edited by D. Brown and L. Brooks. San Francisco: Jossey-Bass: 102–44.

Brandstätter, H. 1991. Emotions in Everyday Life Situations: Time Sampling of Subjective Experience. In *Subjective Well-Being*, edited by F. Strack, M. Argyle, and N. Schwartz. Oxford, U.K.: Pergamon.

Bronfenbrenner, U. 1961. The Changing American Child. *Journal of Social Issues* 17:1–15.

Bumpass, L., and J. Sweet. 1989. Children's Experience in Single-Parent Families: Implications of Cohabitation and Marital Transitions. *Family Planning Perspectives* 21:256–60.

Cameron, S., and J. Heckman. 1993. Nonequivalence of High School Equivalents. *Journal of Labor Economics* 11:1–47.

Cicourel, A. V., and J. I. Kitsuse. 1963. *The Educational Decision-Makers*. Indianapolis: Bobbs–Merrill.

Coleman, J. S. 1988. Social Capital in the Creation of Human Capital. *American Journal of Sociology* 94:S95–S120.

Coleman, J. S. 1990. *Foundations of Social Theory*. Cambridge: Belknap Press of Harvard University Press.

Coleman, J. S., et al. 1974. *Relationships in Adolescence*. Boston: Routledge & Kegan Paul.

Coleman, L. J. 1994. Being a Teacher: Emotions and Optimal Experience While Teaching Gifted Children. *Gifted Child Quarterly* 38:146–52.

Cookson, P. W., Jr., and C. H. Persell. 1985. *Preparing for Power: America's Elite Boarding Schools*. New York: Basic Books.

Coontz, S. 1992. *The Way We Never Were: American Families and the Nostalgia Trap*. New York: Basic Books.

Cooper, C. R., H. D. Grotevant, and S. M. Condon. 1983. Individuality and Connectedness in the Family as a Context for Adolescent Identity Formation and Role-taking Skill. In *Adolescent Development in the Family*, edited by H. D. Grotevant and C. R. Cooper. San Francisco: Jossey-Bass.

Csikszentmihalyi, M. 1975. *Beyond Boredom and Anxiety: The Experience of Play in Work and Games*. San Francisco: Jossey-Bass.

Csikszentmihalyi, M. 1990. *Flow: The Psychology of Optimal Experience*. New York: Harper & Row.

Csikszentmihalyi, M. 1993. *The Evolving Self: A Psychology for the Third Millennium*. New York: HarperCollins.

Csikszentmihalyi, M. 1996. *Creativity: Flow and the Psychology of Discovery and Invention*. New York: HarperCollins.

Csikszentmihalyi, M. 1997. *Finding Flow: The Psychology of Engagement with Everyday Life*. New York: Basic Books.

Csikszentmihalyi, M., and I. S. Csikszentmihalyi. 1988. *Optimal Experience: Studies of Flow in Consciousness*. New York: Cambridge University Press.

Csikszentmihalyi, M., and J. LeFevre. 1989. Optimal Experience in Work and Leisure. *Journal of Personality and Social Psychology* 56:815–22.

Csikszentmihalyi, M., and R. Larson. 1984. *Being Adolescent: Conflict and Growth in the Teenage Years.* New York: Basic Books

Csikszentmihalyi, M., and R. Larson. 1987. Validity and Reliability of the Experience Sampling Method. *Journal of Nervous and Mental Disease* 175:525–36.

Csikszentmihalyi, M., and K. Rathunde. 1993. The Measurement of Flow in Everyday Life: Towards a Theory of Emergent Motivation. In *Developmental Perspectives on Motivation,* edited by J. E. Jacobs. Vol. 40 of *Nebraska Symposium on Motivation.* Lincoln: University of Nebraska Press.

Csikszentmihalyi, M., K. Rathunde, and S. Whalen. 1993. *Talented Teenagers: The Roots of Success and Failure.* New York: Cambridge University Press.

Damon, W. 1983. *Social and Personality Development.* New York: Norton.

Darling-Hammond, L. 1995. Restructuring Schools for Students' Success. *Daedalus* 124 (2): 153–62.

Deci, E. L., and R. M. Ryan. 1985. *Intrinsic Motivation and Self-determination in Human Behavior.* New York: Plenum.

Delle Fave, A., and F. Massimini. 1992. Experience Sampling Method and the Measuring of Clinical Change: A Case of Anxiety Syndrome. In *The Experience of Psychopathology,* edited by M. W. deVries. Cambridge, U.K.: Cambridge University Press.

Diener, E. In press. Subjective Well-being: The Science of Happiness and Some Policy Implications. *American Psychologist.*

Dunne, F., R. Elliott, and D. Carlsen. 1981. Sex Differences in the Educational and Occupational Aspirations of Rural Youth. *Journal of Vocational Behavior* 18:55–56.

Eccles, J. S. D., and B. L. Barber. In press. Student Council, Volunteering, Basketball or Marching Band: What Kind of Extracurricular Involvement Matters? *Journal of Adolescent Research.*

Featherman, D. 1980. *Social Stratification and Mobility: Two Decades of Cumulative Social Science.* Madison: Institute for Research on Poverty, University of Wisconsin.

Fraser, J. 1962. *Industrial Psychology.* Oxford, U.K.: Pergamon.

Furnham, A. 1991. Work and Leisure Satisfaction. In *Subjective Well-Being,* edited by F. Strack, M. Argyle, and N. Schwartz. Oxford, U.K.: Pergamon.

Gamoran, A., and R. Mare. 1989. Secondary School Tracking and Educational Inequality: Compensation, Reinforcement, or Neutrality? *American Journal of Sociology* 94:1146–83.

Garrison, H. H. 1979. Gender Differences in the Career Aspirations of Recent Cohorts of High School Seniors. *Social Problems* 27:170–85.

Green, P., B. Dugoni, S. Ingels, and E. Camburn. 1995. *A Profile of the American High School Senior in 1992.* Washington, D.C.: U.S. Department of Education, National Center for Education Statistics.

Green, P. J., B. L. Dugoni, S. J. Ingels, and P. Quinn. 1995. *Trends Among High School Seniors, 1972–1992.* Washington, D.C.: U.S. Department of Education, Office of Educational Research and Improvement. NCES 95-380.

Greenberger, E., and L. D. Steinberg. 1981. The Workplace as a Context for the Socialization of Youth. *Journal of Youth and Adolescence* 10:185–210.

Greenberger, E., and L. D. Steinberg. 1986. *When Teenagers Work: The Psychological and Social Costs of Adolescent Employment.* New York: Basic Books.

Hafner, A., S. Ingels, B. Schneider, and D. Stevenson. 1990. *A Profile of the American Eighth Grader*. Washington, D.C.: U.S. Department of Education.

Hahn, S. 1988. The Relationship Between Life Satisfaction and Flow in Elderly Korean Immigrants. In *Optimal Experience: Psychological Studies of Flow in Consciousness*, edited by M. Csikszentmihalyi and I. S. Csikszentmihalyi. New York: Cambridge University Press.

Hallinan, M. T., ed. 1995. *Restructuring Schools: Promising Practices and Policies*. New York: Plenum.

Hallinan, M. T., and A. Sorensen. 1986. Student Characteristics and Assignment to Ability Groups: Two Conceptual Formulations. *Sociological Quarterly* 27 (1):1–13.

Hallinan, M. T., and R. A. Williams. 1989. Interracial Friendship Choices in Secondary Schools. *American Sociological Review* 54:67–78.

Hannah, J. S., and S. E. Kahn. 1989. The Relationship of Socioeconomic Status to the Occupational Choice of Grade 12 Students. *Journal of Vocational Behavior* 34:161–78.

Hauser, S. 1991. *Adolescents and Their Families*. New York: Free Press.

Havighurst, R. J. 1982. The World of Work. In *Handbook of Developmental Psychology*, edited by B. B. Wolman. Englewood Cliffs, N.J.: Prentice-Hall.

Hektner, J. M. 1996. Exploring Optimal Personality Development: A Longitudinal Study of Adolescents. Ph.D. diss., University of Chicago.

Herr, E. L., and T. Enderlein. 1976. Vocational Maturity: The Effects of School Grade, Curriculum, and Sex. *Journal of Vocational Behavior* 8:227–38.

Hormuth, W. E. 1986. The Sampling of Experience in Situation. *Journal of Personality* 54 (1): 262–93.

Hotchkiss, L., and L. Dorsten. 1987. Curriculum Effects on Early Post-High School Outcomes. *Research in Sociology of Education and Socialization* 7:191–219.

Inghilleri, P. 1999. *From Subjective Experience to Cultural Change*. New York: Cambridge University Press.

Irwin, C. E., ed. 1987. *Adolescent Social Behavior and Health*. San Francisco: Jossey-Bass.

Jackson, S. A. 1992. Athletes in Flow: A Qualitative Investigation of Flow States in Elite Figure Skaters. *Journal of Applied Sports Psychology* 4:161–80.

James, S. A., D. S. Strogatz, S. B. Wing, and D. L. Ramsey. 1987. Socioeconomic Status, John Henryism, and Hypertension in Blacks and Whites. *American Journal of Epidemiology* 126:664–73.

James, W. 1890. *Principles of Psychology*. New York: Holt.

Jepsen, D. 1984. The Developmental Perspective on Vocational Behavior: A Review of Theory and Research. In *Handbook of Counseling Psychology*, edited by S. D. Brown and R. W. Lent. New York: Wiley.

Kegan, R. 1982. *The Evolving Self*. Cambridge: Harvard University Press.

Konner, M. 1990. Human Nature and Culture: Biology and the Residue of Uniqueness. In *The Boundaries of Humanity*, edited by J. J. Sheehan and M. Sosna. Berkeley: University of California Press.

Kubey, R. W., and M. Csikszentmihalyi. 1990. *Television and the Quality of Life: How Viewing Shapes Everyday Experience*. Hillsdale, N.J.: Erlbaum.

Lamborn, S. N. Mounts, L. Steinberg, and S. Dornbusch. 1991. Patterns of Competence and

Adjustment Among Adolescents from Authoritative, Authoritarian, Indulgent, and Neglectful Families. *Child Development* 62:1049–65.

Larson, R., and M. H. Richards. 1994. *Divergent Realities: The Emotional Lives of Mothers, Fathers, and Adolescents.* New York: Basic Books.

Lee, R. B., and I. DeVore. 1975. *Man the Hunter.* Chicago: Aldine.

Loevinger, J. 1982. *Ego Development.* San Francisco: Jossey-Bass.

Maccoby, E. E., and J. A. Martin. 1983. Socialization in the Context of the Family: Parent-child Interaction. In *Socialization, Personality, and Social Development,* edited by E. M. Heatherington. Vol. 4 of *Handbook of Child Psychology,* edited by P. H. Mussen. New York: Wiley.

Mannell, R. C., J. Zuzanek, and R. W. Larson. 1988. Leisure States and Flow Experiences: Testing Perceived Freedom and Intrinsic Motivation Hypotheses. *Journal of Leisure Research* 20:289–304.

Marcia, J. 1980. Identity in Adolescence. In *Handbook of Adolescent Psychology,* edited by J. Adelson. New York: Wiley.

Marsh, H. W. 1992. Extracurricular Activities: Beneficial Extension of the Traditional Curriculum or Subversion of Academic Goals? *Journal of Educational Psychology* 84 (4): 553–62.

Maslow, A. 1971. *The Farther Reaches of Human Nature.* New York: Penguin.

Massimini, F., and M. Carli. 1988. The Systematic Assessment of Flow in Daily Experience. In *Optimal Experience: Psychological Studies of Flow in Consciousness,* edited by M. Csikszentmihalyi and I. S. Csikszentmihalyi. New York: Cambridge University Press.

Massimini, F., M. Csikszentmihalyi, and M. Carli. 1987. The Monitoring of Optimal Experience: A Tool for Psychiatric Rehabilitation. *Journal of Nervous and Mental Disease* 175:545–49.

McClelland, D. C. 1961. *The Achieving Society.* Princeton, N.J.: Van Nostrand.

Mead, G. H. [1934] 1974. *Mind, Self, and Society from the Standpoint of a Social Behaviorist.* Chicago: University of Chicago Press.

Mickelson, R. 1990. The Attitude-Achievement Paradox Among Black Adolescents. *Sociology of Education* 63: 44–61.

Moneta, G. B., and M. Csikszentmihalyi. 1996. The Effect of Perceived Challenges and Skills on the Quality of Subjective Experience. *Journal of Personality* 64 (2): 275–310.

Morrison, B. 1994. Letter from Liverpool. *New Yorker,* February 14, 48–60.

Mortimer, J. T., and K. M. Borman. 1988. *Work Experience and Psychological Development Through the Lifespan: AAS Selected Symposium.* Boulder: Westview.

Mortimer, J. T., M. D. Finch, T. J. Owens, and M. Shanahan. 1990. Gender and Work in Adolescence. *Youth and Society* 22:201–24.

Mortimer, J. T., M. D. Finch, K. Dennehy, C. Lee, and T. Beebe. 1995. Work Experience in Adolescence. Paper Presented at the biennial meeting of the Society for Research in Child Development.

Murnane, R., and F. Levy. 1996. *Teaching the New Basic Skills: Principles for Educating Children to Thrive in a Changing Economy.* New York: Free Press.

Myers, D. 1992. *The Pursuit of Happiness.* New York: Morrow.

National Center for Education Statistics. 1995. *Digest of Educational Statistics of 1995.*

Washington, D.C.: U.S. Department of Education, Office of Educational Research and Improvement. NCES 95-029.

National Center for Education Statistics. 1994. *National Education Longitudinal Study of 1988: Second Follow-Up: Student Component Data File User's Manual*. Washington, D.C.: U.S. Department of Education, Office of Educational Research and Improvement.

National Research Council. 1998. *Protecting Youth at Work: Health, Safety and Development of Working Children and Adolescents in the United States*. Washington, D.C.: National Academy Press.

Oakes, J. 1985. *Keeping Track: How Schools Structure Inequality*. New Haven: Yale University Press.

Parsons, T. 1952. The Superego and the Theory of Social Systems. *Psychiatry* 15:15-25.

Powell, A. G., E. Farrar, and D. K. Cohen. 1985. *The Shopping Mall High School: Winners and Losers in the Educational Marketplace*. Boston: Houghton Mifflin.

Rathunde, K. 1996. Family Context and Talented Adolescents' Optimal Experience in School-Related Activities. *Journal of Research on Adolescence* 6 (4): 603-26.

Reiss, D. 1981. *The Family's Construction of Reality*. Cambridge: Harvard University Press.

Rheinberg, F. 1995. Flow-Erleben, Freude an Riskantem Sport und andere "unvernünftige" Motivationen. In *Motivation, Volition, und Handlung: Enzyklopädie der Psychologie*, edited by J. Kuhl und H. Heckhausen. Göttingen: Hogrefe.

Rohlen, T. P. 1983. *Japan's High Schools*. Berkeley: University of California Press.

Rosenbaum, J., S. Miller, and M. Krei. 1996. Gatekeeping in an Era of More Open Gates: High School Counselors' Views of Their Influence on Students' College Plans. *American Journal of Education* 4:257-79.

Ryan, R. R. 1992. Agency and Organization: Intrinsic Motivation, Autonomy, and the Self in Psychological Development. *Nebraska Symposium on Motivation* 40:1-56.

Sato, I. 1988. Bosozoku: Flow in Japanese Motorcycle Gangs. In *Optimal Experience*, edited by M. Csikszentmihalyi and I. S. Csikszentmihalyi. New York: Cambridge University Press.

Savickas, M. 1995. Current Theoretical Issues in Vocational Psychology: Convergence, Divergence, and Schism. In *Handbook of Vocational Psychology*, edited by W. B. Walsh and S. H. Osipow. 2d ed. Mahwah, N.J.: Erlbaum.

Savickas, M., amd R. W. Lent, eds. 1994. *Convergence in Career Development Theories: Implications for Scienec and Practice*. Palo Alto: CPP Books.

Scheier, M. F., and C. S. Carver. 1992. Effects of Optimism on Psychological and Physical Well-being: Theoretical Overview and Empirical Update. *Cognitive Therapy and Research* 16:201-28.

Schmidt, J. 1998. Overcoming Challenges: Exploring the Role of Action, Experience, and Opportunity in Fostering Resilience Among Adolescents. Ph.D. diss., University of Chicago.

Schneider, B., S. Knauth, and E. Makris. 1995. The Influence of Guidance Counselors: School Patterns. Paper presented at the annual meeting of the American Educational Research Association, San Francisco.

Schneider, B., and J. Schmidt. 1996. Young Women at Work: A Life-Course Perspective. In *Women and Work: A Handbook*, edited by K. Borman and P. Dubeck. New York: Garland.

Schneider, B., and D. Stevenson. 1999. *The Ambitious Generation: America's Teenagers Motivated but Directionless*. New Haven: Yale University Press.

Schneider, B., C. Swanson, and C. Riegle-Crumb. 1998. Opportunities for Learning: Course Sequences and Positional Advantages. *Social Psychology of Education* 2:25–53.

Schneider, B., and J. S. Coleman, eds. 1993. *Parents, Their Children, and Schools*. Boulder: Westview.

Schorr, E. 1988. *Within Our Reach: Breaking the Cycle of Disadvantage*. New York: Anchor Press/Doubleday.

Secretary's Commission on Achieving Necessary Skills. 1992. *Learning a Living: A Blueprint for High Performance*. Washington, D.C.: U.S. Department of Labor.

Seligman, M. E. P. 1991. *Learned Optimism*. New York: Knopf.

Sewell, W., and R. Hauser. 1975. *Education, Occupation, and Earnings*. New York: Academic Press.

Slavin, R. E. 1983. *Cooperative Learning*. New York: Longmans.

Stein, G. L., J. C. Kimiecik, J. Daniels, and S. A. Jackson. 1995. Psychological Antecedents of Flow in Recreational Sport. *Personality and Social Psychology Bulletin* 21:125–35.

Steinberg, L., S. Fegley, and S. M. Dornbusch. 1993. Negative Impact of Part-time Work on Adolescent Adjustment: Evidence from a Longitudinal Study. *Developmental Psychology* 29:171–80.

Steinberg, L., S. Lamborn, S. Dornbusch, and N. Darling. 1992. Impact of Parenting Practices on Adolescent Achievement: Authoritative Parenting, School Involvement, and Encouragement to Succeed. *Child Development* 63:1266–81.

Stevenson, D. L., K. S. Schiller, and B. Schneider. 1994. Sequences of Opportunities for Learning. *Sociology of Education* 67:184–98.

Super, D. 1976. *Career Education and the Meanings of Work*. Monographs on Career Education. Washington, D.C.: Office of Career Education, U.S. Office of Education.

Super, D., et al. 1957. *Vocational Development: A Framework of Research*. New York: Bureau of Publication, Teachers College, Columbia University.

Third International Mathematics and Science Study (TIMSS). 1996. *A Splintered Vision: An Investigation of U.S. Science and Mathematics Education*. Dordrecht: Kluwer Academic Publishers.

Third Mathematics and Science Study. 1998. *Mathematics and Science Achievement in the Final Year of Secondary School*. Boston: Kluwer Academic Publishers.

Thompson, E. P. 1963. *The Making of the English Working Class*. New York: Viking.

Trevino, L. K., and J. Webster. 1992. Flow in Computer-mediated Communication. *Communication Research* 19:539–73.

Turnbull, C. M. 1972. *The Mountain People*. New York: Simon & Schuster.

U.S. Department of Commerce. 1991. *Statistical Abstract of the United States*. Washington, D.C.: Bureau of the Census.

U.S. Department of Commerce. 1993. *Statistical Abstract of the United States*. Washington, D.C.: Bureau of the Census.

U.S. Department of Commerce. 1997. *Statistical Abstract of the United States*. 117th ed. Washington, D.C.: Bureau of the Census.

U.S. Department of Education. 1991. *Youth Indicators*. Washington, D.C.: Office of Educational Research and Improvement.

U.S. Department of Education. 1994. *Strong Families, Strong Schools*. Washington, D.C.: U.S. Government Printing Office.

U.S. Department of Labor. 1986. *Youth Unemployment*. Washington, D.C.: Bureau of Labor Statistics.

U.S. Department of Labor. 1993. *Geographic Profile of Employment and Unemployment, 1992*. Bulletin 2428. Washington, D.C.: Bureau of Labor Statistics.

U.S. Department of Labor. 1994. *Occupational Outlook Handbook*. Washington, D.C.: Bureau of Labor Statistics.

U.S. Department of Labor. 1995. *Occupational Outlook Handbook*. Washington, D.C.: Bureau of Labor Statistics.

U.S. General Accounting Office. 1991. *Characteristics of Working Children*. GAO/HRD–91–83BR, June. Washington, D.C.: U.S. Government Printing Office.

Vondracek, F. 1995. Vocational Identity Across the Life Span: A Developmental-Contextual Perspective on Achieving Self-Recognition Through Vocational Careers. *Man and Work* 6:85–93.

Vygotsky, L. S. 1978. *Mind in Society: The Development of Higher Psychological Processes*. Cambridge: Harvard University Press.

W. E. Upjohn Institute for Employment Research. 1973. *Work in America; Report of a Special Task Force to the Secretary of Health, Education, and Welfare. Subcommittee on Employment, Manpower, and Poverty of the Committee on Labor and Public Welfare, United States Senate*. Washington, D.C.: U.S. Government Printing Office.

Washburn, S. L., and C. S. Lancaster. 1975. The Evolution of Hunting. In *Man the Hunter*, edited by R. B. Lee and I. DeVore. Chicago: Aldine.

Weber, M. [1922] 1930. *The Protestant Ethic and the Spirit of Capitalism*. London: Allen & Unwin.

Webster, J., and Martocchio, J. J. 1993. Turning Work into Play: Implications for Microcomputer Software Training. *Journal of Management* 19:127–46.

Webster, J., L. K. Trevino, and L. Ryan. 1993. The Dimensionality and Correlates of Flow in Human-computer Interactions. *Computers in Human Behavior* 9:411–26.

Wells, A. J. 1988. Self-esteem and Optimal Experience. In *Optimal Experience: Psychological Studies of Flow in Consciousness*, edited by M. Csikszentmihalyi and I. S. Csikszentmihalyi. New York: Cambridge University Press.

White, R. W. 1959. Motivation Reconsidered: The Concept of Competence. *Psychological Review* 66:297–333.

Won, H. J. 1989. The Daily Leisure of Korean Adolescents and Its Relationship to Subjective Well-Being. Ph.D. diss., University of Oregon.

Yankelovich, D. 1981. *New Rules: Searching for Self-fulfillment in a World Turned Upside Down*. New York: Random House.

Youniss, J., and M. Yates. 1997. *Community Service and Social Responsibility in Youth*. Chicago: University of Chicago Press.

INDEX

and classroom experiences, quality of, 142–143, 150, 154, 162

and the family environment, 117, 118–119, 122, 126

and images of work and play, 69, 83, 84, 91

and moments of flow, 99–100

and paths after high school, 208, 223

Extracurricular activities, 220–221

Extrinsic rewards: and challenging experiences, 98, 109

and envisioning the future, 57–59, 61

and families, influence of, 119

and Maslow's hierarchy of needs, 59

F

Factory workers, 89–90

Fairness, 158

Fall, the, 11

Families, 4–6, 228–229

and adolescent attitudes and experience, 117–118

and college enrollment, 210–211

and experience while doing school-related activities, 126–128

fragmentation of, 14– 15

and goals, 116, 118–119, 126, 129, 134, 138

growing instability of, 4

high challenge/high support, 117, 130–133

high challenge/low support, 117, 133–134

high support/low challenge, 117, 134–136

influence of, overview of, 113–139

life among, narratives of, 128–130

low support/low challenge, 117, 136– 137

and motivation, 119, 122, 128, 133–134

and optimism, 118, 119, 124, 125

and school outcomes, 119–125

supportive aspects of, measuring, 116–117

types of, selected variables related to, 118–119

Family income, median, 173, 187

Farmers, 7, 51, 89–90

and task motivation, 58

and the work ethic, 9, 10. *See also* Agriculture

Fashion models, 46, 217

Fast-food workers, 89–90

Feedback, 97, 155

Feldnor, 24, 187–188, 239. *See also* Grove high school

Fitscore, 110, 119, 255

Flow experiences, 96–102

and classroom experiences, quality of, 142, 148–149, 153, 158–162, 164

in different activities, 102–106

intensity of, activities which induce, 104–105

overall benefits of, 224–225

percent of time in, in various activities, 103–104

and personal growth, 106–111

and the presence of others, 106

and the quality of experience, 99–102

Forest Bluff high school, 24, 239

France, 16

Freud, Sigmund, 96

Friends Sociometric Form (Friends Form), 27, 29–30, 34

Future, 5, 167–198

careers, learning about, 51–52

envisioning the, 39–64

and images of work and play, 83, 86

and occupational values, 48–51

orientation, measures of, 107, 108–109

what students say about school subjects in relation to, 154–156

and work-related motivations, 56–60. *See also* Expectations Goals

G

Games: and challenging experiences, 97, 101, 102, 103

and images of work and play, 76

and intrinsic rewards, 12

{ A NOTE ABOUT THE TYPE }

Becoming Adult has been set in ITC Mendoza, an old-style type designed by French typographer José Mendoza. Unlike many digital types, which undergo a process of computer interpolation, each character in the Mendoza family was hand drawn by the designer. The result is a handsome, low-contrast typeface that is highly readable without being pedestrian. This type is all the more remarkable in light of José Mendoza's lack of formal training, which he once summarized in the credo, *self-taught, no school, no master, no instruction received.*

Book design and composition by Mark McGarry
Texas Type & Book Works